STREET
POISON

Also by Justin Gifford

*Pimping Fictions: African American Crime Literature
and the Untold Story of Black Pulp Publishing*

DOUBLEDAY

New York

London

Toronto

Sydney

Auckland

THE
BIOGRAPHY
OF
ICEBERG
SLIM

STREET
POISON

JUSTIN GIFFORD

All rights reserved. Published in the United States by Doubleday,
a division of Penguin Random House LLC, New York, and distributed
in Canada by Random House of Canada Ltd., Toronto.

www.doubleday.com

DOUBLEDAY and the portrayal of an anchor with a dolphin are
registered trademarks of Penguin Random House LLC.

Book design by Maria Carella
Frontispiece photograph courtesy of Holloway House
Jacket design by Michael J. Windsor
Front jacket image: photo of Iceberg Slim courtesy of Diane Beck; spine image:
northeast corner of Clark and Madison Streets, Chicago, Illinois (detail). Chicago
History Museum / Getty Images

Library of Congress Cataloging-in-Publication Data
Gifford, Justin.
Street poison : the biography of Iceberg Slim / Justin Gifford.
pages cm
ISBN 978-0-385-53834-3 (hardcover)—ISBN 978-0-385-53838-1 (eBook)
1. Iceberg Slim, 1918–1992. 2. African American authors—Biography.
3. African Americans—Illinois—Chicago—Biography. 4. Pimps—Illinois—Chicago—
Biography. I. Title.
PS3552.E25Z64 2015
813'.54—dc23
2014037252

MANUFACTURED IN THE UNITED STATES OF AMERICA

10 9 8 7 6 5 4 3 2 1

First Edition

FOR MY SISTER, JESSIE GIFFORD,
the most courageous woman I have ever known

So, as I started to read that Iceberg Slim, I started to learn how to quote it, you know, all his little poetry and stuff. "I was branded the beast, I sat down at the feast," you know what I'm saying? So I would say it, and my friends would say, "Say some more of that Iceberg stuff, T. Drop that Iceberg stuff, T."

—ICE-T

Iceberg Slim's *Pimp: The Story of My Life* was the book that determined the ghetto persona, which has massively influenced popular culture through music and film. In terms of that influence he's probably the most dominant writer since Shakespeare.

—IRVINE WELSH

Iceberg Slim—Truth, still shining down.

—ANDREW VACHSS

CONTENTS

PREFACE

Robert "Iceberg Slim" Beck—a pimp for twenty-five years, who went on to become a writer of bestselling paperback originals, including *Pimp: The Story of My Life*—might at first glance seem like an appalling choice for a biography. After all, he abused hundreds of women throughout his lifetime, and he is practically unknown to the American mainstream. His books, which were marketed as trashy pulp fiction, have been sold in mom-and-pop stores in inner-city neighborhoods, and they have been read primarily in America's forgotten corners: prisons, ghettos, and military bases. However, Beck has had an enormous influence on contemporary black music, film, literature, and popular culture. Starting in the late 1960s, his pen name, Iceberg Slim, became synonymous with black urban cool, and entire cultural industries grew up around his work. He is arguably one of the most influential figures of the past fifty years, and yet, apart from what he reveals in his own writings, very little is known about this fascinating and contradictory character.

I encountered Beck's influence many times, and in many forms, before I comprehended his significance as a writer and cultural force. Growing up in a working-class family in Seattle during the age of Reaganomics, I listened to as much gangsta rap as grunge. In my twenties, I developed a manic, obsessive relationship to underground American literature. I dropped out of college for a while in an attempt to write the next great American novel, and after reading Jack London, John Steinbeck, and Jack Kerouac, I hitchhiked from Seattle through parts of Mexico and the American South to New

York. I constructed a giant cartoonish thumb out of cardboard and duct tape—it was the size of a medieval shield—and I set out to have my own reckless literary adventure on the road. It was a dangerous trip, full of peril, but the road was full of transgressive pleasures, too. Someday I intend to write about it.

It was on that trip to New York that I made a discovery that would pay off many years later in my search for Beck's books. I was walking down Lenox Avenue after eating a plate of chicken and waffles at Sylvia's, the famous soul food restaurant, when I spied a table on the corner of 125th Street piled high with books. I was on the hunt for Beat literature, so I stopped to scan the selection. I didn't see anything I was looking for, just some beat-up paperbacks with lurid cover illustrations and names I didn't recognize. To be honest, in my ignorance of African American crime literature, I failed to see the archive of literary treasures that sat before me. It would be a full seven years before I would return to this street to discover the works of Beck and the genre he inspired.

I first heard Beck's name when I moved to his old stomping grounds on the South Side of Chicago a few years later. My research had become more focused on issues of race in American literature, and I had come to the University of Chicago to study under, among other brilliant writers, Nobel Prize–winning author Toni Morrison. My life in Chicago was divided between two worlds. In the mornings, I took classes from intellectual luminaries such as Homi Bhabha, Terry Eagleton, and Morrison herself. In the afternoons, I worked in the Chicago public schools as a technology coordinator, helping teachers integrate computer and Internet technology into the classroom. I worked at nine schools located throughout Chicago's economically devastated South Side; the schools lacked basic necessities such as desks and textbooks, and many of the students lived in public housing projects, like the notorious Robert Taylor Homes.

One day I was working with a group of teenagers who asked me what I studied at the university. I told them that I read the classics of African American literature, Zora Neale Hurston, Richard Wright, and Ralph Ellison. They admitted that while they knew of these writers, they were more interested in the books of a former pimp–turned–writer from Chicago named Iceberg Slim. One of them produced a dog-eared copy of *Pimp*, and I thumbed through the autobiography for a few minutes before the teacher came back into the room. In those brief few moments, I didn't really understand what I was looking at. The gold cover had "Pimp" emblazoned in purple letters across the front and a hand-drawn silhouette of a man's hardened face underneath. It reminded me of a Harlequin-style romance novel. Here again, I missed an opportunity to expand my knowledge of African American literature. *Pimp* was certainly not being taught or read at the University of Chicago, and I was so focused on my research of the "canon," I forgot all about the book for the next five years.

Finally, in the summer of 2003, I made a discovery that would entirely change the direction of my life's work. I was now a PhD candidate at the University of Virginia, and I was composing a dissertation on crime and detective fiction—Edgar Allan Poe, Mark Twain, Raymond Chandler, Dashiell Hammett, and Chester Himes. I had come to New York City to search for rare and out-of-print copies of paperback books; those were the days when used bookstores still survived in Manhattan. I was particularly interested in tracking down the works of Chester Himes, the only African American detective novelist that I knew of. I haunted the usual spots—the Strand on Broadway, The Mysterious Bookshop, the Hue-Man Bookstore in Harlem—and then I remembered the book table that I had encountered years earlier. The table was no longer there on 125th and Lenox; but down 125th Street, in front of the Apollo Theater, there was another table, stacked with black-authored paperback novels. They had garish, blaxploitation-style covers, with exaggerated drawings of pimps and gangsters, and prostitutes busting out of their skimpy outfits. I was fascinated with the titles, such as *Whoreson*, *Black Gangster*, *Trick Baby*, *The Jones Men*, *Ghetto Sketches*, and *The Scene*. I had never heard of any of these writers: Donald Goines, Nathan Heard, Vern E. Smith, Clarence Cooper, and Odie Hawkins. In fact, the only book that was the least bit familiar was Robert Beck's *Pimp: The Story of My Life*, the autobiography I had encountered years earlier in Chicago, but had overlooked. Now here it was in front of me again at the center of a puzzle that would take me another decade to solve. I pushed Hammett and Poe to the side and focused on reconstructing the story of Beck and African American crime literature.

———

Over the next year, I spent all of my spare time and money tracking down rare and out-of-print copies of Beck's novels, as well as books by other black writers in the genre. I learned quickly that these were not books one could find in mainstream bookstores or libraries, so I did a lot of searching on used-bookstore websites. One resource in particular proved more useful than any other. A new online auction site called eBay had just recently become popular, and I found hundreds of pulpy paperbacks in my search for first-edition black crime novels. In the summer of 2004, I was doing my usual search for Iceberg Slim materials when I came across a number of auctions selling the former pimp's actual suits, silk shirts, and alligator shoes. I researched further and discovered that his widow, Diane Beck, was selling all of his clothes to raise money for a children's charity. I followed these auctions for days, and at the last minute I swooped in and bought two matching velvet suits, a flannel suit, a red silk shirt, and four pairs of dress shoes. After the auction, I contacted Mrs. Beck and asked her if I could come interview her in Los Angeles. She agreed, and we met at a Starbucks in Silver Lake near her home. We talked for many hours, and she told me about Beck's passion for writing, the radical political views that he shared with the Black Panthers, and his ongoing struggles over royalty payments with his white publisher, which lasted until his death. This was just the first of many meetings I would have with Mrs. Beck, and over the years she provided me with Beck's unpublished writings, his royalty statements, book contracts, and fan letters. More important, she offered her personal insights and heartfelt stories about her late husband, which would shape the direction of my research for ten years. Most recently, she shared with me Beck's unpublished novel *Shetani's Sister*, which had been locked in a drawer for twenty years, and which now, due to her generosity, is being published by Vintage Books in 2015.

It was about this time that I also met Bentley Morriss, the man who was almost single-handedly responsible for bringing Beck's works into the public consciousness. Somewhere along the line, I realized Beck had published all of his works with Holloway House Publishing Company, a white-owned, Los Angeles–based imprint that had put out works by many black crime writers, including Odie Hawkins, Donald Goines, Omar Fletcher, Amos Brooke, and a few dozen others. The company had also published black romances, biographies of famous African Americans for grade school children, and the first commercially successful black *Playboy* spinoff, titled *Players*, which had been edited by Los Angeles's "unofficial poet laureate," Wanda Coleman, as well as Emory Holmes and Joseph Nazel. The magazine, together with the company's so-called "black experience" novels, made Holloway House an important but underappreciated niche publisher of African American materials. I interviewed owner and CEO Bentley Morriss in 2004, and he was surprisingly forthcoming about his original motivations for publishing black-themed literature. He didn't do it for political reasons; he did it, like all savvy businessmen, for the money. Although he met resistance from racist distributors in the 1960s, who didn't believe that blacks read books, he pushed ahead because he, and his business partner Ralph Weinstock, believed that there was a market for African American paperback originals. He was right. Beck's works alone had sold six million copies by the time of his death in 1992, and Holloway House had published about four hundred titles by the time it sold off its assets to Kensington Publishing in 2008.

I continued to search for "black experience" novels and *Players* magazine both online and in my travels. I scoured used bookstores and thrift shops in Philadelphia, Los Angeles, Brooklyn, San Francisco, and Cleveland. *Players* magazine was particularly difficult to find. There were only a handful of issues stored on microfilm at the venerable Schomburg Center for Research in Black Culture in New York, and everyone else I talked to regarded it as smut. As a last resort, I drove from my home in Reno, where I was now a professor, to San Francisco, where there is a vintage pornographic magazine store called simply The Magazine. When I arrived and asked if they had copies of *Players*, the owner smiled knowingly and then headed down a steep staircase into the basement, where he apparently kept the good stuff. When he came back with a few employees, they were carrying four large boxes—a nearly complete collection of the magazine that a guy had sold them just the day before. In my excitement at having located this literary fortune, I bought the whole collection and loaded it into the back of my Explorer, before I realized I now didn't have any money for a hotel. So I parked my truck at the dead end on Belgrave Avenue, unfurled my sleeping bag, and crawled into the back among my giant piles of porn. And as I lay there with my flashlight, illegally camping while thumbing through dozens of African American men's magazines, I realized that I would have a difficult time explaining to any cop who came by that I was doing "research."

Perhaps my biggest break came in 2008, when I was contacted by Jorge Hinojosa, the longtime manager of Ice-T. He was making a documentary film about Beck entitled *Iceberg Slim: Portrait of a Pimp*, and he had heard through Diane Beck that I was a scholar of black crime literature. He asked if I wanted to appear in the film as a literary expert. I agreed, but on the condition that he would allow me access to documents, interviews, and other materials that I couldn't track down on my own. This turned out to be one of the greatest additions to my research I could have hoped for. Mr. Hinojosa has for the past six years provided me with more significant research materials than any other person or institution involved in this project, apart from Mrs. Beck. He copied countless documents for me, including FBI files and prison records; gave me access to interviews with Beck's friends and family members, some of whom are now deceased; and he tracked down rare television interviews and appearances that I simply did not have the clout to retrieve on my own. Long after the film was completed, as recently as the summer of 2013, Mr. Hinojosa invited me into his home time and time again, allowing me to sit in his office and pore over documents and other materials he had tracked down in his own obsessive pursuit of knowledge about

Beck's life. I owe him a great debt of gratitude, as this project would be incomplete without him.

In the years since I worked on the film, I have pursued information on the life and works of Beck in a number of other unconventional ways. I conducted interviews with black writers who at one time worked for Holloway House, including novelists Odie Hawkins and Roland S. Jefferson, as well as *Players* magazine editors Emory Holmes and the late Wanda Coleman. I traveled to Detroit, where I met Eddie B. Allen, the biographer of Donald Goines. Goines had been a pimp in his own right in Detroit's Paradise Valley in the 1950s, and he looked to Beck as his literary mentor. After reading Beck in prison in 1970, he went on to write sixteen books for Holloway House in the next four years, before unknown assailants murdered him and his girlfriend in front of their children. Mr. Allen was gracious enough to provide me with Goines's book contracts, his unpublished writings, and his personal correspondence, thus enlarging my understanding of the literary landscape in which both Beck and Goines worked. At the Mayme A. Clayton Library in Los Angeles, the Chicago Historical Society, and the Schomburg Center in New York, I tracked down articles on Beck, his ancestors, and his associates in significant black newspapers, such as the *Los Angeles Sentinel*, the *Chicago Defender*, and the *New York Amsterdam News*. Spending hundreds of hours relentlessly searching through these sources, as well as on genealogy websites such as ancestry.com, I was able to reconstruct a vivid picture of Beck's life and the world from which he came.

In January 2014, I flew to Chicago to put the final pieces of research together for the book. During one of the coldest winters on record, I rented a car and drove all over the Midwest, searching for the last shreds of missing evidence I needed to tell Beck's full story. I went to his childhood home in Rockford, Illinois, where librarians helped me track down his junior high school yearbook and enrollment cards. I drove to Milwaukee, where school officials uncovered transcripts that had been locked away in a basement for nearly eighty years.

And on a -20-degree day at the Wisconsin Historical Society, with the invaluable help of archivist Lee Grady, I uncovered Beck's psychiatric field-service mental and physical examinations, conducted during his incarceration at both Wisconsin State Reformatory and Wisconsin State Prison. Like many of the other documents I found, these files had never been viewed by the public, and I had to get special written permission from Diane Beck to have them opened. The documents provided me a fascinating glimpse not only into Beck's early psychology as an aspiring pimp, but also into the institutionalized racism of the prison system in which he was incarcerated.

The most intriguing breakthrough I made during my research at the Wisconsin Historical Society, however, was the discovery of Beck's first common-law wife, Mattie Maupins. Because the files were listed alphabetically, Mrs. Maupins's records were stored next to her husband's (Beck went by the name Maupins until 1962). When we pulled the file, I recognized her address as that of Beck's mother's house in Milwaukee, and I realized that he had had an early common-law wife whom he only barely mentioned in his autobiography. Not only did her file provide extensive documentation of her record as a prostitute and pickpocket—including court transcripts of her arrest for nearly cutting off a man's thumb in a fight—but it filled in important details of Beck's life between 1947 and 1951, details that were omitted in his memoir. Mattie's own heartbreaking story (she ended up going to Texas state prison for murder) provided me with the final information I needed to understand the complex life of Robert Beck.

For more than a decade, I have worked to combine paperback pulp novels, interviews, prison records, political essays, FBI files, newspaper articles, unpublished fiction, and letters into a single narrative of a man who was, by all accounts—even his own—corrupt and perverted. At the core of my biography have been Beck's own works: his autobiography, an essay collection, a short story anthology, the album of spoken word poetry, five published novels, and two unpublished ones. Although Beck more often than not provided a thorough and accurate confession of his life in his writings, as a master teller of tales, he also occasionally embellished the truth, switched around events in his life, and outright lied to protect his ego and reputation. Wherever possible, I have tested his stories against the historical record as well as the available prison files and interviews, and I have tried to provide the most accurate account possible of Beck's life. This is not to undermine his word or call him out on the page. On the contrary, the facts, stories, and documents I uncovered in my decade-long search for the story behind *Pimp: The Story of My Life* only add to the complexity and ambiguous allure of one of the most influential renegades of the twentieth century.

Beck was, throughout his life, a mess of contradictions: student at Tuskegee Institute, Chicago pimp with connections to the black mafia, amateur scholar of psychoanalysis, pulp paperback writer, family man, Black Panther Party sympathizer, Hollywood darling of the blaxploitation era, and godfather of hip-hop. He was all these things and more, and *Street Poison* attempts to make sense of these seemingly incongruent identities. This is not a story without tragedy. Beck's life was characterized by failed relationships, sexual trauma and abuse, and fleeting glimpses of fame followed by obscurity. But it is a story of redemption and breathtaking creativity, too. As a pimp, artist, and mentor, Beck was first and foremost a storyteller, arguably one of the most insightful and darkly funny we have ever seen. I have tried to tell his tale the way he might have wanted: clearly, honestly, and without moralizing.

INTRODUCTION

On the afternoon of April 29, 1992, America was shocked to learn that the four white police officers accused of brutally beating Rodney King had been acquitted of assault and excessive force charges. A year earlier, King, an African American construction worker, had led the officers on a high-speed chase through Los Angeles. It had ended with four policemen beating King with batons for over a minute, inflicting bruises all over his body and breaking his ankle and facial bones. A local man had recorded the whole incident, and the ninety-second tape was played and replayed across the globe, making it arguably the world's first viral video. Police brutality—a problem that had plagued black urban communities in secret throughout the twentieth century—was finally out in the open, and except for the most hardened racists, everyone seemed to agree that the officers were guilty. Black America wanted justice, and in a rare moment, it seemed like they just might get it. When the police were acquitted of nearly all charges, much of black Los Angeles reacted with what many viewed as justifiable rage. Looters raided businesses across South Central Los Angeles and then set them ablaze. Commuters were pulled from their vehicles and beaten with bricks, car stereos, and ball hammers. By nightfall, the riot was completely out of control. It continued for six days, and when the smoke finally cleared, over fifty people were dead and the city had suffered a billion dollars in damage.

Across town at Brotman Medical Center on the first night of the riot, Robert "Iceberg Slim" Beck watched the violence unfold on television from his hospital bed. "It looks like the revolution is starting," he said to his second wife, Diane. He wondered if he would live long enough to see it unfold. Born less than a year before Chicago's July 27, 1919, riot, the most violent of the twenty-five race riots that exploded during a season known as the "Red Summer," Beck had lived through all the major clashes between whites and blacks during the twentieth century. Since the late 1960s, he had been an admirer of the radical literature of James Baldwin and the philosophies of the Black Panther Party. In his own writings, he had been calling explicitly for a black revolution since the publication of his essay collection, *The Naked Soul of Iceberg Slim*, in 1971. Now it seemed like revolution was finally here, and he was both eager and fearful to witness the birth of a new social order.

Gangrene had taken hold in his foot, however, and the doctors told him that, based on how it looked, they would have to amputate his leg to save his life. He was reluctant. He wanted to wait to see what the medical tests said about the gangrene's severity before allowing them to take the leg. He would not live long enough to see the results. Despite his seventy-three years of age, Beck was still a bit vain about his good looks. It was the last holdover from his glory days as a pimp. He almost never left the house in anything but a silk shirt and a pair of trousers with a razor-sharp crease ironed into the front. When he was still healthy, he walked six miles a day through the sprawling streets of Los Angeles in an effort to keep his six-foot-two-inch frame trim. For a man who had pimped across the Midwest for twenty-five years, served four prison sentences in reformatories and federal penitentiaries, and survived to tell his tale in a collection of epic novels, the idea of living out his final days as a one-legged man was both terrifying and humiliating. He didn't want to let them amputate unless it was absolutely necessary. As it turned out, it was. The next day—as South Central Los Angeles burned, and smoke filled the skies like some ancient funeral rite—black America's bestselling writer, the literary godfather of hip-hop, and definitive icon of pimp cool Robert Beck passed away after his long struggle with diabetes.

The transformative moment of Beck's life came in 1967 with the publication of his memoir, *Pimp: The Story of My Life*, under the pseudonym Iceberg Slim. He and his first wife, Betty, a white woman from Texas, originally conceived of the book as a type of living-room theater to entertain and educate their young children. *Pimp* was Beck's masterpiece. A gritty, mostly autobiographical account of his childhood and his criminal enterprises as a pimp for a quarter of a century, *Pimp* evokes a vivid picture of black America's urban underworld from the Great Depression to the turbulent 1960s. It is written in black street slang so obscure that there is a glossary in the back to translate words like "mudkicker" (prostitute), "crumb crusher" (baby), and "Hog" (Cadillac). Beck was a born observer and mimic, and he educated himself in subjects ranging from psychoanalysis to macroeconomics. With his perfect memory for dialogue, and encyclopedic knowledge of topics he had mastered from reading in prison libraries, he gave a voice to what he called the "street people" of America.

A strong case can be made that more than any other cultural figure of the past fifty years, Beck transformed American popular culture and black literature. *Pimp* became a potent symbol of subversive style and one of the most influential works of antiestablishment literature of the twentieth century. It sold millions of copies during its first few years of publication in its mass-market paperback edition, and according to its publisher it is the best-selling book by a black American author of all time. It became a classic on military bases, in American prisons, and in black neighborhoods coast to coast. It inspired dozens of black authors, such as Donald Goines, Odie Hawkins, Joseph Nazel, and Omar Fletcher, to write their own stories of pimps, hustlers, and Black Panther revolutionaries. In the process, these literary apostles launched an underground literary renaissance of black crime fiction through Holloway House in Los Angeles. In the twenty-first century, writers like Sister Souljah, Vickie M. Stricker, and Wahida Clark reimagined the style and content of Beck's pimp autobiography for a female audience, thus giving rise to "street fiction." Often self-published, and sold on street corner tables and online, street fiction is now one of the driving forces of the black book market, with hundreds (and perhaps even thousands) of titles by dozens of authors.

Beck invented the figure of the pimp that is now an ever-present fixture in hip-hop songs and videos. The first gangsta rappers, Ice-T and Ice Cube, chose their monikers in honor of Iceberg Slim, and they modeled their ultra-cool gangsta rap personas after the protagonist of *Pimp*. Jay-Z, the most successful rap mogul of all time (who even has connections to the White House), referred to himself as Iceberg Slim when he was getting his start as a rap artist. The comedian Dave Chappelle featured Iceberg Slim in his standup routines, calling *Pimp* the "capitalist manifesto." Chris Rock, at the wrap of every one of his movies, hands out copies of *Pimp* to all cast and crew members, telling them: "All the questions of life can be answered if you read this book." A paperback original that has been translated into a dozen languages and has never gone out of print, *Pimp* remains one of the most important pieces of American literature of the twentieth century, but one that is still widely overlooked by the American mainstream.

Beck's triumph with the publication of *Pimp* was overshadowed by the poverty and isolation in the final years of his life. At the height of the blaxploitation era of the 1970s—an era in part ushered in by white screenwriters who stole outright from *Pimp*—Beck enjoyed the public spotlight for a brief moment. In the dozen years following *Pimp*, he produced an impressive and influential canon: five novels, a short story collection, and an assortment of essays. He appeared on a variety of talk shows and was profiled in numerous newspaper and magazine articles. Anthropologists interviewed him for PhD dissertations on the world of the black pimp, and he served as narrator for documentaries on the dangers of street life. His second novel, *Trick Baby*, was made into a big budget film starring veteran actor Mel Stewart in 1972, and he even released a prototypical hip-hop album titled *Reflections* in 1976. In it, Beck delivers pimp toasts in his haunting baritone voice over the jazz stylings of the Red Holloway Quartet. Ice-T regularly cites this album as one of the main influences on his hip-hop style. Despite these successes, Beck could never quite cross over into the mainstream. He published solely with the same mass-market paperback press, and his books were not reviewed in any major publications. They could be found at liquor stores, newsstands, and barbershops, but were rarely sold at bookstores. They were marketed by the white owners of Holloway House as sensationalist pulp fiction, like blacked-up Harlequin romance novels or pulp detective magazines of the 1930s. In one of the many ironies of his life, Beck was ultimately pimped out by a literary industry that treated him and his works as a disposable commodity.

Beck's frustrations with his publishers finally drove him into hiding in the late 1970s. He stopped publishing his books, and he disappeared from public view altogether to write in solitude. He wrote two unpublished novels at the end of his life. The first was titled *Shetani's Sister*, which he composed in longhand and then gave the pages to Diane, who typed them up. Part pimp autobiography and part detective novel, *Shetani's Sister* was to be one of Beck's greatest triumphs of popular fiction. He didn't want Holloway House to publish the book, and he died before he could find another publisher. Diane promised him that she would never allow Holloway House to get its hands on it, so *Shetani's Sister* was locked away in a drawer for twenty years. The second novel was titled *Night Train to Sugar Hill*, which Beck dictated to Diane in the late 1980s after his eyes started to fail. A rougher manuscript than *Shetani's Sister*, *Night Train* is nonetheless a deeply personal reflection on Beck's own life. It is written from the perspective of an aging criminal, who, like the author, wants to document all of the good and bad things he has done in his life before he passes away. Beck copyrighted the manuscript in 1990 and then passed it over to his oldest daughter, Camille, telling her also not to allow Holloway House to publish it. She died of a drug overdose in 2010, and the book remains unpublished to this day.

For the last ten years of his life, Beck lived in seclusion in a second-floor studio apartment on Crenshaw Boulevard in South Central. Beck had lived with Diane early in their marriage, but as he got older, he just felt more comfortable living alone. After all the years living in solitary pimp pads and prison cells, he came to prefer the quiet seclusion of his tiny room on Crenshaw. His apartment had an east-facing picture window; from that vantage, he could look out at the happenings in the neighborhood. His daughters from his first marriage—Camille, Melody, and Misty—still visited him. Mike Tyson regularly came around seeking advice after he became heavyweight champion of the world. Despite the public perception that Tyson was a thug, he was actually a ravenous reader of philosophy and history, and he loved *Pimp*. He looked to Beck as a kind of surrogate father figure, and the aging pimp tried to advise him on money, women, and crafting a public persona. Diane would come down from her home in Silver Lake to bring him groceries and pick him up from doctor's appointments. She also drove him around South Los Angeles in his 1948 Lincoln Continental, the last relic of his days as a famous author. Even though he was in his seventies, people still recognized him on the street, and they ran up to the car to pay homage to the man they knew as Iceberg Slim.

To a wide range of readers—black entertainers, hip-hop artists, street fiction authors, prisoners, would-be hustlers, military personnel, and white hipsters—Iceberg Slim is the definitive voice of black urban life. To his critics—many feminists, the literary establishment, some Black Panther radicals, and much of mainstream America—Iceberg Slim is a misogynist who wrote trashy paperbacks that promote violence against vulnerable young women. Each of these conflicting outlooks has some truth to it. However, the real story of Beck's life is more complex and contradictory than either of these simplistic views suggests. He was a victim of sexual trauma, convict scholar, drug addict, Chicago pimp, bestselling author, father, and would-be revolutionary. His life story, which spans from the start of the Great Migration to the Rodney King Riots of 1992, provides a dark reflection of black America's urban development and decline in the twentieth century.

CHAPTER 1

CHILDHOOD (1918–1931)

The writer known as Iceberg Slim was born Robert Lee Moppins Jr. on August 4, 1918, in Chicago to Mary Brown and Robert Moppins Sr., two young newlyweds from Tennessee. Mary and Robert Sr. migrated from the Edgehill area in Nashville, a working-class neighborhood perched on the southern border of the infamous Black Bottom. Named for the thick mud, sewage, and stagnant water that covered the streets after floods from the Cumberland River, the Black Bottom was the first African American settlement in the city and a notorious slum. It was crowded with dilapidated houses, saloons, and brothels, and it lacked indoor toilet facilities. As many as six people crowded into the one-room flats that lined the streets, and most of these apartments were infested with rats. At the same time, the Black Bottom was one of the first thriving black urban communities of the South. It had an elementary school and a number of churches, including the important African Methodist Episcopal, St. Paul. The Black Bottom featured a city market, an ice-cream factory, a clothing store, and numerous black businesses. There were boat rides on the river and movies in the downtown theaters, and African Americans could attend circuses and plays put on by traveling acting troupes.[1]

Edgehill developed into a distinct neighborhood following the establishment of the Black Bottom, and residents there regarded themselves as respectable working-class blacks, socially and economically better off than their unruly neighbors in the poorer section. Many of the people who came to Edgehill were transplants from rural parts of Tennessee, including Beck's ancestors. Mary

Brown was born in March 1897, the second of six children, to Frank and Susan Brown.[2] Mary's parents were both born in Tennessee in the mid-1870s, and were themselves likely the children of former slaves. After Susan and Frank married sometime in their late teens, they lived in Giles County right in the center of Tennessee's declining sharecropping region. Frank worked as a farmhand—a job held by most African American men in this area—and he made around fifty cents a day working sunup to sundown. In the early 1900s, as the plantation system began to erode, Frank and Susan decided to move their growing family to Nashville. It was the destination of thousands of black migrants looking for work in the city's growing manufacturing sector. The Browns moved to 299 Eleventh Avenue on the northern border of Edgehill, and Frank got a job working as a laborer on the steam railroad.[3] Unlike many of the industries in Nashville, the three major railroad companies hired black workers regularly, though only as unskilled laborers. Skilled jobs, such as clerks and linemen, were reserved for whites. Nevertheless, railroad work paid better than sharecropping, and the family quickly became adjusted to their new community. Mary attended school, completing the tenth grade, and the family became members of the Bethel African Methodist Episcopal Church, the oldest and most important church in their neighborhood. They threw dinner parties, and their pastor, Reverend S. J. Howard, was a regular guest in their home.

Beck's father, Robert Sr., was born in 1897 just two months after Mary and grew up in Tullahoma, a railroad town in south-central Tennessee that once served as the headquarters for the Confederate Army. Records are incomplete and often dubious, but it appears that Robert moved to Nashville in his teens, perhaps by way of Buffalo, New York. He became a member of the Mid Frolic Social Club, one of the many black working-class social clubs that had emerged since the Civil War. Nashville's black elite had their own organizations, but black civic and party clubs for everyday people also existed in every black neighborhood in Nashville. They had names like the Housekeepers' Club, the North Pole Club, the We Mean Pleasure Club, and the Ladies' Thimble Club, and their proceedings were reported in the African American newspaper the *Nashville Globe*. The club season usually ran from winter until spring. Members attended formal dinners and played parlor games, and they lavishly decorated their homes for dances, and prayed and sang together.[4] At the end of each event, they usually served an ice course, which was fashionable during an era in which people lacked the means to refrigerate food.[5] Robert regularly attended club meetings.[6] He had an exceptionally good voice, and he opened and closed these proceedings with a song.[7]

Mary and Robert lived in the same neighborhood on the border between the Black Bottom and Edgehill, and they probably met either in church or at one of the clubs' social events. They married on September 19, 1917, to great fanfare. A family friend named Mrs. Murdix gave Mary a linen bridal shower, which received plenty of attention in the *Globe*'s society pages: "This enjoyable affair will always be remembered by those who attended the same. The parlor was beautifully decorated with sunflowers and honeysuckle vines. Delicious ices were served and games were played."[8] The couple took a honeymoon tour of the Eastern Seaboard, and they planned to settle down in Buffalo, New York. For some reason, they never made it to New York, but instead headed for Chicago.

In doing so, Mary and Robert joined what has since become known as the Great Migration. It was the largest voluntary migratory movement in America to that point, one that would dramatically change black America's social, political, and cultural lives in the twentieth century. Ultimately, six million blacks would leave the South over the course of six decades. It would change the very composition of the American city, and it would set the stage for the African American culture that served as the seedbed for such popular figures as Iceberg Slim. Mary and Robert, like other black migrants from this period, left the South for a variety of reasons. Working conditions in Nashville were less than ideal. Half of black men worked in menial labor positions or as wagon drivers, while half of black women labored in domestic service.[9] Blacks during this era grew up in what was called the "age of accommodationism," during which they were expected to surrender their civil rights to legalized segregation. Mary and Robert had been born only a year after the famous Supreme Court decision *Plessy v. Ferguson*, in which the court ruled that separate but equal public facilities did not violate the Constitution, nor did they violate the civil rights of black citizens. After this, legalized racial segregation was the rule of the land below the Mason-Dixon Line, and blacks were forced to conform to Jim Crow laws or risk imprisonment or even lynching. Jim Crow—a formalized racial caste system named after a cruelly stereotypical black character portrayed by antebellum white minstrel performers—had been created after the Civil War and Reconstruction, as state legislatures all across the South passed laws restricting the civil liberties of African Americans in housing, transportation, education, and every other area of social life. Under this arrangement, blacks were expected to accommodate white racist views of black social, political, and economic inferiority, and in return whites made some concessions, such as funding black trade schools. *Plessy v. Ferguson* gave these laws federal sanction, and there was little blacks could do except flee to states north of the Mason-Dixon Line. In Nashville, blacks who attempted to resist this racism were met with hostility and violence. They boycotted streetcars in 1905 in an effort to end segregation, though failed because black workers feared the retaliation of white employers. The Ku Klux Klan built a sizeable presence in Tennessee, publishing the *Klan Krusader* in Robert's hometown of Tullahoma, and they murdered a number of black citizens in Nashville.[10]

During World War I, Robert and Mary, along with tens of thousands of other African Americans, left the South for Chicago, lured by the promise of factory work and better living conditions. With white factory workers now serving in the military, and the flow of low wage–earning immigrants from Europe stemmed by the conflict overseas, blacks suddenly found themselves allowed into factories for the first time. Granted, they were often hired for the dirtiest and most dangerous jobs. They shoveled coal into hot furnaces, treated animal hides with lye, and cleaned up industrial waste. Nevertheless, in Chicago they earned higher wages in the meatpacking houses, rail yards, and steel mills than they could anywhere in the rural South. A typical wage in the sharecropping South was about fifty cents a day. In Chicago, a black worker could make as much as five dollars a day.

Chicago offered blacks better schools, voting rights, access to public facilities and black-owned amusements. Perhaps most important of all, in Chicago, blacks did not live under the constant threat of lynching. The immensely popular black newspaper the *Chicago Defender* played a central role in spurring the migration, extolling the virtues of the urban North and criticizing the violence of the Jim Crow South. Between 1916 and 1919 alone, between fifty thousand and seventy-five thousand African Americans settled in Chicago. Most of those rode the Illinois Central rail line up through the Mississippi Valley to Chicago, following the same route that escaping slaves had traveled on the Underground Railroad. They came to Chicago in droves, and the city quickly became known as "the promised land."[11]

But as migrants like Mary and Robert quickly discovered, Chicago was not quite the promised land. They moved to a tiny apartment at 2155 South LaSalle Street, in one of the oldest sections of a narrow strip of neighborhood known as the Black Belt.[12] Most black Chicagoans—85 percent of the one hundred thousand black inhabitants of the city—lived there. The Black Belt was a row of dilapidated tenements on Chicago's South Side, near the vice district and the railroad tracks that stretched from Twenty-Second Street to Fifty-Fifth Street. The borders of the ghetto were heavily policed by neighboring whites in a variety of ways. Real estate brokers, banks, and white homeowners entered into formal agreements—known as "restrictive covenants"—not to sell homes to blacks outside of the Black Belt. Between July 1917 and March 1921, white people bombed the homes of fifty-eight black families who tried to move out of the rectangular neighborhood, an average of about once every three weeks.[13] White violence against Chicago's black population spiraled out of control on July 27, 1919, as the city witnessed the most destructive race riot it had ever seen. After an African American teenager named Eugene Williams crossed the invisible but inviolable line separating black and white territory at the Twenty-Ninth Street beach along Lake Michigan, white youths stoned him to death. A policeman on the scene refused to arrest anyone for the crime. Whites and blacks started hurling rocks at one another, and the violence escalated quickly. By nightfall, gangs of white hooligans invaded the Black Belt with bricks and shotguns, killing black residents and lighting houses on fire. People were pulled from streetcars and horse-drawn carriages and beaten by angry mobs. The press on both sides of the color line exacerbated the conflict by reporting unconfirmed instances of racial violence. In an August 2 article, "Ghastly Deeds of Rioters Told," the *Chicago Defender* reported, "An unidentified man, young woman, and a three month old baby were found dead on the street at the intersection of 47th Street and Wentworth Avenue. She had attempted to board a car there when the mob seized her, beat her, slashed her body into ribbons and beat the baby's brains out against a telegraph pole. Not satisfied with this, one rioter severed her breasts and a white youngster bore it aloft on a pole, triumphantly, while the crowd hooted gleefully."[14] The riot went on for a week until the state militia finally stepped in and ended it. When the smoke finally cleared, thirty-eight people were dead, over five hundred injured, and a thousand people, most of them black, had been burned out of their homes.

Despite the racial violence and urban segregation, black Chicago also offered some of its citizens a world of prosperity and entertainment. With the exception of upper Manhattan, home of the Harlem Renaissance, Chicago's Black Belt was the most vibrant and prosperous African American community during the 1920s. There were black policemen and firemen, city and state officials, lawyers and doctors. Black Chicago was home to a number of banks, newspapers, and law firms, as well as dozens of grocery stores, restaurants, and funeral parlors. Before it would later move to Forty-Seventh Street, black social life centered on State Street, between Twenty-Sixth and Thirty-Ninth, in an area known as "the Stroll." This was just four blocks from where Mary and Robert lived. The great African American poet Langston Hughes described the scene in 1918, the year of Beck's birth: "South State Street was in its glory then, a teeming Negro street with colored theaters, restaurants, and cabarets. And excitement from noon to noon. Midnight was like day. The street was full of workers and gamblers, prostitutes, pimps, church folks, and sinners."[15]

In 1912, vice reform movements succeeded in closing down prostitution and gambling houses in red-light districts across the country, including Chicago. As the police cracked down on these illegal enterprises, vice moved into African American communities, where white police didn't bother to enforce the laws as strictly. Because blacks were excluded from most commercial amusements, such as dance halls and nightclubs, they created their own network of nightlife: taverns, gaming houses, cabarets, and so-called Black and Tan clubs, which were famous for catering to mixed-race couples as well as homosexuals, prostitutes, and other individuals not welcome in mainstream bars. Chicago in particular had a reputation for these underground clubs, which were focal points of public outrage. By 1920, the Black Belt housed more of the vice industries than any other section of Chicago, and by the late twenties, 80 percent of the prostitutes in Chicago were black.[16] One unintended result of the Great Migration and the reform movement was that many sex industries became predominantly African American enterprises during the formative years of America's modern urbanization.

Even when he was an infant, Beck's life was influenced by Chicago's prostitution and other vice rackets. When Robert and Mary arrived in Chicago, they found jobs in one of the hotel kitchens downtown. They couldn't save any money, however, as Robert's father was taken in by the neighborhood's glimmering underworld scene. Having been part of Nashville's upwardly mobile and respectable black working-class society, he had been, for the most part, shielded from these alluring and dangerous subcultures. According to Beck's memoir, "My idiot father had come to the city and gone sucker wild. He couldn't stay away from the high yellow [i.e., light-skinned] whores with their big asses and bitch-dog sexual antics. What they didn't con him out of he lost in the cheap crap joints."[17] Reportedly, Robert was also physically abusive. When Beck was a few months old, he suggested to Mary that they leave the infant on a church doorstep. "Mama naturally refused," Beck reported, "so he hurled me against the wall in disgust."[18]

Mary and Robert divorced shortly after this incident, and the young mother struck out on her own with her son. For the next few years, they moved around from city to city across the Midwest.

Mary found work wherever she could. She was determined to make sure that she and her son survived. She had dreams of him becoming a doctor or lawyer; this was the north, after all, and such things were now possible. She cooked and sewed for various white families. She was also a talented hairstylist, and she went door-to-door with her pressing irons and waving combs, drumming up work. She carried her son in her arms in a blanket, and while she flashed his face in a prospective customer's direction, she delivered her sales pitch. "Madam, I can make your hair curly and beautiful. Please give me a chance. For fifty cents, that's all, I will make your hair shine like new money."[19] Mary kept her son alive, and in the course of his early childhood, Beck formed a profoundly close bond with his mother, one that would shape his dynamic with women for the rest of his life.

In a range of writings and interviews he gave in the early 1970s, Beck theorized that it was the pimp's relationship to his mother that defined his approach to the profession. "The best pimps that I have known, that is the career pimps, the ones who could do twenty, maybe thirty years as a pimp, were utterly ruthless and brutal without compassion. They certainly had a basic hatred for women. My theory is . . . if we are to use the criteria of utter ruthlessness as a guide, that all of them hated their mothers. Perhaps more accurately, I would say that they've never known love and affection. I've known several dozen in fact that were dumped into trash bins when they were what? . . . only four or five days old."[20] Beck did not hate his mother as a child, unlike the successful pimps he so admired. His hatred for her emerged during his teenage years, when she abandoned his stepfather for a neighborhood hustler and betrayed the only stable family structure he would ever know.

Beck's first experience with sex also occurred during these early, volatile years. Mary worked all day at a laundry, and he was left with a babysitter. At about the age of three, he had what he later recalled as his first memory. After Mary left for work one day, the babysitter made him perform oral sex on her. "I remember more vividly the moist, odorous darkness and the bristle-like hairs tickling my face and most vividly I can remember my panic, when in the wild moment of her climax, she would savagely jerk my head tighter into the hairy maw."[21] The event deeply scarred Beck—as his hateful language suggests—and he later attributed his anxious and violent relationships with the women he pimped to this incident. He also conjectured that pimping provided him with temporary relief from the psychological distress he experienced as a result of the event. At the height of his career, he would intentionally draw upon his traumatic memories—especially of the babysitter, as well as of his mother's betrayal during his teenage years—to fuel his cruel treatment of his prostitutes. Even after years as a seasoned pimp, this memory of that first sexual abuse still had a grip on his psyche. "I thought about the first bitch who had Georgied [extracted sexual favors without paying money] me and how she had flim-flammed me out of my head. She would be old and gray now, but if I could find her I would sure get the bitch's unpaid account off my conscience."[22]

—

Despite his early ordeals, Beck had an otherwise happy childhood. In 1922, Mary married a man named Henry Upshaw. She was determined to raise Beck in a stable household, and although Henry wasn't particularly handsome or charming, he was the perfect model for the young boy. He owned a cleaning and pressing shop in Rockford, Illinois, a small industrial town about ninety miles west of Chicago. Henry married Mary and moved his new bride and son to 1123 Green Street near downtown Rockford. Beck's years with Henry were the most peaceful of his life. He described him in countless writings and interviews as the only father he ever knew and one of the only people he ever truly loved. "He fell instantly in love with my lissome beautiful mother," Beck remembered years later. "His name was Henry Upshaw, and I guess I fell as hard for him as he fell for Mama."[23]

Compared with Nashville's and Chicago's, Rockford's black community was small and scattered throughout the growing city. African Americans occupied a low rung on the social and economic ladder in town, a position to which they had been relegated since the city's founding. Two of the very first inhabitants of Rockford were Lewis

Lemon, a black slave, and Germanicus Kent, his owner. They started a settlement on the banks of the Rock River in 1835. Lemon later bought his freedom from Kent for eight hundred dollars and lived out the rest of his life as a farmer. During the late 1830s, a handful of ex-slaves migrated to Rockford and set up the city's first barbershops, barbering being one of the few professions that free black people were allowed to pursue in the pre–Civil War years. The first barbers were located on Madison Street, down along the waterfront in central downtown. The shops were ornate rooms with walnut floors, high ceilings, and metropolitan furnishings. One of the first black barbers of Rockford was Daniel Hale Williams, who later went on to perform one of the earliest open-heart surgeries in history. But barbering in Rockford was taken over by whites by the turn of the century, as African Americans were increasingly pressured into unskilled and domestic work in the town's competitive job market.[24]

During World War I, Rockford's manufacturing sector grew with the production of furniture, knitting, and farm implements. For whites, Rockford gained a reputation as a peaceful midwestern town where people could find good jobs. Rockford blacks, on the other hand, were restricted mostly to unskilled labor and domestic service jobs. According to the 1930 census, only a handful of the black community owned businesses in town. Resentment toward blacks grew over the course of the Great Migration. White ethnic groups regularly committed violence against African Americans, and in 1918 a riot erupted between blacks and Italians. The Ku Klux Klan opened a local chapter in Rockford at about the time Henry moved his new bride and stepson to the city. The Klan hosted several rallies throughout the 1920s in Rockford. They were held on the Fourth of July, and they attracted crowds of thirty to fifty thousand people. It is little wonder, then, that the black population in Rockford grew slowly compared to the general population and to black populations in other cities. Between 1920 and 1930, the black population doubled, but the total was still relatively small; it grew from 490 to 1,010 people, while the city's population as a whole grew from 65,000 to 85,000 during that same time. By 1930, blacks still made up only 1 percent of the total population. The Irish, Italians, and Swedes far outnumbered blacks and asserted their racial superiority by subordinating them in labor as well as housing. Unlike African Americans in Chicago, who were concentrated in the tight-knit community of the Black Belt, blacks in Rockford were spread throughout the city, dispersed into small pockets by white hostilities.[25]

Within the confines of this environment, though, Henry Upshaw was a respected businessman and leader of the black community. He was born November 16, 1891, in Trenton, Tennessee, the second youngest of five brothers.[26] In 1893, his father, Berry, and his mother, Minerva, moved the family to Rockford, among some of the first African Americans to come to the growing town. Henry's father got work in the sawmill, and over the years the family became an essential part of Rockford. During World War I, Henry's brother Samuel was given a hero's parade as he walked down to the train station to ship off for war. Likewise, Henry was industrious and worked steadily to improve himself. He completed high school, and during his early twenties he worked as a laborer in a box factory and as a baggage man at a hotel. In 1920, he opened Royal Cleaning and Pressing Shop at 110½ Church Street; the shop was modest, but Henry was full owner. The first ads for the business appeared in the *Rockford Republic* on September 18, 1920. They stated simply: "Altering and repairing for ladies and gentlemen. Work called for and delivered."[27] By 1925, Henry had opened a second laundry called Forest City Cleaners at 315 South Main Street, across from the Nelson Café in downtown Rockford.[28] The shop was the only black-owned business in the downtown area.

Henry was also active in community events and organizations. He contributed money to the efforts to revitalize the downtown business section.[29] In the early 1920s, the papers reported that he and other local black leaders met to consider solutions to the housing shortage for black residents. "A number of Colored citizens of the city met at the headquarters of the local Colored branch of the American Legion for the purpose of discussing ways and means of bettering the housing conditions of the Colored population already here and to properly house who may come in from time to time."[30] In this meeting, they resolved to build and purchase apartments to provide housing for blacks coming in to Rockford. Henry also promoted leisure activities to build a sense of community. In March 1922, he and his younger brother Samuel helped establish the Lincoln Athletic Club. A month later, they announced that they would put a colored baseball team in the field, which would practice at South Rockford Park. Henry was elected captain of the team.[31]

Mary also rose to social prominence during these years in Rockford. She was the president and chairman of many clubs, including the Missionary Society of the Allen Chapel, the first black church in Rockford. The church was established in 1892 and began with only seven members. In 1917, they erected a larger building, replacing the stone house that sat on the property. By 1927, Mary had become a leader in the church. She sponsored society parties,[32] represented her church at national conventions,[33] and hosted political debates concerning the future black vote.[34] Mary was also a major proponent of outreach and charity, working with the Nora F. Taylor Missionary Society to sponsor dinners at her home and her church. During Christmas of 1929, at the beginning of the Great Depression, she put on a charity dinner at the church. In the *Daily Register Gazette*, Mary placed an announcement encouraging people of all races to attend. "All needy people are invited, regardless of race, to the dinner which is free. A special invitation is extended to children."[35] Mary Upshaw was in fact so well loved in the community that when her father, Frank Brown, died in 1931, the local paper reported on her trip home.[36]

In this stable, middle-class environment, Beck was the most content he would be in his whole life. "Henry treated Mama like she was a princess. Anything she wanted, he got for her. She was a fashion plate all right. Every Sunday when we all three went to church in the gleaming black Dodge, we were outstanding as we walked down the aisle in our fresh neat clothing. Only the few Negro lawyers lived as well, looked as well. Mama was the president of several civic clubs. For the first time, we were living the good life."[37] Within the structures of family, church, and school, Beck was a happy and industrious child. He worked with his father in the pressing shop during the summer, and he joined the Boy Scouts at his school. He dreamed of one day owning a pony that for some reason he wanted to call Bo Mee. There are few records of Beck's performance in school, but the ones that do survive suggest he was a good student in his preteen years. He went to Barbour Elementary School and then transferred to the Theodore Roosevelt Junior High School starting in January 1931. Although his IQ was measured at only 97 on the National Intelligence Test, which is about average, he scored a B minus in Scholarship, a B in Social, and an A in Physical.[38] At Roosevelt, Beck was among the thirteen best male spellers in the seventh- and eighth-grade classes at the semifinal intraschool spelling contest.[39] As far as everyone was concerned, young Beck was developing into an influential young member of the community, just like his mother and stepfather. "My reputation coming up before I got street poisoned—all of my mother's friends [and] all of my mother's and father's associates—They all thought I was the most charming, the sweetest. They use to talk about, 'Oh your son is so sweet. Oh he is such a gentleman.' "[40]

During this period, Beck even reestablished a relationship with his father, who worked in Chicago as a chef for the mayor, "Big Bill" Thompson. Considered by some to be one of the most corrupt politicians in history, Thompson served as mayor from 1915 to 1923 and then again from 1927 to 1931. He was known for his affinity for bribes and for his connections to organized crime bosses, such as Al Capone. He was also famous for his spectacular political stunts, such as staging an election debate between himself and two live rats (who were supposed to represent his opponents), and he organized an expedition to the South Seas to search for a mythical tree-climbing fish. He was also an accomplished yachtsman, who had won boating competitions and served as the commodore for the Associated Yacht Club.[41]

Toward the end of his second term, Thompson spent a lot more time on his yacht entertaining guests, and it was then that Robert Sr. worked aboard the ship. Young Beck visited his father at times there, and he later remembered a moment that stood out above the rest. While Robert Sr. was preparing dinner for the guests, Thompson stumbled drunkenly into the galley, shouting that the meal was late, and he even shoved Robert Sr. Rather than cowering before these threats, Robert Sr. did something his son did not expect. "And then you, Papa, nigger from a plantation outside Nashville, Tennessee, had the courage, had enough raw heroism left in your battered black balls to clench your fists and scream out to the feared Croesus of Chicago's corruption and crime, 'Don't you never put your hands on me, sonuvabitch. Don't you never call me no boy. You get your big fat red ass out of my kitchen before I go plumb crazy and whale the shit outta' you.'"[42] Much to Beck's shock, Thompson merely laughed at the threat and retreated from the kitchen. Although Beck, when he became a pimp, would maintain an infrequent relationship with his father, this early experience made a powerful impression on him. Forty years later, he reflected that this was one of the cornerstones of his radical political views, as well as of his lifelong abhorrence of white power structures. "For on that occasion and at that shining moment," Beck wrote, "the jewels of your manhood coruscated in a star burst of pride and courage that was, in that ultra-repressive era and circumstance, the purest heroism."[43]

The end of Beck's childhood and the beginning of his life of crime coincided with his first encounter with pimps. In 1930, his mother opened a beauty shop on Winnebago Street called the Vole Bura Beauty Parlor; the name is based on a Romanian word for a type of flowering weed from Europe.[44] The business was a gift from Henry, and the interiors recalled the luxurious black barbershops of antebellum Rockford. It was meant to be an extension of Henry and Mary's social and economic success in the community, a visible symbol of their business and personal partnership. Instead, it became the starting point for Beck's pursuit of criminal notoriety. As he remembered it, "It was a four stall, opulent beauty shop. Its chrome gleamed in the black-and-gold motif. It was located in the heart of the Negro business section and it flourished from the moment its doors opened. Her clientele was for the most part whores, pimps, and hustlers from the sprawling red-light district in Rockford. They were the only ones who always had the money to spend on their appearance."[45] Growing up under the supervision of Henry and his mother, Beck had never seen pimps and prostitutes before. He was mesmerized by their flashy clothes and their jewelry. At his first sight of the only black people he had ever witnessed so flamboyantly styled, he decided he wanted to become a pimp. "The first phases of my own street poisoning happened when I was a boy. My mother had a beauty shop and she catered to a colony of black hookers and pimps. And these fellows would be decked out in all their finery with all their diamonds and all the rest of them and of course their women. And I was so impressed. The options for young black people at that time were not the way they are now to get some of the so-called finer things of life. So I just started admiring these fellows. And ultimately, I wanted to become a pimp, so I could have all these beautiful clothes and the diamonds and the women. You know, groups of women. And that's how I got street poisoned."[46] As a teenager, Beck started to notice the poverty and lack of opportunities in the black community around him. Although Henry provided him with a model of hard work and respectability, pimps seemed to offer an easy and glamorous pathway to money and power. Legitimate work for a black man during the early 1930s was becoming even more limited with the onset of the Depression, and Beck was increasingly turned off by his available choices. "The chances were so narrow. Your opportunity was so narrow. You either had to be a doctor or a lawyer or a successful businessman. That was it. Otherwise you could be a maintenance man, could be a shoe shiner, a porter or a pants presser and the like."[47]

In the fall of 1931, just before Beck's eighth-grade year was about to begin, Mary made a decision that would forever change her son's life. She fell for one of the smooth-talking hustlers from her beauty shop, a man Beck names "Steve" in his autobiography. Much like her son, Mary was bewitched by the counterfeit glamour and dangerous charm of the street criminal. She made the fateful choice to leave Henry and follow Steve to Milwaukee. On September 15, Mary withdrew her son from Theodore Roosevelt Junior High School and had his records sent to Chicago. Beck would never make it to the Chicago public schools, and he would remain absent from any school for three more years. Years later he remembered the final good-bye between his mother and Henry. For him, that last scene signaled his mother's ultimate betrayal of Henry and the life they had built as a family. "Henry fell down on his knees and bawled like a scalded child pleading with Mama not to leave him, begging her to stay. He had welded his arms around her legs, his voice hoarse in anguish as he whimpered his love for us. I will never forget her face, cold as an executioner's, which she was, as she kicked and struggled loose from him."[48] Henry was so hysterical, Beck thought, "in his state she was lucky he didn't kill her and me, and bury us in the back yard."[49]

Although Beck claimed in *Pimp* that his stepfather died of a broken heart a year after, in truth, Henry eventually got over the loss of Mary and her son. He remarried a few years later to a woman named Ruth, sixteen years his junior. In 1935, they moved to Metropolis, a small town deep in the southern part of Illinois. He moved his cleaning and pressing shop there and worked in the laundry profession for the next two decades. He remained an active member of his Presbyterian church, hosting community events like ice-cream socials with his wife until he died from an injury he sustained in his pressing shop in 1954. Until the end, Henry was a respected and beloved member of the communities where he had lived. Weeks after his death, his family posted the following announcement in the newspaper: "The Henry Upshaw family of Metropolis and Rockford, Illinois wishes to thank their friends for florals, telegrams, and cards received during our bereavement."[50] Despite the monumental loss of Mary and Beck, Henry had managed to carve out a happy life following their departure.

However, Beck's hopes for this kind of normal life were over. He was on his way to Milwaukee, where he would enter the world of street crime. Never again would he look to his mother as a stable source of trust and support. "Somehow after that cross Mama just didn't seem like the same honest sweet Mama that I had prayed in church with back in Rockford."[51] Mary's fateful decision to leave the secure life in Rockford with Henry was a tragic one for her son, as this motivated him even further to adopt the lifestyle of the pimp. For just as she was seduced by the toxic charms of the well-dressed player, so too would the impressionable Beck fall victim to the spell of the pimp in Milwaukee's vice district. Separated from

Henry's positive influence, and without formal schooling to keep him grounded, Beck would turn to the streets of Milwaukee's red-light district for his education during his teenage years. Ironically, or perhaps quite logically, he looked to pimping as a creative outlet in the face of a home life shattered by a gambler and street hustler. Reflecting on this choice many years later, Beck remarked: "I only wish I had understood my potential when I was younger and channeled my energies into more constructive areas. I was actually much quicker in multiple areas when I was younger, because my mind was unfettered with criminal intent. You see, when a young individual has not become street poisoned—in other words, he has not devoted all his intellectual energies to becoming a pimp, for instance, or to becoming a stuck-up man—then he can use his mind constructively. But, when a young mind has become street poisoned, the individual can think of nothing else but his own particular chosen criminal pursuit."[52] "Street poisoned" was the term Beck used again and again in his writings and interviews to describe this critical transition moment from childhood to young adulthood. In the teenage years to come, he would find perverse comfort on the street corners and in the alleyways of Milwaukee's Bronzeville, and these experiences would lay the foundation for a lifetime pursuit of pimping.

CHAPTER 2

EDUCATION (1931–1937)

When Beck arrived in Milwaukee in the fall of 1931 with Mary and Steve, he was deeply depressed. Everything that he had ever known and cared for—his church, school, home, and family—was gone. For the next year, he and his mother rented a house with Steve. Beck remembered him as an absolute maniac. Mary worked as a cook, leaving Beck home alone with him. Steve was an alcoholic and a compulsive gambler, who lost their furniture piece by piece in crap games. He frequently threatened Beck, telling him, "You little mother-fucker, you. I'm going to beat your mother-fucking ass. I am telling you, if you don't run away, I'm going to kill you."[1] Beck claimed that Steve even killed his kitten one day, smashing its head against the concrete steps behind their house. At first Mary ignored the warning signs. She was in love, and she also felt guilty for taking her son away from Henry. These two conflicting emotions created an emotional impasse, so she simply closed her eyes to the impending danger. According to Beck, it was in August 1932 that Steve sent Mary to the hospital with a broken jaw. He disappeared after that, and Mary finally came to terms with her mistake. "As worthless as that bastard was otherwise, he sure must have been a son-of-a-bitch in bed," Beck stated years later. "After all he had done to us, she still had a terrible itch for the bastard. That beating was good for her. It cured the itch."[2] Beck and Mary were free from Steve, but they were on their own again in a new city. They couldn't go back to Rockford; it was too late. In an attempt to start over, Mary and her son started going by the last name "Maupins," an altered version of Beck's surname. They rented a hotel room in Milwaukee's small black neighborhood, and it was here that Beck would make his first entrance into the criminal underworld. Although it might seem counterintuitive, Steve's cruelty and violence would prove powerful motivators to the young Beck. In an unjust system where good men like Henry were abandoned and forgotten, while hustlers like Steve bullied their way through life, Beck emulated the man who refused to be victimized by a corrupt world. He would ultimately become an abusive man himself in the decades to come, and he did so in response to the traumas he had experienced on a daily basis during his formative years.

Milwaukee was a booming metropolis compared to the tiny Rockford. Once known as "The Machine Shop of the World," Milwaukee was the second-largest industrial city in the United States during the early twentieth century. It was a factory city of foreign-born European immigrants who came to work in the numerous tanneries, meatpacking plants, and steel and iron industries. Milwaukee had the largest wheat market and hide-tanning center in the world. Miller, Pabst, and Schlitz established it as the beer capital of the United States, and prolific machine shops and foundries supported a massive metal fabrication industry. Companies like Harley-Davidson, Allis Chalmers, and A. O. Smith made bicycles, machine parts, engines, and motorcycles.[3] During the Great Migration, blacks arrived from the South seeking work. Black women were refused entry into factory jobs altogether; they mostly ended up in low-paying and unstable domestic work. Black men were allowed in factories, but they worked in the dirtiest, lowest-paying, and most dangerous jobs. They fed blast furnaces in steel foundries. In meatpacking factories they slaughtered animals, while in the tanneries they burned hair from hides using lime. Racism in the factories extended from rank-and-file management staff to the white industrial workers of Milwaukee's unions. Blacks were the most susceptible to layoffs, and industrialists often used them as scabs in an attempt to weaken the unions. During a strike at the Wehr Steel mill, the police were called in by management to protect black strikebreakers. Instead, they helped white workers attack blacks. According to official reports, "Police had been summoned to protect those who cared to enter but in turn joined in with the strikers in overturning an automobile filled with Negro workers."[4] Despite these numerous dangers, African Americans still came to Milwaukee for the generous wages that were impossible to earn in the South.

Milwaukee's black community was small compared to that of other major northern cities. Because of Milwaukee's proximity to Chicago, many migrants simply ended their journey at the Windy City, rather than travel another ninety miles to the north. They also headed to Detroit, where the Ford auto plant had exceptionally tolerant policies on hiring black workers. In 1930, Milwaukee had a black population of only 7,500 people out of nearly 580,000, a little over 1 percent. Although not a large black city, Milwaukee was still similar to Chicago, New York, Philadelphia, Cleveland, and other major Great Migration destinations in many ways. It had a sharply defined and heavily regulated Black Belt, albeit on a smaller scale. When blacks began arriving in Milwaukee in larger numbers in the 1920s, the city's white business and civic institutions joined together to maintain strict control over growth of the black neighborhood. The Milwaukee Real Estate Board met in 1924 and vowed to establish policies to promote the creation and maintenance of a Black Belt. As in Chicago, restrictive covenants were widely used by homeowners and real estate agents alike. They prohibited the sale, lease, or occupancy of property "to any person other than of the white race." A full 90 percent of housing deeds filed with the county after 1910 had some kind of language prohibiting sales to black buyers. Banks refused to lend to black customers seeking a loan for a house outside the Black Belt. By the time Beck and his mother moved to Milwaukee, an astonishing 97 percent of black people lived in the northern Near Downtown district, an area sixteen blocks long and eight blocks wide. During the Depression, nearly every black person lived in a neighborhood bordered by Highland Avenue to the south and North Avenue to the north, Third Avenue to the east and Twelfth Avenue to the west.

The conditions of the neighborhood were deplorable. The buildings were located in the oldest part of the city's original settlement, and most of the largely derelict housing had been built before the turn of the century. Only about 1 percent of blacks owned their own homes; the rest rented, and were at the mercy of unscrupulous landlords, who let the properties fall into ruin. Racism was common among white landlords, who believed that blacks "were quite careless and in many instances very destructive and made no effort to beautify the homes in which they lived."[5] In reality, most of the properties suffered a range of structural problems that absentee landlords neglected to fix: standing water in basements, broken and unserviced furnaces, leaky roofs, and rat infestations. Because of these problems, African Americans were more susceptible to disease, higher infant mortality rates, and death. There were a total of fifteen junkyards throughout the Black Belt, which gave off an intolerable stench, especially during hot and humid summer days.[6] In the 1920s, the neighborhood was officially designated a "slum district" by the Mayor's Housing Commission after the agency deemed two-thirds of the housing "unfit" for human habitation. These conditions only worsened in the 1930s, as whites policed the borders of the Black Belt.

But even while facing these issues—substandard housing, dangerous work conditions, and an atmosphere of racism—black Milwaukee still managed to flourish as a new kind of urban community. Walnut Street became the main stroll during the 1920s. It was disparagingly called "Chocolate Avenue" by whites, but for its black citizens it was *the* scene. Blacks owned dozens of businesses along this corridor, including garages, barbershops, beauty parlors, storefront churches, dentists' clinics, doctors' offices, boarding houses, moving companies, bars and restaurants. The black-owned Columbia Building and Loan Association, started by Wilbur Halyard and his wife, Ardie, in 1924, financed many of these businesses. It served as the backbone of black Milwaukee's economic development during the 1920s and '30s, providing low-interest loans for small business owners. The neighborhood featured a National Urban League chapter, which offered a free employment service; a day nursery; health education; and classes in black history, art, and drama. There was a local chapter of the NAACP, a Negro Professional and Business Men's League, and a Black Chamber of Commerce, dedicated to black economic growth. Barred from white social clubs, black Milwaukeeans created a number of their own, including the Elks Club, Dramatic Club, the Cream City Medical Society, the Chatterboxes, the Flamingoes, the Top Hat Club, and the Variety Boys.[7] They had their own newspaper, *The Blade*, which advocated on behalf of black businesses and black citizens. Like their Chicago neighbors, black Milwaukeeans named their city Bronzeville to commemorate an emerging black pride in their modern urban community.[8]

Bronzeville featured many forms of entertainment for its inhabitants. Because blacks were excluded from white spaces of leisure—theaters, amusement parks, taverns, dance halls—they created their own institutions within the borders of Bronzeville. The Booker T. Washington Center held formal dances for high school students, while the Columbia Theater on Walnut Street accommodated black audiences. Just down the street, the Regal Theater—known as "the flicks"—became a popular hangout for teenagers. On the weekends, people could spend nearly the entire day at the theater, watching a triple feature of cartoons, westerns, and serial adventure stories. In 1938, African American attorney James Dorsey purchased the Regal and turned it into a centerpiece of Walnut Street. He hung a new marquee over the sidewalk, and installed matching red velvet curtains and carpeting in the interior. On Friday and Saturday nights, local talent held jitterbug contests and piano shows. Jazz clubs—venues such as the Flame, the Plantation Club, the Blue Room, and the 711 Club—dominated the musical scene in Bronzeville. The Metropole was the first jazz club in Milwaukee, springing up in the late 1920s. The Moon Glow opened in 1930 and commanded the top spot in Milwaukee until 1936, when the Congo Club became the place to be seen in. The Congo Club was the classiest of them all; the establishment had a doorman, hatcheck girl, and headwaiter. The popular group Tommy Fox and His Clever Little Foxes was the top billing at the club, drawing large crowds.[9] Over time, the African American district of Milwaukee earned the nickname "little Harlem."

Mary and her son scraped out a living in this new city. It was the Great Depression, and the black population in particular struggled during this economic downturn. Half of black Milwaukeeans were unemployed during the Depression, which was three times the percentage of unemployed whites. Further, one third of the African Americans were on government relief, compared to only 2 percent of whites.[10] Once a month, Beck and his mother walked a few blocks down Galena Street to the relief station, where they filled a gunnysack with a month's worth of potatoes, prunes, and onions. It was a haunting scene for the young Beck. "Tattered paupers filed past the cubicles. Anemic joy lit their drawn faces as bored county clerks shoved a month's ration of relief groceries across the dusty cubicle counters. They would eagerly fill their gunny sacks and shuffle away to the street with their treasures." Although he was a bit embarrassed by their poverty, Mary told him to carry himself with a sense of pride, even in the face of destitution. "We'd be on our way to a gigantic barn-like building. Mama would always proudly square her shoulders before she stepped inside. When our turn came, Mama would hold her chin high in the manner of a queen accepting gifts from her subjects."[11]

Mary continued to work long hours as a cook to support the family, and Beck spent his free time exploring the thrilling new terrain around him. He was a teenager now, and he felt drawn to the rebelliousness and swank style of the neighborhood pimps and hustlers. He often sat in his room or up in the attic of his house and spied on them as they made the rounds. "We lived across the street from a 'ho house. I'd sit in my room and watch the pimps, in silk shirts and yellow toothpick shoes, come to get their money with satchels. Damn! I'd get excited when they'd pack their hoes into Duesenbergs, Lincolns, and Caddies and cruise away on joy rides. I ached to be a pimp."[12] Beck found Bronzeville exhilarating, and he wanted to be part of it, to escape the oppressive poverty of his everyday life. His mother had warned him many times to stay out of the streets, so he simply waited until she went to work and then ventured out. He loitered outside of bars and pool halls, and he learned how to play craps in the alleys. He was fascinated by the street theater acted out by local hoodlums and drunks. The most well known of these forms was "playing the dozens," a type of verbal combat in which two opponents insult each other's family members (especially their mothers) in the most creative and vulgar ways possible. Playing the dozens privileges outrageous humor, clever turns of phrase, and raunchy poetics, and Beck loved listening to this game. He had a knack for memorization, and he began stashing away the dirty ditties in his mental bank. "Your mama is a freakish bitch that hasta crap in a ditch 'cause she humped a railroad switch." "Your raw ass mammy had bad luck. That drunk bitch got platoon raped in an army truck."[13] His favorite street game, however, was "Mock Murder." In this performance, opponents pretended to fight each other with blades and guns until one man was dead. For Beck, it was electrifying and a little bit dangerous. "I'd watch old drunk buddies horse around down on the sidewalk in front of Steve's Bar. Even though it was almost always drunken play, it was still exciting to see their knives and pistols flashing under the street lamps. I guess it was so exciting because at first I couldn't ever be sure that it wasn't for real. Let me tell you, when those savage pranksters bared their teeth and rolled their eyes in fake madness it was hard to tell. Often one of the phony victims would flop around on the sidewalk like a dying chicken."[14]

Beck's entrance into Milwaukee's criminal underworld began a new era in his life. Mary tried to convince him to return to being the dutiful son he had been in Rockford. She herself started going to church again, and she made a promise never to go anywhere near a character like Steve again. Beck remained unmoved. He had found a new outlet for his inquisitive mind, and that was the street. "Mama was desperate to save at least fragments of her image, to hold fast the love and respect I had for her in Rockford. I had seen too much, had suffered too much. The jungle had started to embalm me with bitterness and hardness. I was losing the fine rules of thought and deed I had learned in church, from Henry, from the Boy Scout Troop in Rockford. I was sopping up poison from the street like a sponge."[15] Mary had many aspirations for him, and it is unclear why she didn't insist that he go to school during this period. Perhaps she still felt guilty about leaving Rockford and decided not to press the issue. Perhaps in Bronzeville's stimulating urban scene, she simply couldn't control him anymore. In any case, Beck decided not to go back to school, and Mary appears to have been powerless to do anything about it. Instead, he began spending all of his spare time in the streets.

Beck cultivated relationships with many outlaw mentors throughout his lifetime, but the first was a small-time con artist he calls Joe "Party Time" Evans in his autobiography: "The slide was greased. I started by long plunge to the very bottom of the grim pit. I guess my trip downward really was cinched when I met a petty hustler who was really likeable and we became pals."[16] An exhaustive search of prison files, city directories, and other records turned up no evidence of anyone named Joe Evans. However, it is still likely that he was a real person. Beck used pseudonyms in his autobiography in order to conceal the identity of anyone he knew from the old life. There was a code of protecting anonymity among criminals and con artists, and he took this code seriously. Furthermore, one of the consistent patterns of Beck's life is that he was always seeking out surrogate father figures. With the almost total absence of his biological father and the loss of Henry, Beck again and again reached out to older male role models in the criminal life. They served the dual purpose of teaching him the rules of their world and fulfilling his emotional need for fatherly affection. It is likely Beck started this search as early as fourteen, right after Steve's departure. Until the end of his life, Beck carried a picture of himself at about the age of fifteen with a companion he always claimed was Party Time. In the photo, they are both wearing black wool suits and staring at the camera with a look of cool indifference. Beck sports a pencil mustache, looking a bit like Clark Gable, while his friend wears a pair of sunglasses that appear to be aviator specs. They look like two aspiring con artists, testing out the stylistic flourishes of the hustler for the first time. "Joe was likeable and I was hungry for a pal," Beck recalled later. "He had a head full of wild risky hustles he wanted to try. He needed a partner. He tried all of them on me for size."[17]

Joe introduced Beck to the world of grift and con, or at least as much as he knew of it. He usually set up in Milwaukee's vice district, located south of Walnut Street near Seventh Avenue. He mainly targeted white people who were slumming there. He frequented the Black and Tan clubs—the speakeasies that allowed interracial dancing and dating—and he skimmed money from white women in exchange for sex. He robbed white men who came in from the outlying neighborhoods to find prostitutes. This was easy to do, as the neighborhood was flooded with white men on the weekends. Beck described the scene as lousy with white suckers: "The vice section was overrun with Johns. It seemed like every white man in town was out there, scratch in one hand and rod in the other, ripping and running after the black whores with the widest, blackest asses."[18] Joe's favorite swindle was the Murphy. Beck learned much later that "Real Murphy players use great finesse to separate a mark from his scratch. The most adept of them prefer that a trick hit on them. It puts the Murphy player in a position to force the sucker to 'qualify' [or prove] himself and to trim the mark not only for all of his scratch, but his jewelry as well."[19]

The sophisticated version of the con goes like this: The Murphy man sets up in the heart of a red-light district. When a white mark approaches him looking for a prostitute, the Murphy man delivers a prepared speech designed to hook the mark. "I know a fabulous hot house not more than two blocks away. Brother, you ain't never seen more beautiful, freakier broads than are in that house. One of them, the prettiest one, can do more with a swipe [penis] than a monkey can do with a banana."[20] While steering the mark to a respectable-looking apartment building, the Murphy man uses the white man's own racism to distract him from the swindle. He tells him: "The house don't have nothing but high-class white men coming to [it]. No Niggers or poor white trash. You know, doctors, lawyers, big-shot politicians. You look like a clean-cut white man, but you ain't in that league are you?"[21] By challenging the white man's sense of racial superiority, the Murphy man pricks his ego. The mark, in turn, ignores the signs that this is a double-cross; the con works precisely because of the mark's own deeply held prejudice toward blacks. He is blinded by two things: "First his desperate need to relieve himself into a black body, the second was his complete inability to conceive that the black boy before him was intelligent enough to fool him, to fashion the Murphy dialogue."[22] In the lobby of the dummy whorehouse, the Murphy man finally separates the mark from his valuables. He produces an official-looking envelope, and he insists that the mark check all of his loot. Prostitutes are known thieves, the Murphy man would tell him, and the mark should check his valuables or potentially lose them. "Only fools trusted whores, right?" the Murphy man would challenge. "The mark wasn't a fool, right? Right!"[23] In the ideal scenario, the mark hands over all his money and jewelry to the Murphy man. He walks away thinking the Murphy man has done him a favor.

Beck would learn this sophisticated version of the Murphy later in life, in Chicago in his twenties, and would immortalize this underworld scene of the short con in his first work of fiction, *Trick Baby*. Beck would only later realize, "I didn't know [Joe's] version was crude and dangerous, and only a weak imitation of the real Murphy."[24] Beck and Joe set up their con in the vice district. Beck dressed in a red cotton dress, red satin shoes, and a scraggly wig. While he stood at one end of an alley "aping a whore's stance," Joe steered the mark to the other end of the alley and collected his fee. When the mark got halfway between the two con men, they disappeared in opposite directions and met up elsewhere to split the take. It was a dangerous game they were running, but Beck felt a brotherhood in this partnership. In reality, Joe was not a sophisticated con man. He was a talented talker, and Beck was drawn mostly to his boasts and toasts. After a big score, Joe liked to brag at the local bar, "All right you poor ass bastards, it's party time and Joe Evans is in port with enough scratch to burn up a wet elephant. All you studs stop playing stink finger with these long-cock whores and everybody belly up to the log and get twisted on me."[25] To Beck's inexperienced ears, these ditties seemed like epic poems, much like the dozens he heard in the streets. He hung out with Joe in order to soak up all the street knowledge that he could.

During his teenage years in Milwaukee, Beck was arrested half a dozen times for charges ranging from larceny to immoral conduct. In 1932, he had his first encounter with the law when he was picked up for suspicion of rape. He was only thirteen or fourteen. He was held for a day and questioned, but admitted to nothing and was finally released. Beck later confessed in his memoir that during this period he was becoming reckless and violent. He was already over six feet tall, thin, and he had a handsome face. With his good looks and some slick dialogue he had picked up in the streets, he proved irresistible to many of the young women in the neighborhood. Beck wanted to have sex with all of them: "Dangerously, I was frantic to sock it into every young girl weak enough to go for it. I had to run for my life one evening when an enraged father caught me on the back porch punching animal-like astraddle his daughter's head. I had become impatient with the unusual thickness of her maidenhead."[26] Beck acted on his aggressive impulses in other ways as well. On November 3, 1933, he climbed up into the attic of his house with a BB rifle. He had gotten it as a gift from a friend of his mother. Normally, Beck used it to kill the vermin who lived in his neighborhood. "I enjoyed blasting the brains of hunchback rats nesting in our cellar."[27] But on this day in early November, Beck took aim at his neighbor's windows and shot them out. He was arrested and reprimanded, but the police released him after he finally surrendered the gun.[28] More and more, Beck was lashing out, and his mother saw this as a sign that she needed to take action.

After the shooting incident, Mary moved with her son to the outskirts of the Black Belt at 1705 North Fifteenth Street. She hoped that, away from the gambling joints and street corners, he might stay out of trouble. She redoubled her efforts to get him to go back to school. Beck felt guilty for the pain he had caused his mother on account of his arrests, so in the fall of 1934, he begrudgingly decided to give school a chance. On September 20, 1934, he started his first and only year of high school at the age of sixteen, at Lincoln High School.[29] Although Beck claimed at various points to have attended four years of high school, all the records I uncovered indicate that he went but a single year. There were six high schools in Milwaukee at the time: Riverside East, West Division, North Division, South Division, Bay View, and Lincoln High School, and only Lincoln shows records of his attendance. Located three miles across town from home, and over the Milwaukee River, Lincoln High School might as well have been on another planet. Beck was one of just a few black students, and although he had attended a predominantly white school before in Rockford, the divide between whites and blacks in Milwaukee no doubt felt sharper to him. Like all the other high schools in Milwaukee, Lincoln was an intensive college preparatory institution with a focus on classic liberal arts education. Only scraps of Beck's school records still exist, but they indicate that he struggled in this academic environment. His elective records show that he passed just one course, Commercial Arithmetic, with a 70 percent. He scored a 60 in Physical Training, a 50 in both Mechanical Drawing and English, and a 45 in Citizenship.[30] This is a far cry from the 98.5 average that Beck always claimed to have graduated with. To complicate matters further, he again received an average score on the National Intelligence Test while attending Lincoln (a 103 this time). That his school grades were so low but his intelligence was relatively average suggests that he never applied himself in the classroom. He had spent two years learning the con games, the lingo, and styles of Bronzeville's streets, and high school probably seemed irrelevant to him at this point.

Beck had a particularly difficult time fitting into the social world of the white school, as it primarily centered on its many clubs. Blacks were for the most part excluded from these clubs, and he had little interest in them anyway. Lincoln had an honor society, student council, law society, German club, band and orchestra, and a camera club. It boasted a literary and public debate club called Philomilia, and two clubs, the Blue Domino and the Harlequin, dedicated to drama. Finally, there was something called the Creative Leisure Club. In the yearbook description, the members explain what a Creative Leisure Club does: "The meetings are given over to book reports, talks on different occupations, the discussion of possibilities of travel for culture and education."[31] While once these extracurricular activities might have interested the studious Beck, now none could have remotely engaged a young man who had felt the illicit excitements of the street.

Beck skipped a lot of school during the year. Lincoln bored him, and he kept being drawn back to the world of pimps, prostitutes, and hustlers. In fact, during the school year at Lincoln, he was arrested for more crimes than in any other period of his life.

September 19, 1934—the day before school even started—he was arrested for "immoral conduct." Although no further documentation exists about the case, it is likely that it was for inappropriate sexual conduct, as this is the common infraction associated with the charge. Furthermore, such a charge is consistent with his history of repeated sexual aggression toward women. Beck denied all wrongdoing, and there was no evidence against him; the matter was closed the next day with a reprimand. In December 1934, he was arrested for juvenile larceny when he was caught stealing fountain pens from Woolworth's. He was held in the Milwaukee Detention Center and then appeared in juvenile court a few days later, where he received probation. Only two weeks later, two days after Christmas, he was charged with juvenile delinquency for disorderly conduct in a movie theater. This charge was ultimately dismissed. That spring, in April 1935, his probation officer took him to the Milwaukee Detention Center on another complaint of immoral conduct. As always, Beck admitted to nothing, and the case was closed after a reprimand. Suggestively, Beck did not mention any of these incidents in his autobiography, nor did he admit to having attended Lincoln High School. Instead, he focused on his exploits with Joe Evans and his sexual conquests. Beck's crimes at this formative age ranged from the erratic to the bizarre, and collectively they reveal a personality that is deeply troubled. Stealing pens, interrupting movies, and compulsively stalking young women are not the exploits of a criminal mastermind. They are the actions of a young man who is angry, self-destructive, and on a collision course with prison.[32]

Beck had thus far been lucky. Although he had been arrested a number of times, he had managed to avoid conviction. His good fortune started to run out in the spring of 1935 at the end of the school year. On May 6, he was arrested for juvenile truancy and incorrigible and immoral conduct. No doubt he had skipped school. He was also constantly getting in trouble for his sexual activities, as outraged fathers found him deflowering their daughters. As he described one such incident among many: "I yowled and leaped straight up out of the squishy valley like a black tomcat from the top of a red-hot stove. I slipped through his clutching hands like a buttered eel. He didn't have even a remote chance of catching me. I vaulted over the back fence and torpedoed down the alley. I heard his angry bellowing and pounding of his feet die in the sultry spring air."[33] However, in May 1935, Beck was apprehended for one of his incidents of sexual misconduct. He appeared in juvenile court on May 10 and was found guilty. He was given a choice: he could choose to be committed to the Industrial School for Boys in Waukesha, a reform school for juvenile delinquents, or he could take a job with the Civilian Conservation Corps, a branch of the Works Progress Administration in charge of creating parks and maintaining forests. The U.S. Army ran the camps, and the workers followed a strict military regimen. Beck chose the CCC. He spent seven months digging ditches, planting trees, and clearing brush.

After all this hard manual labor, Beck was ready to do anything else. Through her deep involvement with her church, Mary had built a relationship with the Tuskegee Club in Milwaukee, and she asked them to help her son. They agreed to use their influence, and Beck gained admission to the historic black college for the fall of 1936. It is unclear how exactly Beck was able to pull this off, given that he never graduated from high school. However, it was quite common for teenagers at this moment to leave school, especially in industrial cities such as Milwaukee, in order to work in factories or enter vocational training programs. Even though Beck did not have a degree, the Tuskegee Club's influence could have been enough to gain him entrance. In July, he boarded a train headed for Alabama. He had never been south of Indianapolis before. Now he traveled against the tide of the Great Migration to return to the rural South where his parents were born and raised. It would be his last chance at an education and perhaps a middle-class life.

⌐

In late summer of 1936, Beck arrived at the Tuskegee Institute in the center of Alabama. He was known to police in Milwaukee as a criminal and sexual predator. He had to stay away from the city, and Tuskegee presented the perfect place to lie low for a while. Mary was thrilled. She had been saving money in order to pay for his school-ing, and thanks to her connections with the Milwaukee Tuskegee Club, her son was now a college man. She convinced herself that her son would pursue a law degree, but Beck had more modest goals. He knew that the next time the Milwaukee police picked him up, he would be heading to prison. He would try his best to fit in at Tuskegee, but he didn't feel like he was cut out for college life. As he characterized it, "The alumni went into debt and sent me down to their hallowed school with a sparkling wardrobe. They didn't know I had started to rot inside from street poisoning. My mental eyes had been stabbed blind by the street. I was like a freakish joker who had gotten clap in his eyes from a mangy street whore."[34]

Tuskegee's importance in the history of African American strug-gles for freedom cannot be overstated. The college is located near Alabama's capital, Montgomery, in the heart of the South's Black Belt, a crescent-shaped expanse of land about twenty-five miles wide that stretches from Tennessee to Georgia and cuts through large swaths of Alabama. The region's rich sedimentary soil made it perfect for planting cotton. Planters had flocked to the area in a movement known as Alabama Fever after future president Andrew Jackson forcibly removed the Creek Indians from these lands in the Creek War of 1813–1814. The slave economy grew rapidly following Alabama's achievement of statehood in 1819, and in the years pre-ceding the Civil War, central Alabama emerged as the cultural, eco-nomic, and political epicenter of the South. In the 1850s, new modes of transportation—the steamboat and the train—greatly expanded the slave trade in Alabama. In Montgomery, slaves arrived by the hundreds at import stations located downtown along the banks of the Alabama River. From there, they were marched up Commerce Street in chains and held in warehouses and depots until they could be sold at auction. By the time that Alabama seceded from the Union in 1861, there were nearly as many slaves as free whites in the state.

Tuskegee Normal and Industrial Institute was created in the tur-bulent aftermath of the South's defeat in the Civil War and the col-lapse of the agrarian economy. After the Thirteenth Amendment abolished slavery and the Fifteenth Amendment gave black men the right to vote, black citizens used their political power to establish long-sought institutions of higher education across the South. Black education directly contradicted ideologies of white control and intellect, and so whites resisted these developments for fear they would undermine the Southern agricultural economy. Tuskegee became one of the most iconic institutions in this struggle to promote black higher education. This success was largely due to the still-controversial leadership of Booker T. Washington. Born a slave in Virginia, Washington attended Hampton Normal and Agricultural Institute, which emphasized the training of young black men and women for vocational jobs in the South. He took this approach to Tuskegee in 1881 as its first president, and established a program that focused on teaching agricultural and trade skills. Washington came to national prominence after his famous 1895 Atlanta Exposition Speech, in which he laid out the Atlanta Compromise, the blueprint of accommodationism. In it, he stated that blacks needed to focus on industrial education and the accumulation of wealth. At the height of lynching in the South and the disenfranchisement of the black vote, he proposed that blacks—only recently emancipated—give up their political and civil rights in exchange for white philanthropy in the form of vocational education. He famously stated, "In all things purely social, we can be separate as the fingers, yet one as the hand in all things essential to mutual progress." Even after his death in 1915, Washington continued to have a strong presence on campus. A statue of him lifting the veil from a slave's face sits in the center of the grounds. The inscription reads, "He lifted the veil of ignorance from his people and pointed the way to progress through education and industry."

The town of Tuskegee was very much a product of this contentious racial history between whites and blacks. The city itself was divided between the Southern white landowning class and the black tenant farmers. During the rush to the Black Belt, whites occupied the floodplain in Macon County, as it provided the richest and most desirable farmland. Following the end of slavery, blacks settled in the hills surrounding the plains, where the agricultural opportunities were limited. This region was incongruously called the "Black Bottom." Unlike Nashville's Black Bottom, which sat on a flood plain, Tuskegee's Black Bottom was located geographically on higher elevation. The rocky soil there provided limited economic possibilities in an agrarian society, and it was therefore referred to as the "bottom." The Tuskegee campus itself was located on a ridge at the highest point of Macon County—the least fertile spot in the Alabama Black Belt—and separated from the town by a series of gullies and ravines. Even the design of the grounds reflected the pervasive racism of the South. While libraries and main administrative buildings on early white college campuses were built facing outward onto the main road, Tuskegee's main buildings faced away from Old Montgomery Road, the main highway leading to town. Instead, the foundry, sawmill, and blacksmith shop were all placed in full view of the main entrance. This was done to reassure white Southerners that teaching trade skills—and not a liberal arts education with its potential to implant subversive ideas of freedom and equality—was the main aim of the college.[35] Although the school had come a long way since the days of Booker T. Washington, offering a more traditional college education starting in the 1930s, it was still standing in the shadow of the racist South and Washington's accommodationist philosophy. Only a month before Beck arrived, future novelist Ralph Ellison left Tuskegee after three years of study, fed up with the stifling atmosphere of the campus. As the author of the classic novel *Invisible Man* later said: "My trip to Tuskegee was my journey into the heart of darkness."[36]

Beck also found Tuskegee to be oppressive. Order and discipline were the two virtues most extolled by university faculty and administration. When Beck entered, he was given a student manual that informed him: "Here you will find every phase of your life systematically regulated and supervised for the purpose of aiding you in getting the most from your courses."[37] Each dinner was a formal affair with tablecloths, napkins, and a host. Male students were considered cadets, under the supervision of an official commandant and overseen by the U.S. Army. Men could not escort women to or from Tuskegee, the nearby town, or ride in cars with them. Tuskegee emphasized that work, not leisure, was the driving philosophy. The school manual promised: "Tuskegee is a vast workshop. Work is the chief element awaiting you at every turn."

Beck ignored his classes and instead spent his time trying to seduce the young women on campus. Confined to the grounds, Beck exploited the dorm-style living arrangement of the men and women. "On the campus, I was like a fox in a chicken coup. Within ninety days after I got down there I had slit the maidenhead on a half dozen curvy coeds."[38] Because the campus was so small, Beck started to get a reputation. He became worried that he might get sent home, back to the Milwaukee Police Department. "My notoriety was getting awful. The campus finks were envious, and it was too dangerous to continue to impale coeds on my stake."[39] Beck started exploring the hills around campus. He followed the informal footpaths that ran past the Tuskegee campus and all over the hills of Macon County. First slaves and then sharecroppers had created and used these paths to travel between plantations and home. At the crossroads of some of these trails, Beck discovered jook joints, which were ramshackle buildings that were set up on the edge of rural towns in the South by African Americans following emancipation. They featured dancing, gambling, and blues music. Jook joints were really the first private spaces for African Americans following slavery, and they became important places of leisure where sharecroppers socialized. As famous black novelist and anthropologist Zora Neale Hurston described it in her 1934 essay "Characteristics of Negro Expression," "Jook is a word for a Negro pleasure house. It may mean a bawdy house. It may mean the house set apart on public works where the men and women dance, drink and gamble. Often, it is a combination of all these."[40] Beck felt right at home in the jooks. They reminded him of the underworld bars in Milwaukee, and the women there found him attractive and urbane. "I started going into the hills near the campus to juke [*sic*] joints. With my slick Northern dress and manner I was prince charming in spades to the pungent hot-ass maidens in the hills."[41]

What happened next is a matter of some dispute. In his autobiography and in interviews, Beck claimed to have been expelled for bootlegging whiskey after finding a moonshine connection in one of the jook joints. His federal prison record, on the other hand, states that he was involved in a gambling incident and asked to leave.[42] Tuskegee reported that he left voluntarily after only one quarter of school. Given Beck's criminal activity from the early 1930s onward, it seems likely that he was forced from Tuskegee for doing something illegal. Whatever the case, by December 1936, he lamented, "I was on the train going back to the streets for good."[43] When Beck returned home, his mother was heartbroken. She told him, "Bobby, apparently you like to run and associate with bad people, with street people. You can become a criminal lawyer and make them pay you. Bobby, get your education. Become a criminal lawyer, and get a license to associate with the people you like and admire so much."[44] It was wise advice to be sure, but Beck's days as a student were over. He was eighteen, an adult, and there was no keeping him away from the pimp game now. Years after Mary's death, Beck remembered his mother's advice, and realized that she was right. "I couldn't understand it. But it haunts me now. Of course, I could have become a criminal lawyer. But it was too late. I was already street poisoned. And I wanted that thrill, that voluptuous sensation of controlling a stable of women."[45] He set out to get it.

CHAPTER 3

PRISON (1936–1942)

Beck returned to Milwaukee in December 1936 and immediately began his pimp career. He knew he was never going back to school. Tuskegee, with its military-style discipline and air of bourgeois self-importance, had shown him that. The education he sought was hidden away in the minds of those boss players who frequented Milwaukee's jazz joints and cabarets. Beck was determined to infiltrate these clubs and steal secrets from well-heeled pimps. He knew he would have to be careful; he had already been arrested eight times between the ages of fourteen and seventeen. He was a notorious small-time criminal with a lengthy rap sheet. As a minor, he had always managed to talk his way out of prison, but he was a legal adult now, and for his next offense he would likely be sent to the Wisconsin State Reformatory or prison. He didn't really care; he was young and handsome, overconfident, and ignorant of the double-crosses that awaited him in the complex world of sex work. "I was eighteen now, six feet two inches tall, slender, sweet, and stupid. My maroon eyes were deeply set, dreamy. My shoulders were broad and my waist as narrow as a girl's. I was going to be a heart breaker all right. All I needed was the threads and a whore."[1]

Beck moved back in with his mother, who now lived at 1865 Eleventh Street in Milwaukee. He had no money to live on his own, and Mary always had room for him. She worked as a domestic servant and nurse for an older white woman. Domestic service was one of the few jobs available to black women during the first half of the twentieth century. Even in the industrial powerhouse of Milwaukee, over 60 percent of black women worked in domestic labor. Domestic and personal service was grueling and often humiliating work. Women were required to wash clothing and bedding, scrub floors, cook and serve meals, dust homes, and perform dozens of other tasks. Wages were as low as five dollars a week, and a typical workday lasted between twelve and fifteen hours. At the height of the Depression, jobs were so scarce in northern cities that many black women gathered at so-called "slave markets" or "slave pens" each morning to seek daily employment. White employers drove up in cars and hired whichever woman bid her services at the lowest price. This forced black women into competition with one another for already limited work, driving down their wages during one of the greatest economic crises in American history. Like many women in this line of work, Mary lived in her employer's servant's quarters six days a week. She was a caregiver as well as a housekeeper, so she lived on the property to fulfill her many duties.[2]

Mary's absence gave Beck the perfect chance to explore the gambling dens and taverns in Milwaukee's red-light district. He had neither the money nor the flash to try to break luck at any of the big-name clubs like the Congo Club and the 711 Club, so he made for the underground speakeasies instead. In one unnamed dive, Beck found a fraternity among a group of has-been pimps and gamblers. The old men had enjoyed moments of glory as the neighborhood's top ass-kickers, but now they were broken down from a lifetime of prison, drugs, and scheming. They had stories to tell, though, and Beck memorized as many of them as he could. Diamond Tooth Jimmy, so named for the "two-carat stone wedged between the upper front rotting teeth," used to brag "he was the only Nigger pimp on Earth who had ever pimped in Paris on French girls."[3] Another character, named Weeping Shorty, was a notorious "gorilla" pimp, who controlled his women through brute force. He was a longtime junkie; he shot heroin regularly to cope with the stress of the pimping. Even at the relatively young age of fifty-five, Beck recalled, Weeping already looked like a "breathing corpse." He was reputedly so cruel that, when it rained, he told his prostitutes, "Get out there and work. Don't worry about the rain. Walk between the raindrops, bitch."[4]

Beck found a second home in this gambling joint, and got his first real glimpse into the complex rules of the pimp game. He got a job cleaning up the bar for the nine o'clock opening. He slept on an old army cot in the back room rather than return to his mother's hotel room. The old pimps introduced him to marijuana in after-hours rap sessions, and they often stayed up until dawn telling stories about the glory days. Beck kept quiet and listened, mostly. He had an ear for dialogue, and he mentally copied down their stories and jokes for his future interactions with prostitutes. This informal mentorship came with a price, however. The veterans berated him constantly; Beck, in order to learn the rules of the game (have his "coat pulled"), put up with a steady string of insults and name-calling. Weeping Shorty was particularly vindictive in this regard, naming him "the whore's pet and the pimp's fret."[5] During this era, pimp mentorship was a complex hazing ritual. The teacher tested the fortitude of the would-be pimp by hurling creative insults at him. If the young pimp could keep his cool, the mentor revealed to him secrets from the legendary "pimp book."

The pimp book—like playing the dozens, toasting, and sidewalk songs—was an African American oral tradition that started around the time of the Great Migration. It was a set of unwritten rules, run-downs, gambits, and codes of conduct created by the first pimps who came to northern cities after the end of slavery. They adapted the physical and mental cruelty of the slave system in order to control a stable of women. These strategies were handed down to younger pimps through oral storytelling and instruction. Although Jimmy and Weeping were no experts in the ways of the book, they knew some of the basics. For example, the pimp had to be, above all else, cool. "The career pimp lives by a rigid code of self-discipline which projects an image of icy composure in the face of constant stresses, and threats of the turf. He keeps his cool despite the voluptuous sexual temptations within his stable or in the streets."[6] Furthermore, it was not the pimp's electric sexuality that attracted women to his stable, but rather the fantasies of fame and wealth he concocted for them. Because would-be prostitutes were usually working-class women with little access to wealth or social capital, they were drawn to the pimp who provided the illusion of success. "I also discovered that whores need and use the flashy front, notoriety and phony glamour of pimps to get a sense of personal importance and worth," Beck remarked later in life. "I don't think I ever got a dime from a whore because of any sexual prowess I possessed."[7] Finally, Beck learned in these early rap sessions that there was a high turnover rate of sex workers. "[The pimp] doesn't try to keep a stable of whores happy, either. He can't even keep himself happy. What he does is keep them conned, confused, bamboozled and fascinated so that they will continue to hump his pockets fat with greenbacks. Life for a whore if she's got a pimp is around-the-clock-pressure, terror, and constant fear of death traps in the streets."[8] Beck put up with the older pimps' slurs and jabs in order to figure out the essentials of the game. "Weeping Shorty was an old man, and he had gotten past the questions and had worked out a few answers, but even so he knew a thousand times more than I did. So I fought for control. I couldn't show anger. If I did he would cut me loose."[9]

It didn't take long for Beck to find himself in trouble after running with this new crowd. On the morning of March 19, 1937, only a few months after his return from college, he was arrested for "advising a felony." There is no more specific information in the case file, so it is impossible to know for sure what the nature of his crime was. However, it is more than likely that Beck was arrested for some charge relating to the sex trade. Given his own accounts of his activities during this period, as well as his arrest record, it is plausible that Beck was involved in some form of pimping from the age of eighteen onward. Whatever the circumstances, Beck told the judge that he was recently home from Tuskegee, and that he was a laborer looking for work. The judge was lenient and gave him three years' probation on the condition that he take a job with the Works Progress Administration. Beck agreed.

During the Depression, the WPA was the largest and most significant federal agency connected to President Franklin Roosevelt's New Deal program. It was created to put America's massive numbers of unemployed to work building highways, bridges, schools, and parks. Nearly every city and town in America benefited from the

WPA construction projects; the agency employed over eight million people between 1935 and 1943. In Milwaukee, WPA ventures were responsible for laying six miles of sewers and repairing 175 miles of roads. Municipal buildings, museums, and schools were renovated and repaired. There was a sewing project, through which 750 workers fabricated garments for Wisconsin institutions; a toy-lending project, in which workers repaired over forty thousand toys for needy children; and a microfilm enterprise, created for the preservation of the city's journalistic history.[10] Mary herself worked for what would become Milwaukee's most celebrated WPA venture, the Handicraft Project. It was designed to employ women who had not been able to get financial relief. The women made quilts, toys, dolls, and books for underprivileged people in hospitals, schools, and on relief rolls. It was unique among the WPA projects, as it consisted of an integrated workforce of whites, African Americans, and new immigrants. Even unskilled laborers made as much as sixty dollars a month, and amazingly, the WPA made no wage distinctions between black and white employees.[11] Mary worked in the sewing unit, and she no doubt preferred this work over the drudgery of domestic service. Beck, on the other hand, found his job exhausting. He was employed as an unskilled laborer in Milwaukee's ambitious parks project. The city expanded the park system through the construction of playgrounds, swimming pools, pavilions, and numerous ornate buildings. New roads and pathways were created in nearly every park in the county, while miles of parkways were laid in and around Milwaukee. Beck most likely worked as a common laborer for these projects, digging ditches and clearing brush.

Beck used the WPA job to plan new and exciting heists. Sometime in the summer of 1938, he met a burglar and ex–con man named Orin Brasted while working at the WPA. Beck was fifteen years younger than Brasted, and he looked up to the older man as a mentor. Beck had a plan to rob a jewelry store owned by a local businessman named Herbert L. Palzer, and he decided to bring Brasted in on the plan. In December 1938, Beck put the scheme in motion; it was only later that he realized it had been foiled from the beginning. According to Beck's statement to the police, "I planned a job with a white fellow while we were working together on WPA. Told him of a jewelry store and how we might tie up the proprietor and rob him. He was a former inmate at WSP [Wisconsin State Prison] and told me of the jobs he'd pulled, but I didn't know he had a brother on the police force. The police were waiting for us when we went to rob the store. He tipped them off and two weeks later got a job as a health officer."[12] Although Beck had been the mastermind of the caper, he tried to convince the judge that he was a victim of Brasted's influence. It seemed like a plausible enough story to the judge, given Brasted's age and his former record. Besides, nothing had actually been stolen, so he decided to continue Beck's three-year probation.

During this period in his life, Beck consistently, almost compulsively, sought out the mentorship of older men and women in the pimp game. In each instance, he gained some knowledge, but he also ended up in handcuffs. It was nothing short of a miracle that he had not yet been sent to prison. By now he had been arrested ten times, and on every occasion he had managed to talk his way out of it. This good-luck streak ended only a few days after his botched jewelry heist. On December 8, 1938, Beck was picked up by the police and charged with advising a felony for "having sexual intercourse with a married woman and accepting money tendered him by her but belonging to her husband."[13] In his memoir, Beck called this woman "Pepper Ibbetts," though I could find no record of anyone by that name, or any variation of it. (But again, Beck used few real names in his autobiography.) However, there are records substantiating that Beck was involved with an older married woman at this time, one who had an enormous influence on his life. In his 1945 prison record, for instance, his mother reported that her son met the woman as early as 1936, and that she was even responsible for convincing Beck to drop out of Tuskegee. The file states: "Mother indicates he became involved in his present trouble due to contact with an older woman who influenced him into the life which caused him to become arrested when 17 years of age. This original trouble has caused him to be arrested numerous times."[14]

The woman known as Pepper Ibbetts provided Beck with a significant education in the sex trade, one he could not get from his

pimp teachers. Because of his traumatic past, Beck was drawn to surrogate parents of both genders, and the more mature Ibbetts fulfilled
his deep need for a mother figure. In his memoir, Beck described her
as an "ex-whore who had worked the jazziest houses on the Eastern
Seaboard."[15] He had had extensive sexual experience with girls since
he was thirteen, but Ibbetts was a street veteran who taught him
all the sexual tricks of the industry. It was from Ibbetts that Beck
learned how to use sex as a weapon, and as a form of control. As
he recounted later, "I was just a hep punk, I wasn't in her league,
but one of my greatest assets has always been my open mind. That
freak bitch cajoled and persuaded me to do everything in the sexual
book, and a number of things not listed."[16] With her, Beck snorted
cocaine, and he learned the art of "circus love," an exhausting ritual
in which every possible erotic act was performed. "She was a hell
of a teacher all right, and what a performer," he later exclaimed. "If
Pepper had lived in the old Biblical city of Sodom the citizens would
have stoned her to death. She nibbled and sucked hundreds of tin-
gling bruises on every square inch of my body. Fair exchange, as the
old saw goes, is never robbery."[17] After a few weeks of this routine,
Beck was exhausted. He was staying up all night, and his nerves were
shot from constantly snorting cocaine. "When I got home and looked
into the mirror, a death's head stared back at me. That vampire bitch
was sucking my life's blood all right. I also knew that crystal cocaine
wasn't exactly health tonic."[18]

Beck finally realized that he was being played. He was breaking
one of the first rules of the book: a pimp always gets his money up-
front from his woman. He knew now he had handled it all wrong
from the beginning. "I was green all right and twice as soft, and
Pepper knew it. Here was a hardened ex-whore who knew all the
crosses, all the answers, who handled lots of scratch and wasn't laying a red penny on me."[19] Beck went back to his mentors seeking
advice. They all told him the same thing: he was wasting his time. As
one pimp put it, "The suckers in Hell want ice water, but it's late for
them. They ain't never going to get no ice water. The way you start
a bitch is the way you end with a bitch. You can start pimping hard
on a bitch and then sucker out and blow her. But ain't no way you

can turn it around and pimp on Pepper after starting with her like a sucker. Forget her and get down on a fresh bitch."[20] This was one of the well-known axioms of the pimp book, but Beck wouldn't listen. He was ashamed that he had let Pepper manipulate him, and he was angry at himself for betraying the pimp code. Beck was determined to make some money off of her.

According to his own account, Beck first tried to muscle the money out of Ibbetts. He had seen neighborhood pimps do it before. He waited until he was in bed with her, and then he asked her for money to buy a new suit. When she refused as usual, Beck went into action. "I reached down and slapped her hard against the side of her face. It sounded like a pistol shot. On impact a thrill shot through me."[21] For a brief moment, Beck felt power and a sense of control. He felt he understood now why pimps hit their women. It gave him a feeling of omnipotence, and all of his insecurities drained out of him. However, the feeling lasted just a split second, as Ibbetts fought back like an old pro of the streets. "I should have slugged her with a baseball bat," Beck said later. "The bitch uncoiled from that bed like a striking yellow cobra, hooked her arms around my waist, and sank her razor sharp teeth into my navel."[22] Bleeding and bruised, Beck left Ibbetts to devise another plan. Little did he realize that she was already putting together a con that would land him in prison.

What happened next is not entirely clear, as records are scant and contradictory. According to the police report of December 8, he was caught "keeping company with a married woman and receiving three hundred and eighty dollars from her."[23] In his memoir, Beck explained that he was arrested for these charges after he and Weeping tried to blackmail Pepper for five hundred dollars. They supposedly took photographs of her having sex with Beck without her knowledge and then threatened to show them to her husband. Beck got the payoff, but then the police immediately arrested him. He suspected that Pepper and Weeping had together set him up for a fall, but he couldn't be positive. In the official prison records, we find Beck giving a slightly different version of events: "I was placed on probation but got to running around with a married woman and was sent here when her husband turned me in for accepting $380 she had taken from his private gambling fund, and which we planned to get married on as soon as she could get a divorce."[24] Given that Beck many times embellished and exaggerated his stories in both his autobiographical writings and his testimony to prison officials, it is difficult to say what exactly happened here. Adding further to the mystery is the fact that Beck had attempted to rob a jewelry store two days before he was arrested for the Ibbetts situation. Did he do this to finance his marriage to Ibbetts? Did she give him the money because of blackmail or because she was trying to help him after his jewelry store arrest? We will probably never know the whole truth. However, in light of Beck's lengthy rap sheet, as well as his writings about this period in his life, the most likely scenario is that he was trying to run a variety of swindles all at the same time, and they all backfired on him at once. That Brasted ratted him out to the police is clear from records, but it also appears that Ibbetts also helped get him busted days later by informing on him to her husband. Beck could no longer hide behind the defense that his actions were merely youthful shenanigans; this time he was going to jail.

For two weeks, Beck awaited his trial. His mother wrote him every day, and she came to visit once per week at the Milwaukee Detention Center. She was becoming more religious, and threatened him with fire and brimstone if he didn't change his ways. In Rockford, Mary had attended church, but she had never been a religious zealot. Now she was so saddled with guilt that she had an actual nervous breakdown. "I realized that poor Mama was becoming a religious fanatic to save her sanity," Beck remarked in retrospect. "The pressures of my plight must have been awful."[25] On the day of his trial, December 23, 1938, Beck pleaded guilty to the charge of advising a felony. He had been caught red-handed with Ibbetts's money, and he hoped that if he threw himself on the mercy of the court, the judge would be lenient. Instead, the judge sentenced him to one to two years at Wisconsin State Reformatory, a prison for first-time offenders. Mary was sick with grief, and she sobbed as Beck was taken away in handcuffs. He felt a stab of guilt for what he had done, but it was too late to change anything now. For five days, he was locked up in county jail while he waited for the bus to take him upstate. The older cons tried to scare the new prisoners with tales of horror about the reformatory. He was so worried about his mother that he just ignored them. "There were several repeaters from the reformatory on my tier at county jail, who tried to bug the first offenders with terrible stories about the 'hard time' up at the reformatory, while we were waiting for the van to take us upstate. I was too dumb to feel anything."[26] Three days after Christmas, Beck boarded a bus heading for Wisconsin State Reformatory.

Originally commissioned in 1897 for the purpose of treating first-time offenders, Wisconsin State Reformatory was created as a model of prisoner rehabilitation in Wisconsin. Prior to the late nineteenth century, American prisons were based on the Pennsylvania model—named after America's largest prison of that era, Eastern State Penitentiary in Philidelphia—which emphasized isolation and prisoner penance. Early American prisons like Eastern State were fashioned after Jermey Bentham's panopticon design, in which a single watchman in a tower observes all of the prisoners in the institution at once, without their knowing if they are being watched. The fact that prisoners cannot see the guard motivates them to police themselves. Penal philosophies shifted in the 1890s during the Progressive Era and began instead to emphasize discipline, group labor, and vocational training as the path to prisoner self-betterment. Wisconsin State Reformatory was created to keep young, impressionable convicts away from the harsh realities of the mainstream prison system and provide them with the educational and vocational tools to rebuild their lives once they were released. It was a system that stressed the possibility of parole over a strictly punitive flat sentence, and in the decades between its opening and Beck's arrival in the late 1930s, WSR increasingly focused on education, psychiatric treatment, and vocational training for prisoners.[27]

The reformatory was set up like an experimental city. It was built on the banks of the Fox River in northern Wisconsin between Green Bay and De Pere. The convicts themselves had built all of the buildings on the prison grounds. In the first few decades of its construction, WSR added a power plant, hospital, school, machine shop, tailor shop, and a farm. In the years just preceding Beck's arrival, new trade schools were implemented for automobile repair, plumbing, cabinet making, and painting. As the first superintendent of the prison, James Heg, envisioned it, discipline and hard work were the key components to rehabilitation at WSR. A prisoner's normal day consisted of a strict schedule. "Five hours of some productive work for the state, three hours of technical training in some industry whereby a trade may be acquired, one hour of military drill and setting up exercises and one and one-half hours of school, wherein at least the rudiments of education [are learned]."[28]

On a snowy, frigid day in late December, Beck arrived at WSR. The sight of the prison unnerved him. A twenty-two-foot concrete wall completely encloses the prison on four sides. Two massive cellblocks made of granite spread out nearly two hundred feet in each direction like wings from a central administration building. This building, which also serves as the entrance to the prison, is an imposing example of Romanesque architecture, four stories tall and also made of solid granite. It features arched gothic windows adorning the front, and a pair of eagles perched ominously over the front door. As Beck's bus made its way up the long drive through rows of trees to the main entrance, the terror of this fortress city struck him. "When those high slate grey walls loomed grimly before us it was as if a giant fist had slugged the breath from us all. The van went through three gates manned by rock-faced hacks carrying scoped, high-powered rifles. Three casket-gray cell houses stood like mute mourners beneath the bleak sunless sky. For the first time in my life, I felt raw, grinding fear."[29]

Beck was processed into the prison in the central administration building. In the intimidating central rotunda, the floors are made of rose terrazzo, a durable form of composite marble imported from Italy. The columns are made of the same marble, and they stretch from floor to ceiling, nearly twenty feet high. The rotunda is a massive open rectangle, seventy feet by seventy feet, featuring poured concrete staircases and ornate spindles. The room is filled with a number of twelve-foot-high murals of dramatic natural landscapes painted by prisoners: Mount McKinley, Mount of the Holy Cross, and the Wisconsin Dells. It looks like the entrance to a mausoleum. As Beck would learn during his incarceration, the classical architecture and beautiful artwork hid darker realities within the so-called reformatory. "This was part of the shiny, clean skin of the apple. The inside was rotting and foul."[30]

Beck spent the next few weeks in quarantine, and his every move was documented and recorded. He was given a medical exam and dental checkup. His medical history was thoroughly documented, as his chart indicates: "Measles, mumps, chicken pox, pneumonia 1928, small pox vaccination, circumcision." Upon entering the prison, Beck was rail thin; he stood at well over six feet, and he weighed only 145 pounds. He had a few cavities and high blood pressure, and he scored a 109 on his IQ test.[31] He was interviewed by the vocational director, psychiatrist, and chaplain. He did not leave the psychiatrist with a positive impression; the chief examiner wrote, "His delinquency was due to deferred mental development of reasoning powers and judgment with indications of mental defectiveness and possible morbid impulsiveness or psychopathic personality."[32] The report went on to state, reflecting the subtle institutional racism of the period, "This colored boy is introverted, shallow, superficial, and lacking in moral and social sense. He has poor reasoning, insight, and judgment. His home environment, training, and race, have been against proper socialization in the past. He is defective in appreciation of his past societal behavior. With a period of training and discipline he may develop sufficiently to make a more proper adjustment in the future."[33] Beck was given a temporary work assignment—probably performing manual labor—and then observed by the Social Service staff and assistant superintendent, who assessed his work habits, attitudes, and adjustments. Finally, before being released into the general population, he was given a stern warning by the Warden: "We are here to punish you smart-alec bastards, so if you fuck around, two things can happen to you, both of them horrible. We got a hole here that we bury tough punks in. It's a stripped cell without light, twenty feet below ground. Down there, two slices of bread and a pint of water twice a day. You can go out that North gate in a box for your second choice."[34]

After quarantine, Beck was moved into cellblock B. This was where he realized that WSR was a reformatory in name only. The design of the cellblocks was based on the so-called Auburn or New York system. In this model, seventy prison cells are lined up side-by-side in a row, and then these rows are stacked on top of one another four tiers high. The cells face a concrete wall, and guards patrol the narrow corridors between the cells and the wall. This design minimizes contact between prisoners and maximizes guard control when transporting inmates from cell to workplace or mess hall. The conditions in cellblock B were absolutely vile. It was racially segregated, and the only one without toilets. The prisoners used buckets that they dumped in a trough behind the cellblock. Furthermore, the food was barely edible. On his first night, Beck discovered why inmates wolfed down their rations so fast. "It was barley soup with a hunk of brown bread. It would have made great shrapnel in a grenade. I was new and learning, so instead of just gulping it down, I took a long close look at the odd little things black-dotted at one end. I puked until my belly cramped. The barley in the soup was lousy with worms." At night, guards shined their lights on inmates once per hour in order to monitor any potential escapes or interrupt any masturbating. Convicts also fought off bedbugs, as the cellblock was infested with them. Night after night, countless bedbugs invaded the cells. "I slapped the itching sting on my thigh. I pulled the sheet back. Lord, have mercy! How I hated them. It was a bed bug I had smashed, but he was only a scout. When that flashlight jarred me awake an hour later, a division of them was parading the walls."[35]

Movement and socialization were tightly controlled. First of all, prisoners were marched in silent lockstep to and from every location. The sound of hundreds of feet shuffling in the cavernous hallways made a haunting impression, one Beck would never forget. "I heard it before I saw it. A loud scraping, thunder laced with a hollow roar. Never before had I heard anything like it. Hundreds of gray-clad cons were lock-stepping from the mess halls into the three cell houses. They were an eerie sight in the twilight marching mutely in cadence like tragic robots. The roaring thunder was the scrape and thump of their heavy prison brogans."[36] This would have been particularly haunting, as the prison followed a silent rule. Convicts were not to speak to one another while marching, in their cells, or at places of work. They could talk for ten minutes during the evening meal, but otherwise the prison was quiet except for the sound of prisoners marching in unison.

There was an air of violence about the entire place. All the rules were strictly enforced by the prison's guards, an all-white staff who wore dark blue uniforms in order to emulate the police. They were a violent, uneducated lot of thugs with a propensity for racism. They put prisoners in solitary confinement for crimes like "gazing about while working" and "general crookedness." Beck remembered that one poor inmate went into the hole for looking at a guard the wrong way: "One of those arrogant repeaters went to the hole for a sassy look in his eyes. His charge was visual insubordination."[37] More often than not, however, the guards corrected inmate behavior with a swat of a wood cane with a brass tip.[38] When Beck encountered a guard with a cane for the first time, the guard didn't even speak. He just directed the prisoners with the motions of his weapon. "A tall silent screw, dazzling with brass buttons and gold braid on his navy-blue uniform, slashed his lead-loaded cane through the air like a vocal sword directing us."[39] Beck privately called this guard the Dummy, because he never spoke. However, his instructions were always clear to Beck. "He didn't pass out an instruction leaflet running down the lingo of that cane. If you misunderstood what it said, the Dummy would crack the leaded shaft of it against your skull."[40] Although designed to operate as a center for rehabilitation, WSR was not much better than the punitive systems of the nineteenth century. Forced to work and eat in silence, sleep in bug-infested cells, and march under constant threat of physical violence, the prisoners at the reformatory were terrorized into compliance.

For the year that Beck spent in the reformatory, he kept to himself and tried to stay out of trouble. He spent a lot of his time in the prison library, reading fiction and civic theory. His records do not indicate which works he read. However, his writings and interviews suggest that his tastes were wide-ranging, from the philosophical works of Aristotle to the romantic poetry of John Keats and Percy Bysshe Shelley. He loved the fin de siècle novels for their decadence and perversity. He admired Oscar Wilde's novel *The Picture of Dorian Gray*, the story of a young man whose face stays young forever, but whose cursed portrait grows more hideous as he gets older and more corrupt. Unsurprisingly, Beck also had a deep respect for George du Maurier's 1894 *Trilby*, which introduced the character of Svengali, a swindler who seduces and controls young women through hypnosis. Like Malcolm X and Claude Brown, Beck used his time in prison to educate himself by reading a broad range of literary texts, and this reading would later serve him in his respective careers as pimp and author.

He participated in other prison activities as well. He played basketball, as well as bass in a beginners' band. He was written up once, on March 20, 1939, for "leaving place of work," but committed no other transgressions during his stay.[41] As for his social life, Beck mostly hung out with the aspiring pimps and petty hustlers in the prison. They gathered in a self-segregating racial clique out in the prison yard during recreation time. These self-described "mack-men" were sent down from the overcrowded state prison to serve out their terms, and Beck attempted to learn everything they had to teach. He followed them and listened quietly to their rap sessions. "I was fascinated by the yarns they spun about their pimping ability. They had a lot of bullshit, and I was stealing as much of it as I could from them to use when I got out."[42] He memorized their speeches, and started practicing his own performances. "I would go back to my cell excited. I would pretend I had a whore before me. I would stand there in the cell and pimp up a storm. I didn't know that the crap I was rehearsing wouldn't get a quarter in the street."[43]

Beck served out his time this way, sharpening his reading skills, improving his proficiency as a pimp, and learning to adapt to the discipline of prison life. Over the course of a few months, he gained about five pounds and his blood pressure dropped from dangerously high into the normal range. On August 16, 1939, he had a parole hearing. Parts of the review reported Beck's strengths, noting that he studied hard in classes and was generally "well adjusted."[44] The chief medical examiner, Peter Bell, however, didn't believe that he had really changed. In the report, he wrote, "This individual possesses normal intelligence and demonstrates no symptoms that would indicate the presence of mental disease. In makeup he is rather weak and shallow, but appears honest and truthful. He is rather flighty and his moral judgment is defective. He is devoid of proper insight into the fallacy of crime and we believe can be further benefited by continuation for a longer period of time of his present detention."[45] Despite this recommendation to keep Beck longer in prison, on December 9, 1939, he was paroled for good behavior. He had learned a bit of self-control and restraint, and was eager to test his new skills. In truth, Beck was about to learn that the ideas he had picked up in prison were "half-baked criminal, pimping theories" from a bunch of amateurs—or, as they were known in the business, "chili pimps."[46] These were "small-time one-whore pimps," and there was a reason that prisons were crowded with these wannabe players. Beck would soon find out why.

When Beck was released from Wisconsin State Reformatory on December 9, 1939, he had served just shy of one year of his one- to two-year sentence. He returned to Milwaukee hungrier than ever to crack the pimp code. He moved back in with Mary, who now lived at 730 West Walnut Street, right in the heart of black Milwaukee's main thoroughfare. Living on Walnut Street, Beck got a firsthand look at the city's top players and pimps. From the window of his apartment, he could see the famous 711 Club just across the street. At the time, the 711 Club was one of the cultural centers of black Milwaukee, and it was a hip spot for players and pimps. It was owned by Clinton "Joe" Harris, who controlled Milwaukee's illegal gambling operation, known as "policy." Using the 711 Club as a front, he used policy to become one of the richest black men in America.

Much like Beck's parents, Harris had been born in rural Tennessee in the late nineteenth century. He migrated to Milwaukee in 1920, and at first worked as a laborer in a steel mill. He opened a billiard parlor at 1435 North Sixth Street, and then, in 1935, bought the tavern at 711 Walnut Street. Soon it became the cornerstone of the neighborhood, with a mix of respectable and notorious clientele.[47] In this tavern, Harris even held court in order to resolve daily neighborhood disputes.[48]

Policy was a form of lottery that appeared in black communities in New Orleans, New York, and Chicago during the 1880s and then spread nationwide. The bettor chose three numbers between 0 and 77. Bets were collected by numbers runners, who took wagers in pool halls, taverns, or in alleys hidden from public view. Three numbers were then picked at random from the wheel, a drum-shaped receptacle. A customer had to hit all three numbers to win, which was nearly impossible, as the odds against this were 456,456 to 1. However, the game offered the opportunity for a bettor to turn a bet of a penny into five dollars, which could feed a family of four for a month. It therefore earned the name "policy," as in an insurance policy for the future. For poor blacks in urban areas during the first half of the twentieth century, policy was a way of life. Policy stations could be found on most street corners. People carried dream books, which promised to translate names and phrases into winning numbers. Some of the more popular were *Aunt Sally's Policy Players Dreambook, Three Witches*, and *Combination Dream Dictionary*.[49] Bettors consulted psychics and attended storefront churches, looking for signs of what numbers to play. Although they faced impossible odds, hundreds of thousands of people gambled away what little money they had in hopes of a hit.[50]

Like prostitution, policy was an illegal economy that was primarily controlled by African Americans. The popularity of policy in black communities across America made policy operators, or "bankers," unbelievably wealthy. During the 1930s and '40s, policy was the biggest black-owned business in the world, with combined sales of one hundred million dollars annually. Joe Harris made millions from his policy operation and other illegal activities, but he was also known as a community philanthropist. He directly combated black poverty by donating to local organizations, and to nearly every black church in Milwaukee.[51] He was also a part of the community-wide movement sponsored by the Milwaukee Urban League to erect a monument in honor of those who served in the armed forces.[52] Like most policy operators in black America during the pre–civil rights era, Harris was both a humanitarian and an opportunist.

At first, Beck tried to stay away from this world. As a gesture of respect to his mother, he looked for other work besides hustling in the streets. In January 1940, as part of the conditions of his parole, he got a job playing basketball for Paul J. Shubert, a white man who managed the Central States Booking Agency. Shubert coached a basketball team in his spare time, and he employed Beck to play on the team for twenty-five dollars a month and a room.[53] However, watching the pimps and gangsters parade in and out of the 711 Club made Beck more eager than ever to pimp again. Fresh out of prison, he didn't quite have the cash or style to compete with the more experienced players, so he decided to target teenage girls in his neighborhood. They were inexperienced and insecure, and therefore more susceptible to his poisonous charms. He was twenty-one years old, dashing, and felt he could manipulate young girls easily. This strategy immediately led to his return to prison.

As Beck told the story, "For several months I had been screwing the luscious daughter of a popular band leader. She was fifteen. Her name was June and she had a wild yen for me."[54] Despite the fact that he knew the girl's father in the club scene, he tried to take advantage of her anyway. This was a risk that proved disastrous. One day, Beck asked her, "Do you love me enough to do anything for me?" When she said yes, he pressed her, "Even turn a trick?" She responded, "Anything." Beck suddenly saw a way to be like those pimps coming out of the 711 Club. "I put my clothes on and went to the street and saw an old gambler whom I knew was a trick and told him what was upstairs. Sure enough he gave me a five-dollar bill, the asking price, and I took him upstairs and let him in on her. She turned him in less than five minutes. My brain reeled. This was still the Depression. I could get rich with this girl and drive a big white Packard."[55]

At the time, the Depression had hit black Milwaukee particularly hard. Over 50 percent of black men in Milwaukee were unemployed, with 30 percent actively looking for work. Even menial jobs like laborer or porter were hard to come by, and Beck decided that he would pimp rather than work a square job. His experiment with teenage girls was short-lived, however, as the next customer turned out to be a friend of June's father. "The father called the local police department and my pimping career died aborning. When the detective came, I was still out there looking for tricks for the down payment on that big white Packard."[56] In the late summer of 1940, Beck was arrested and charged with carnal knowledge and abuse. According to police reports, he as usual tried to deflect attention away from himself. He claimed that he was no pimp; he worked as a garage employee, waiter, and amateur magician. He also told police, "This girl's father didn't like me because I kidded him for serving time once on the same charge himself. I never had anything to do with this girl except that I talked and danced with her occasionally. I was accused of having sexual intercourse with her, but it was a trumped up charge. The girl was a hustler anyway, and got sent to W.I.S.G. [Wisconsin Industrial School for Girls]. She involved a dozen other fellows, but I was the only one set up. Her girlfriend broke probation by some of the escapades the two were out on, and that's what started the ball rolling."[57]

Beck's strategy of misdirection didn't work. The charge stuck, and he had to go back to court. In a way, he was fortunate. He could have been charged with pandering, but the girl's father was reluctant to pursue that charge. "My sentence was for carnal knowledge and abuse, because you can't pander from anything except a whore, and June's old man wasn't about to go for that."[58] When Beck was brought before the judge, he tried to plead his case. He had talked his way out of nearly a dozen arrests already, and he remained confident about his ability to do it here. The judge wouldn't hear it; he told Beck: "You are a vicious young man. Your crime against that innocent girl, against the laws of this state, are inexcusable. The very nature of your crime precludes the possibility of probation."[59] Beck received a two-year sentence in Wisconsin State Prison at Waupun. He felt numb. He had been out of the reformatory for only six months, and now he was heading right back to jail for an even longer stretch. And this time, he wasn't going to an institution for first-time offenders—he was heading to prison for real.

—

Wisconsin State Prison was the first prison built in the state of Wisconsin. In 1851, Waupun was chosen as the site of the penitentiary, because of its proximity to large deposits of limestone perfect for building walls. Stonecutters trained the prison's first convicts in the art of cutting limestone, and they constructed the very buildings that would eventually incarcerate them. The prison itself is a dazzling example of Gothic Revival architecture. The central administration building, which is made entirely of white limestone, looks like an English castle, complete with battlements and parapets. An ornamental tower sits atop the building, an aggressive symbol of surveillance and military might. A twenty-foot-tall barricade of stone and iron surrounds the prison grounds. Behind these walls, the prison is an orderly and self-contained city. During the 1860s and '70s, the prison established a cabinet shop, a shoe shop, a tailor, a blacksmith, and a wagon factory. By 1878, the prison's sales of their manufactured goods produced enough revenue to run the complex without drawing on the state's treasury. Between 1893 and Beck's arrival in 1940, the prison added a twine plant, a cannery, a license-plate operation, a print shop, and a laundry. At various work stations, inmates produced butter, cheese, socks, shoes, and all the license plates for the entire state. They could get training in the foundry, greenhouse, barbershop, paint factory, dairy, bakery, twine plant, mattress factory, and any number of other work sites.[60]

Everything at the state prison was founded on the principle of rehabilitation, with education and vocational training operating as critical elements in the process. Under John C. Burke, the warden in 1940, the typical day for a prisoner was designed around a disciplined regime of work and training:

5:50   Rising bell and whistle.
6:25   March to mess hall for breakfast.

6:50	March to shops or other works.
11:35	Signal for stopping work, wash, and lineup.
11:45	March to mess hall for noon meal.
12:20	March to cells for rest period.
12:30	Whistle announces completion of count and checkup of all inmates.
12:55	March to shops.
4:40	Signal for stopping work, wash, and lineup.
4:45	March to mess hall for evening meal.
5:10	March to cells for evening and night.
5:30	Whistle announces completion of evening checkup.
9:50	Retiring bell.
10:00	Lights out.[61]

Additionally, prisoners followed a strict set of rules designed to keep the institution in order. Inmates were not allowed to draw, paint, or paste pictures in their cells, nor could they talk or call out to men in other cells. They were not allowed to sing, whistle, or make unnecessary noise. The list of items prisoners could own was short: Bible, cup, spoon, face towel, soap, comb, hairbrush, blanket, sheet, pillowcase, nightshirt, mattress, bedstead, chair, table, and water jug. For good behavior, a convict could also keep an electric light, a small bookshelf, and books in his cell. Prisoners could not alter their clothing or shoes, and they were not permitted to have money, jewels, or other valuables.[62]

In 1940, Waupun was an extremely overcrowded prison. Nearly seventeen hundred inmates occupied an institution meant for nine hundred. It was so overcrowded that five hundred prisoners were constantly housed in dormitories on the grounds. The average prisoner was thirty-two years of age, had a fifth-grade education, was in poor health, and had no hobbies.[63] In this environment, a premium was placed on order and discipline. Every inmate was given a copy of "Rules for the Government of Prisoners." This was a manual that instructed prisoners on how to behave in every aspect of prison life. Although rehabilitation was the goal of the prison, obedience was the cardinal rule. Inmates were marched in lockstep formation from their cells to the mess hall and to the workstations. The instruction manual provided detailed directions for the marching procedure. "At every signal to fall in for marching, take your place in line promptly, forming a column of twos. Stand erect in line, arms folded, eyes on the neck of the man in front of you, and keep a distance of sixteen inches."[64]

Meals were rigid and formal events as well. Prisoners ate over tablecloths and were served by waiters. At the beginning of the meal, the prisoners were instructed to "sit erect, eyes to the front, with arms folded until the gong rings to begin eating. Keep your elbows off the table." Prisoners did not talk to the waiters. Instead, a system of silent signaling was used to communicate orders. When a prisoner wanted coffee, he placed his cup right-side-up with the handle away from the waiter. A prisoner holding up his right hand meant that he wanted bread. If he wanted meat, he held his fork up the height of his chin. If he wanted soup, he did the same with a spoon. And if he wanted vegetables, he held up his knife. While eating, prisoners were allowed to talk to the man on his left or right, but not across from him. The administration thought that exchanges across the table would create too much noise and disruption.[65]

Although a tough prison in a lot of ways, Waupun was in the process of some major reforms by the time Beck arrived. The old straw mattresses in the cells had been replaced by cotton-filled ones manufactured at the prison. Prisoners were no longer required to wear formal coats for meals. (The coats were wool, and in the summer they were oppressive to wear, particularly as prisoners were required to fasten all the buttons to the throat.) They were now allowed to smoke hand-rolled cigarettes during leisure times, and they could shave themselves instead of being marched to the barber to be shaved once a week. Furthermore, the twenty-five-watt lightbulb that was a standard part of each prison cell was replaced by a forty-watt bulb in order to encourage the men to read in their cells.[66] The silent system, which had been an integral part of the disciplinary system in Wisconsin since the prison opened, was also partially phased out during the 1930s. As one recent brochure of the prison states: "In early years, along with the striped clothing worn by the inmates, penal practices included the 'silent system' whereby inmates were not permitted to talk to each other or to officers, and officials carrying heavy wooden canes with a brass tip as a symbol of authority used to signal inmates by rapping on the concrete."[67] Waupun changed the policy of the silent system in an effort to promote better job training for prisoners. Starting in 1938, men could talk during vocational training and educational classes. The following year, the silent rule was curtailed further, allowing conversation between inmates during recreation periods.

By the time Beck entered the prison in September 1940, it was an institution that was shifting its focus to more rehabilitation-based practices and attitudes. "Rules for the Government of Prisoners" in the early 1930s used to open with this stern warning: "All necessary means shall be used, under the direction of the Warden, to maintain order in the prison, enforce obedience, suppress insurrections and effectually prevent escapes, even at the hazard of life."[68] Additionally, the manual threatened: "For willful violation of any of the following rules, or for laziness, filthiness or disorderly conduct . . . punishment by solitary confinement on bread and water."[69] Ten years later, the manual opened with a more encouraging message: "Waupun is a prison, but it is not simply a place to 'do time.' It has walls to be sure, but nevertheless it is a place where you have a chance to make good."[70] There were other changes occurring as well. The older General Rules of Conduct section lists dozens of rules, such as "Be quiet everywhere and at all times unless given permission to do otherwise" and "Do not anger another prisoner in any way whatever."[71] As a point of contrast, the section in the newer pamphlet begins with the counterintuitive statement "There are few rules here." It then goes on to try to reason with the inmates. "You would not like others to be loud, boisterous, and insolent in their talk and actions. You don't want others to annoy you or show anger or play tricks on you and perhaps get you into trouble. Be considerate of others and avoid such things yourself."[72] Although the content of the rules is practically the same in both documents, the differences in tone and rhetoric do suggest a modestly improving prison culture occurring in 1940, one focused on reform rather than punishment.

Beck himself found the conditions of this prison to be much better than those of the reformatory. For one thing, he didn't have to defecate in a bucket or sleep in a cell teeming with bedbugs. "Since I was one of the youngest cons in the joint I bunked in a dormitory. It was like a suite in the Waldorf compared to the bug infested tight cells in the reformatory with their odious crap buckets."[73] For another, even though the schedule was brutal and work assignments demanding, the overall conditions were better under this highly organized system. "The Waupun State Prison was tough, but in a different way than the reformatory. Here the cons were older. Many of them were murderers serving life sentences. These cons would never put up with the petty tyranny that was practiced in the reformatory. Here the food was much better. There were industries here. A con could learn a trade if he wanted to."[74] At Waupun, the prisoners were politically active and they voiced their complaints regularly. Just a month before Beck arrived, for instance, a group of forty to fifty prisoners refused to eat their noon meal in protest over the quality of the food.[75] The prison even had its own monthly magazine, entitled the *Candle*, which reported on prisoner complaints over unfair prison laws,[76] praised prisoners who volunteered their services for the war effort,[77] and commented on prisoner participation in events such as charity drives.[78] Beck adapted to this system of discipline well. He studied typing, shorthand, business principles, and bookkeeping. He only got in trouble twice during his entire term. He was written up on June 17, 1941, for loafing in the machine shop, an offense that cost him thirty days of good time.[79] He was also reported for wasting food on August 27 of the same year, though this charge was excused.

The prison staff did not hold out much hope for Beck's rehabilitation, however. This was partly due to his continued desire to pursue pimping, but it was also due to the institutional racism that pervaded the prison administration. Dr. Peter Bell, who had assessed Beck's health status at Wisconsin State Reformatory, was once again his medical examiner upon his admission to prison. He wrote: "Physical examination indicates no pathological condition. This inmate in his intellectual capability is normal and no characteristics are portrayed which would in any respect allow the assumption of mental [defect]."[80] While the examiner applauded Beck because he had "refrained from habits of criminal nature which he had previously displayed," he complained that the prisoner "is to a degree rather resistive in his wholehearted admission of guilt." Bell felt that he was intelligent, could do trade work, and should be placed in classes, but he feared that "his adjustment will, however, at all times be at a mediocre level." The doctor concluded that his "delinquency was due to morbid impulsiveness," and that Beck was a "recidivistic type."[81] Perhaps most damning of all, Bell judged: "His personality makeup is typically negroid, he is irresponsible, superficial, flighty, to a degree rather silly, and despite his intelligence poorly receptive of the necessity for conformity with normal social standards."[82]

These "normal social standards," or rather "white social standards," undoubtedly held little appeal for Beck. In an environment where official reports were often rife with socially accepted racism, it is small wonder that he continued to turn to fellow black pimps as mentors and educators, rather than relying upon the prison's version of social reform. Waupun, like other American prisons of the Jim Crow era, was segregated by race, and black prisoners formed factions in an attempt to protect themselves both from other prisoners and from prison officials. Beck joined one of these groups, and he soon discovered how the older cons adapted the vocational training model of the prison in order to teach various criminal trades. He noticed that after work, a prisoner "could go into the yard during recreation hours and learn other trades and skills. Here the desperate heist men congregated to plot new, more sensational robberies. The fruits and the punks lay in the sun romancing each other. This was a prison of cliques, of bloody vendettas."[83] It was here in the yard that Beck found his community in a gang of "soft-spoken smooth Midwest pimps and stuff players [drug dealers]." They were two-bit hustlers from small towns, mostly. But this community of practiced con men further opened Beck's eyes to the complex order of pimping. As he recounted it later, they were the first men who really taught him mannerisms and lines he would need as a pimp. "I was a member of a clique that talked about nothing except whores and pimping. I began to feel a new slickness and hardness."[84]

Ever the diligent student of the game, Beck studied these older prisoners and memorized their pimp rundowns. The rundown was a poisonous pitch designed to ensnare young and vulnerable women in a life of prostitution. The pimps and players at Waupun knew dozens of these speeches, and Beck set out to memorize them all. The rundowns were created to handle the various stages of the pickup. Beck was told that if a potential prostitute offers to buy a pimp a drink at a bar, he must turn her down. "Tell the bitch no dice. I'll take care of the little things, and if she is qualified maybe I'll let her take care of the big things. Give the bitch a drink on me."[85] If a pimp wants to catch a girl who has been eyeing him all evening, he should suddenly make a move to leave and say to her on his way out the door, "I know your pussy is jumping for me. I know you want me for your man. Some lucky bitch is going to steal me from you. You better toss that bullshit out of your mind. Get straight Bitch, and tell me like it is on the way out. You had your chance. After tonight you don't have any."[86] Most important of all, when a pimp has sex with a prostitute for the first time, she must first give him a respectable amount of money to seal their relationship. If a woman tries to get a pimp into bed without paying him first, he should say, "Bitch, don't put shit in the game. Business always comes before pleasure in my book. I'll take my clothes off with my whore. I don't sucker for the Georgia. Jar loose from respectable scratch, Bitch."[87] According to the glossary of street terms in the back of Beck's autobiography, to be Georgied is "to be taken advantage of sexually without receiving money."[88] For a true pimp, allowing oneself to be Georgied was the ultimate betrayal of the pimp code. Pimps always got their money before getting in bed. Only suckers freaked for free.

Beck learned these rundowns word-for-word. He practiced them constantly in his cell, preparing for when he hit the streets again. He also worked in the laundry, which allowed him to keep his clothes pressed and neat. From this time onward, he always ironed a crease down the front of his pants. It was also in the laundry that Beck learned cunning and self-discipline to balance out his hardness. An older con who also worked there taught the young Beck how to control his emotions. From his many years behind the gray walls, the "old convict philosopher" had developed a method of survival that he called the "screen theory." He advised Beck, "Always remember whether you be sucker or hustler in the world out there, you've got that vital edge if you can iron-clad your feelings. I picture the human mind as a movie screen. If you're a dopey sucker, you'll just sit and watch all kinds of mind-wrecking, damn fool movies. We are the absolute bosses of that whole theater and show in our minds. We even write the scripts. So always write positive, dynamic scripts and show only the best movies for you on that screen whether you are a pimp or a priest."[89] Beck's raw emotions had always been his main liability as an aspiring pimp. They had put him behind bars twice, and he didn't plan on going there a third time. The screen theory provided him with a method for controlling his feelings. And it worked. After serving twenty-one months, Beck was released in June 1942, three months early for good behavior. Armed with the "whorology" he had learned, he decided to light out for the fast track of Chicago. "I was free, hard, slick, and bitter. No more small towns for me. I was going to the city to get my degree in pimping."[90]

CHAPTER 4

CHICAGO (1942–1945)

After his release from Wisconsin State Prison, Beck moved back in with Mary, who had relocated to 1634 North Fifth Street in Milwaukee. The nearly two-year bit at Waupun had done nothing to deter him from the pimp game. In fact, the state prison had provided him with his first substantial education on how to become a better player. Over the period of his incarceration, he had picked up some important lessons from the pimp book. He had learned how to sport his clothes with a sharper sense of style, and he had memorized dozens of rundowns from the older cons. Perhaps most significant of all, the "screen theory" had given him a glimpse of how to control his emotions and focus his hatred toward women. Armed with these new skills, Beck left prison eager to test his knowledge. "When I got back to Milwaukee, Mama, and the street, my mind was straightjacketed into the pimp game."[1]

The most important lesson that he had learned at Waupun was that every pimp needed a bottom woman. A bottom woman was the foundation of any real pimp's enterprise. She was the main woman, and she recruited and controlled all the other women in the stable. If Beck was really going to make a run at the fast track, he would first need to find a genuine mudkicker, a woman with streetwalking pedigree. The high school girls he had attempted to pimp proved dangerously inexperienced and would most likely put him back in prison. No more hardened veterans of the game like Pepper Ibbetts, either. Beck could never handle a woman with so much experience. He had always struggled to get any money from her, and their circus lovemaking left him feeling ashamed and exhausted. After sex with

Ibbetts, Beck lamented, "It took me a week to get the stench of piss out of my hair."[2]

Beck stood a better chance of finding a bottom woman in Milwaukee and then taking her to Chicago. The Windy City was unfamiliar territory, and he knew the hangouts and pickup joints of Milwaukee's underworld. In the Milwaukee Black Belt during the 1940s, prostitution, gambling, and other forms of vice continued to be largely tolerated and even sanctioned by the city, as long as these activities remained confined within the African American Sixth Ward. Beck decided to try his luck at the 711 Club, where he had once watched pimps parade back and forth in their Cadillacs. Ever since he was a teenager, he had wanted to make his name there, and he felt it was the perfect place for finding his first bottom woman, "to get piles of white scratch from that forbidden white world."[3]

When Beck arrived at the 711 Club, he was nervous. He frantically tried to remember the advice of the old players at Waupun. The first rule of approaching a potential prostitute was always to stay cold and brutal. "Chase a whore, you get a chump's weak cop. Stalk a whore, you get a pimp's strong cop," they had said.[4] At the club, Beck zeroed in on an eighteen-year-old girl he named "Phyllis." We have only Beck's testimony of their meeting, so we can't entirely trust his account. However, when he was finally arrested in 1944 for violating the Mann Act, he was charged with transporting two women from Milwaukee to Chicago for the purposes of prostitution.[5] It is likely that the woman Beck called Phyllis was one of the women that testified against him. According to his autobiography, he first hit on her with one of the poisonous pimp monologues that he had memorized while in prison. Essentially a string of stylized insults and come-ons, the rundown is designed to manipulate a would-be prostitute by using a combination of verbal abuse and sexual innuendo to knock her off balance. When she first tried to talk to him at the bar, he responded with: "You stinking black Bitch, you're a fake. There's no such thing as a lady in our world. You either got to be a bitch or a faggot in drag. Now Bitch, which is it? Bitch, I'm not a gentleman, I'm a pimp. I'll kick your funky ass. You gave me first lick. Bitch, you're creaming to eat me up. I'm not a come freak. You are. I'm a freak to scratch."[6]

The second rule Beck had learned was that the pimp had to project an image of glamour and success in order to offset the cruel rundown. Combining flash and front with physical and mental abuse was the way that the pimp attracted women; it was this "kick and kiss" ritual that defined the pimp-prostitute relationship. Newly freed from Waupun, Beck had only fourteen dollars to his name. He retreated to the bathroom of the 711 Club with a desperate plan. "Inside the crapper, I ripped a wad of paper from its holder. I wrapped a sawbuck and four singles around it. Whatever happened out there, I had to show a bankroll."[7] Back at the bar, Beck peeled the ten from the outside of the roll and paid his tab. He made sure that Phyllis got a peek. The deception worked, and she invited him back to her apartment. It was here Beck remembered the most important lesson of his pimp education: Get the money before you get into bed. The veteran pimps used to say, "They'll cut you loose like a trick after they've flim-flammed you. Your scratch cop is the only way to put a hook in their stinking asses."[8]

Beck later recounted that Phyllis sensed his inexperience, and she tried to toss him out of her pad. She told him, "You're pimping too hard skinny ass nigger. I have changed my mind. Get your lid and benny [hat and men's overcoat] and split." Beck became angry and frantic. He decided to resort to violence. After his experience with Ibbetts, he had learned that he couldn't just slap her. The pimps in the joint insisted that he had to physically dominate her, so he became brutal. "I kicked her rear end until my leg cramped. Through it all she just moaned and sobbed. I was soaked in sweat."[9] The older cons had taught him that although a typical woman would recoil from this kind of abuse, a "whore" is not a typical woman. They told him she is most likely the victim of childhood molestation or sexual abuse, and as such, she has a "freakish pain-loving bitch inside her."[10] She is entirely aware of society's contempt for the figure of the whore, and yet she chooses to be an object of scorn anyway. As Beck learned through the decades, she is often motivated by guilt and self-loathing, and therefore "she needs the pimp to drive her, to punish her, to make her suffer so that painful guilt for her bitch dog existence can be relieved. After all, whores are not born."[11] This was Beck's terrible genius. He grasped and could articulate the social, psychological, and cultural forces at work in the creation of pimps and prostitutes in a way few could. He then used this knowledge to further his single-minded agenda of becoming a top pimp.

According to Beck's own testimony, his manipulation and abuse worked. Phyllis agreed to be his bottom woman, which surprised him. Apparently, those old cons were right; he thought, "The tougher a stud is the more a whore goes for him."[12] Now that he had Phyllis hooked, he set out to draw her in even further using psychological manipulation. He asked her endless questions about her childhood, her first sexual experience, her goals, and her traumas. This was because the pimps in the joint had advised him, "There ain't nothing more important than what makes a new bitch tick and why. You gotta scrape her brain. Find out whether the first joker who laid her was her father or who. Make her tell you her life story. If she can remember back to her mammy's ass, good! Fit all the pieces together. Maybe then you'll know if she's a two-day package or a two-year package."[13] Beck and Phyllis stayed in Milwaukee only a week longer. Before turning her on the streets, he explained the last of the rules that he had picked up in prison. He told her to stay away from black men and lesbians. They would try to steal her away from him. White tricks, on the other hand, had deep pockets. "Keep those crack-wise Niggers out of your face. If I see you rapping to a jasper broad I'm gonna put my foot in your ass. Play for cruising white tricks. Spade tricks are trouble. They all want to make a home."[14] Beck warned her about squares who were looking to take a prostitute off the street and make a domestic life with her. He also advised her on how to make the most money possible. "Ask them for a hundred and take ten. You can go down to a price. You can't go up. Don't go to nobody's pad. Flip out of the wheels as much as possible. Flip 'em fast and crack more scratch for over time."[15] Finally, he repeated verbatim the last lines he had heard in the joint: "I want you to work nothing but the street. Stay out of the bars. Don't drink, smoke gangster, or use anything while you're working. Your skull has got to be sharp and clear out there. Otherwise you could lose your life, and almost as bad, my scratch."[16] Beck sent Phyllis to the red-light district, feeling hopeful about having copped his first real prostitute, but he secretly worried. "It was just pimp garbage. What the ninety percent know to tell a whore. What she really needed to protect herself in those terrible streets were daily rundowns for as long as she was my woman. How could I rundown the thousand crosses she'd face?"[17]

It was about this time that Beck began having horrific nightmares. They had started while he was in Waupun, but after copping Phyllis they got much worse. The dreams were always the same. He would be dressed in a rainbow-colored silk suit and jewel-encrusted silver shoes sharpened like daggers. He would kick the women groveling at his feet until they were flopping around like dying chickens. At that point, a gargantuan platinum-haired Christ would come down from the heavens and command him to whip a woman with her back to him. "Eagerly I would grab the heavy whip in both hands. I would bring it down with all my force on the woman's back. She would just stand there. The scarlet would drain down from her slashed back. She would be standing to her knees in a river of blood. She would turn her brown agonized face toward me. It would be Mama. I would be shaking and screaming in my sweat. It was horrible. I could never cut the dream off until its end."[18]

Beck continued to have these dreams about his mother for the next twenty years, until he finally quit the pimp game. The dreams became such a commanding force in his life that they sometimes took the form of daydreams, haunting his waking hours. After each dream, he felt deep regret and was depressed for days. He started snorting cocaine again to ward off these feelings. It helped. "Sudden dark arrows of depression and regret would stab into that open sore in my mind," Beck remembered. "I would get high. The narcotics seemed to ward off like armor the stealthy arrows."[19] These dreams signal Beck's complex relationship to pimping throughout his life. Even though he had an insatiable desire to pimp—a desire born out of early psychological and sexual trauma as well as greed—his dreams reveal deep remorse about the effect his pimping had on him. Beck's many writings suggest that his hatred of his mother was one of the dominant aspects that led to his pimping. Her betrayal of his stepfather, Henry Upshaw, and her ill-fated relationship with Steve created much of his distrust of women. But it was also his tender feelings for his mother that would ultimately inspire him to abandon pimping just before her death in 1962.

Nearly all of Beck's writings are in some way preoccupied with the figure of the mother, as she is the most potent symbol of his guilt about his abuse of women. She appears in various guises in his fiction, essays, and autobiography and occupies the most space in his literary universe. It was Beck's unresolved relationship with his mother, in fact, that drove much of his literary production, which is evident throughout his works. However, back in 1942, Beck repressed all of these divided feelings, which as a result haunted his subconscious, manifesting in his hideous dreams. His mother tried to convince him not to leave Milwaukee and to stay away from pimping. "I had to wrestle out of her arms," he wrote. "I picked up my bags and hit the stairs. When I reached the sidewalk, I looked up at the front window. Mama was gnawing her knuckles and crying her heart out. My shirt front was wet with her tears."[20] Beck and Phyllis (and possibly one other girl) headed to Chicago's promised land, repeating the journey his parents had made a quarter of a century earlier.

⌇

Beck arrived with Phyllis in Chicago in late June or early July of 1942. Since World War I, the South Side of Chicago had been in the process of dramatic growth and transformation. The southern border of the Black Belt had expanded from Fifty-Fifth to Sixty-Third Street, but Wentworth Avenue and Cottage Grove had held firm as the western and eastern edges of the neighborhood. Whites, fearing a "Negro invasion," had fervently policed these boundaries, drawing on the usual practices of bombings and restrictive covenants to keep black neighbors out. During the Depression, the pace of the northern migration had slackened somewhat, but the density of the Black Belt had continued to increase. By the time Beck arrived in

Chicago in the 1940s, the Black Belt was almost exclusively African American. In 1920, there were no neighborhoods that were even 90 percent black; mixed black and white neighborhoods still dotted the city. By 1940, three-quarters of all black Chicagoans were living in areas that were 90 percent or more African American. In just two decades, the black population had become, according to one sociologist, "as concentrated as it could get" in solidly African American territories.[21]

Overcrowding in the Black Belt became an epidemic. Many black citizens were packed into unsanitary kitchenette apartments, dwellings that were partitioned into tiny single-room occupancies by crooked landlords. These tiny spaces often had no running water or other facilities, and an entire floor usually shared a single bathroom. Infant mortality and overall death rates were significantly higher in the Black Belt than in white neighborhoods; tuberculosis and other diseases were a constant threat. In 1940, in response to the all-too-common reports of rats biting and even killing sleeping children in these neighborhoods, the city launched a massive anti-rat campaign. In the first year alone, one and a half million rats were exterminated in the city—almost thirty tons of vermin—in an attempt to stem the plague.[22]

The beginning of World War II witnessed the dawn of the Second Great Migration, as blacks came to the north seeking work in the booming wartime industries that made guns, shells, aircraft engines, rations, and other products. In 1941, A. Philip Randolph threatened to organize an all-black march on Washington, D.C., in response to the segregated wartime workplaces. This gesture was one of the important precursors to the civil rights movement, and it forced President Roosevelt to issue Executive Order 8802, which banned racial discrimination in wartime factories. The following year, an important black newspaper, the *Pittsburgh Courier*, spearheaded the "Double V" campaign, calling for victory over fascism abroad and segregation at home. Given blacks' renewed sense of hope for jobs and civil equality, black migration picked up again in the early 1940s. An astonishing 60,000 blacks migrated to Chicago between 1940 and 1944.[23] The influx of new blacks in cities led to increasing white violence; there were nearly 250 racial incidents and riots in American cities in 1943 alone. In Chicago, racial tension centered on housing, as black families continued to press against the lines that segregated the city. "Improvement associations" sprung up in every white neighborhood; their sole purpose was to keep black families out. In the late 1940s, the Chicago Housing Authority tried to move black families into public housing in white neighborhoods, in an attempt to integrate them. At sites such as Airport Homes and Fernwood Park Homes, mobs of thousands of whites gathered outside the buildings, throwing rocks and firebombs. In some instances, it took as many as a thousand policemen to get the white rioting under control.[24]

Despite these ongoing problems, "Bronzeville," as it was now known by its citizens, replaced Harlem as black America's cultural and political center. A Black Chicago Renaissance flowered in the 1930s and '40s, characterized by a more radical stance than its Harlem predecessor. As an industrial urban city, Chicago boasted a massive working-class population, and the architects of the Black Chicago Renaissance attempted to capture the spirit of this experience by drawing from naturalist literature and the discipline of urban sociology. The creative imagination of the age was defined by a realist perspective and Marxist sensibility; it emphasized the overpowering effect the Chicago environment had on the individual. With connections to the University of Chicago's Department of Sociology, a number of literary writers, academics, and artists articulated a new black cultural identity. These artists and intellectuals emphasized social protest and class and race consciousness in their works. They made Bronzeville life and the Great Migration the subjects of their art.

A number of influential black artists defined this movement and gave voice to the Bronzeville community. Jazz, blues, and gospel all flourished during this era, as Louis Armstrong, Mahalia Jackson, and Muddy Waters redefined black musical genres. Archibald Motley evoked the vibrant nightlife of Bronzeville's cabaret culture in his colorful and moody paintings, such as his masterpiece *Nightlife* (1943), while activist and educator Margaret Taylor-Burroughs represented everyday street scenes in watercolor works like *38th and*

Wabash (1943). Gordon Parks—who is best known for his photo essays in *Life* magazine, as well as for directing the blaxploitation classic *Shaft*—got his start as a documentary photographer, capturing the despair and beauty of the lives of women in kitchenette apartments. In 1945, Gwendolyn Brooks published her groundbreaking book of poetry, *A Street in Bronzeville*. In it, Brooks adapted classical poetic forms in order to expose the alienation and oppression of overcrowded kitchenette buildings and dangerous streets in Bronzeville. A few years later, Brooks became the first African American ever to win the Pulitzer Prize.[25]

However, it was Richard Wright's 1940 novel *Native Son* that became the hallmark of the Black Chicago Renaissance, and one of the most important American novels of the twentieth century. It is the story of Bigger Thomas, a black teenager from the South Side of Chicago who takes a job as a chauffeur for a rich white family and then accidentally kills the teenage daughter, Mary Dalton. Bigger goes on the run through the catacombs of derelict buildings in Chicago's Black Belt, but he is captured and put on trial. The novel ends with Bigger heading toward execution. A touchstone of American social protest literature, *Native Son* dramatizes the violent effects of racism, urban segregation, and economic exploitation in Chicago. Five years later, Wright set out to show that "sincere art and honest science were not far apart," writing a laudatory introduction to St. Clair Drake and Horace Cayton's landmark study *Black Metropolis*. Drake and Cayton were black academics who wanted to expand upon and revise the work of University of Chicago's influential Department of Sociology, helmed by Robert E. Park. Park, who invented modern American sociology, theorized that different races passed through four stages in the process of integration: encounter, conflict, accommodation, and assimilation. This model reflected Progressive Era optimism as well as white privilege, and Drake and Cayton sought to rethink such positivist assertions using clear-eyed racial critique. In *Black Metropolis*, they drew upon a massive archive of field research conducted by over a hundred Works Progress Administration fieldworkers, to provide the most comprehensive study of black urban life in Chicago to date. In his introduction, Wright praised the work as the scholarly equivalent of his protest novel *Native Son*, and admirers have since regarded it as one of the most important pioneering works of American sociology.

Numerous black institutions gave Bronzeville its distinctive character as well. From the 1920s to the early 1940s, the neighborhood had grown to include five hundred black churches and twenty-five hundred black-owned businesses, including beauty parlors, barbershops, groceries, cleaners, and undertakers. Bronzeville also hosted some of the most elegant theaters and clubs in black America. As in Milwaukee, the clubs and cabarets in Chicago were particularly important to black life, because African Americans were excluded from other forms of entertainment such as white nightclubs, dance halls, and amusement parks. The main thoroughfare had shifted from the Stroll on State Street to Forty-Seventh Street, where the legendary Regal Theater and the Savoy Ballroom were located. Jazz legends Louis Armstrong, Cab Calloway, Duke Ellington, Lena Horne, and Billie Holiday all made the rounds at these clubs, and they could also be spotted at smaller—though no less famous—venues, such as the Checkerboard Lounge, Club DeLisa, and the Palm Tavern.

By the time Beck arrived in Chicago, the Palm Tavern was the centerpiece of Forty-Seventh Street. When it opened in 1933, it was immediately hailed by the *Chicago Defender* as "the most high class Negro establishment in America."[26] African American architects Rousseau and Douglas, known for their work on the Liberty Life Insurance Building on Thirty-Fifth and South Parkway (which housed the first African American–owned insurance company in the northern United States), designed the décor, and famed artist C. G. Jackson painted the Masonic mural that hung on the east wall. The Palm featured a neon palm tree and flying birds in its interior. It had leather booths, and the bar was carved from a single piece of an oak tree. It was one of the first places in the nation to introduce boothside jukeboxes, known as "talkies." It served dishes like wild pheasant and duck, and the men who attended the club wore suits, while women wore fashionable dresses. It was a hangout for black doctors, lawyers, politicians, writers, and civic leaders, as well as stage performers from the Regal Theater around the corner.[27] When Joe Louis knocked out James Braddock in the eighth round at Chicago's Comiskey Park and became heavyweight champion of the world in 1937, his first stop was the Palm Tavern. An ocean of people gathered outside, so many, in fact, that they broke the front windows when they were pressed against them.[28]

Bronzeville was also the site of some of the largest black-operated vice and crime syndicates in America. As Drake and Cayton wrote in *Black Metropolis*, Bronzeville contained a whole interlocking network of illegal pursuits that were tolerated by the white establishment. "This complex is composed of the 'policy' business, prostitution, and allied pursuits," they wrote, "and is intimately connected with the legal but none-the-less 'shady' liquor interests and cabarets."[29] Since the late nineteenth century, Chicago had operated as a "wide open" town. Reefer dens, gambling houses, brothels, saloons, and buffet flats (private residences where patrons could sample a buffet of sex shows, drugs, and booze) operated with impunity under the protection of the local government. Bronzeville had developed as Chicago's center of prostitution, starting with the closing of the nearby red-light district in 1912, but especially following the Great Depression, as black women were the most economically vulnerable individuals in the city.

Policy was the biggest black-owned business in Chicago, created out of a complex alliance between and among gangsters, businessmen, judges, cops, and government administrators. During Prohibition, legendary gangster Al Capone made a deal with black policy kings. The mob would stay out of policy as long as black gangsters steered clear of bootlegging alcohol. Throughout the first half of the twentieth century, the policy kings were at the center of black entrepreneurship in America. Black gangsters such as John "Mushmouth" Johnson, Teddy Roe, and the infamous Jones Brothers controlled immense vice and gambling rackets on Chicago's South Side, and they grew wealthier than any other black people in history to that point.[30] The Jones Brothers in particular were known for their riches and extravagance. Starting from humble beginnings, they built a small empire that included policy, gambling establishments, beauty salons, hotels, and a famous variety store on Forty-Seventh known as the Ben Franklin Store. They drove expensive cars, kept their fortune in twenty-five different banks, and often traveled to their villas in Mexico and Paris.[31]

When Beck arrived in Chicago, he was determined to join this world. "I won't give up no matter what happens," he told himself. "If I go stone blind, I'm still going pimp. If my 'props' get cut off I'll wheel myself on a wagon looking for a whore. I'm going to pimp or die."[32] Beck started making the rounds at the clubs throughout Bronzeville. He approached pimping with the same philosophy of self-education that had served him well in prison. "I have to keep my mind like a sponge. I'll use my eyes and ears like suction cups. I have to know everything about crosses and whores. Fast, I got to find out the secrets of pimping. I don't want to be a half-ass gigolo lover like the white pimps. I really want to control the whole whore. I want to be the boss of her life, even her thoughts. I got to con them that Lincoln never freed the slaves."[33] In Chicago, as in other American cities, there were distinct differences between white and black styles of pimping. Whereas white gigolos could seduce rich older white widows and leech off their fortunes, black pimps had to work within the confines of the Black Belt. The aggressive technique and strict code for which Beck would become known were a direct result of the racial segregation that limited the social mobility of black people. He in fact greatly admired the white swindlers and players of the time, such as "Count" Victor Lustig and Joseph "Yellow Kid" Weil, but his black skin limited him to pursuing a more brutal form of stabling and oppressing black women. Everywhere he went, he listened to the rundowns of dozens of would-be pimps. He picked up a few gems, but mostly encountered one-prostitute chili pimps who spouted useless come-ons. "Bitch," one unsuccessful pimp stated to a waitress, "you got a mint between your big hairy legs. I'm gonna show you how to make a grand a week. I ain't never wanted nothing and didn't get it. Bitch, I'm gonna get you."[34] Beck learned very quickly that the most successful black pimps possessed a combination of finesse, ruthlessness, and patience. The chili pimps failed because they usually came on too strong and reeked of desperation.

Beck's big break came when he met Albert "Baby" Bell, an enforcer for the Jones Brothers and a notorious pimp known for violence. Bell was a cultural icon in Bronzeville. He lived in a luxury apartment at 124 East Garfield Boulevard between Michigan and Indiana, near the Michigan Theater. He had DOCTOR A. BELL carved on his door knocker, and he held lavish parties. He was born in Nebraska in 1903, and completed one year of high school. He moved to Chicago around 1935, and soon he was a regular item in the pages of the famous black newspaper the *Chicago Defender*—especially in its gossip columns, "Everybody Goes—When the Wagon Comes!" and "Swinging the News"—and in other papers. They reported when he went to horse races[35] and when he drove his supercharged hot rods late at night.[36] Columnists speculated about the women he dated, and provided detailed descriptions of his evenings out with playboys and local celebrities,[37] including boxing legend Joe Louis.[38] Most of all, the papers loved to gossip whenever Bell flashed his massive bankroll at any of the popular nightclubs he attended,[39] including the It Club,[40] the Terrace, the Ritz Lounge,[41] and the Palm Tavern.

Bell walked the thin line between fame and notoriety. On August 1, 1938, while brandishing his automatic pistol at Club DeLisa, he accidentally shot two patrons. In the trial, Euclid L. Taylor—a black lawyer who had business dealings with various policy kings—argued that Bell was simply playing too much with his gun that night, and it went off unintentionally. The charges were dismissed after the two people he shot mysteriously retracted their complaint against him.[42] On March 14, 1942, Bell threw a party for jazz legend Count Basie. Everyone from blues shouter Jimmy Rushing to George Jones of the Jones Brothers was in attendance. But just a week after the party, Bell was arrested for assault with a deadly weapon with intent to kill, when he pulled a gun on the owner of the It Club, Theresa Elbaum. Once again, Euclid Taylor got the charges dismissed, arguing that Bell was intoxicated and thus had impaired judgment.[43]

A year after this episode, Bell was arrested for murder when he killed his friend Preston Ray in front of dozens of witnesses. According to court testimony, Bell shot Ray six times after they got into an argument in the alley near Bell's apartment. The police found Bell nonchalantly lounging at home wearing a bathrobe with the pistol in a pocket. His guilt was so self-evident, the *Chicago Defender* initially reported that in Bronzeville "they're laying odds 20 to 1 that Baby Bell, alleged bad man, sportsman, and loud talker, will get a long penitentiary sentence for that murder."[44] Three weeks later, those odds increased to 100 to 1.[45]

Miraculously, Bell beat the charge. At his trial, which "resembled a grand opening of a huge tavern with nightlifers from every section present," Bell was again defended by policy king mouthpiece Euclid Taylor.[46] Judge John Sbarbaro presided over the trial. Taylor initially entered a plea of guilty and then somehow got Bell off after only a two-day trial. Many were outraged. One man complained in the *Defender* that only one person came forward to testify against the notorious gangster. "To the public that wonders how could it be a man commits a crime and goes FREE without justice being served upon him so that he may be punished for the crime that he committed? Well this is one of the reasons: it is the people of the public to blame. We do not give a helping hand to put justice back in place whenever the unjust kick it out of place. Such as the case of Albert Bell, alias Baby Bell. There were more than 35 or 40 bystanders at the scene of the shooting by Baby Bell, taking the life of Preston Ray. Out of this crowd of 35 or 40 people there was only one who attempted to put justice back in place."[47]

How Bell beat the murder case against him is a matter of some speculation. Sbarbaro was the same judge who had found Bell not guilty on the assault charge a year earlier, and it is a possibility he was bribed. However, Sbarbaro was no friend to Chicago gangsters. He had sent a lot of mobsters to prison during the Al Capone Prohibition days. More recently, he had been the judge in the "Big 26 Conspiracy Trial" of 1942, in which twenty-six of Chicago's biggest policy operators were tried for criminal conspiracy. In that trial, every single key witness who had sworn a grand jury statement then refused to testify after taking the stand. Behind the scenes, the policy kings had likely threatened or cajoled all of them into silence. Sbarbaro was forced to release the indicted twenty-six policy kings, calling the case "hopelessly hopeless." Afterward, he complained to the press of the "shocking spectacle of witness after witness in case after case before this court and other courts obstructing the administration of justice by taking refuge behind the privilege of a witness against self-recrimination."[48] Sbarbaro recommended that the legislature address the problem of intimidated witnesses, which he saw as common in Cook County criminal trials.

It is much more likely that Bell's lawyer, Euclid Taylor, was pulling the strings behind the judge to get Bell acquitted. From humble beginnings, Taylor had grown to be a powerful and well-respected Chicago lawyer. He was born in 1906 in Coffeyville, Kansas, and his father died when he was only one. His mother worked in a laundry and sewed to keep the family afloat, while Taylor himself started sewing to help out at the age of nine. His stepfather was a military man, and at a young age Taylor became interested in military tactics. He was the first black man to receive an ROTC commission at Fort Leavenworth, the original home of the famous Buffalo Soldiers. He migrated to Chicago in 1924 and worked as a busboy at the Hotel Sherman for a while and then as a mail clerk at the post office. He became friends with Octavius Granady, who was murdered by political assassins while a candidate for the office of the Twentieth Ward. Taylor was in the car with Granady when he was killed, and suffered five gunshot wounds himself.[49] After that, he advocated on the part of black victims of white violence. In 1932, he pursued the arrest of two white police officers for raping two young black girls while they were in jail.[50] A year later, he donated his services to Douglas Porter, a seventeen-year-old youth who had been falsely accused of robbery. Taylor argued that the boy should not be returned to Charlottesville, Virginia, as he would be lynched there.[51] He campaigned tirelessly for anti-lynching bills, and in 1941 he was elected the youngest president of the Cook County Bar Association, the oldest African American bar association in American history.[52]

Taylor was also known as a shady lawyer with ties to organized crime. He defended Ily Kelly, whose brother Walter J. Kelly was a gangland boss.[53] He also successfully defended Jack Blackburn— trainer of the "Brown Bomber," Joe Louis—for maiming a nine-year-old girl in a gunfight.[54] He even formed a business alliance with three Bronzeville businessmen and policy bosses—Charlie Cole, Winston Howard, and Louis "Buddy" Hutchens—in order to buy Bronzeville's Pershing Hotel. At the time, the $550,000 deal was the largest mortgage transfer between African Americans to date, and Taylor was right at the center of it.[55]

Bell and Taylor were also friends. They had been seen hanging out together as early as 1936 at a Joe Louis boxing match, and they were both horse race enthusiasts who could be found together at the track.[56]

The most likely explanation for Bell's acquittal is that Taylor used his connections with the policy kings to intimidate potential witnesses into not testifying. Only one of the three dozen people who saw Bell murder Ray stepped forward to testify. The rest were apparently scared into silence, as Bell's reputation for violence was well known. As one rival put it, "He's killed four studs. He ain't human. He's got every Nigger in town scared shitless. His whores call him Mr. [Bell]."[57] By the time Baby Bell committed suicide in 1949—a suicide perhaps motivated by fatigue after decades in the pimp game—black America's most influential poet, Langston Hughes, clearly regarded him as an essential fixture of black Chicago: "Chicago's wind goes well with the town because it is a big rough-neck city, a kind of American Shanghai, dramatic and dangerous, one of the cradles of the atom bomb, Carl Sandburg's 'hog-butcher to the world' perfumed with stock-yard scents. It is a Baby Bell town whose death by suicide sold out a whole issue of the *Chicago Defender* as soon as it appeared on newsstands."[58]

Beck sought out Baby Bell sometime in 1942, during the heyday of Bell's notoriety. "When I first got to Chicago," Beck later ruminated, "I had this wild dream of picking the brain of the town's top pimp. And eventually I did. In retrospect now, I suppose I could say that I wanted to be like . . . God for whores."[59] Taking on the moniker "Slim Lancaster," he started hanging around the bars on Forty-Seventh Street to find out whose name was ringing. It is likely that he first met Bell at the Palm Tavern or Club DeLisa, two of the clubs both men are known to have frequented. In addition to being a notorious murderer, Bell was also reputed to be a top pimp, a man who pimped by the book, that "unwritten code of the pimp which was handed down by word of mouth from the older men to the younger dudes." As Bell used to boast, "There are thousands of Niggers in this country who think they're pimps. Don't none of them pimp by the book. They ain't even heard about it. There ain't more than six of 'em who are hip to and pimp by the book. You won't find it in the square-Nigger or white history books. The truth is that book was written in the skulls of proud slick Niggers freed from slavery."[60] Beck coaxed and flattered his way into Bell's inner circle over a period of weeks and began to learn from the master himself.

Bell shrouded himself in pimp mythology, and he passed this mythos along to Beck. In Bell's mind, black pimps were heroic figures who defied both white racial oppression and black female betrayal of the race. In Bell's version of the book, pimps emerged on the scene in Chicago because black women coming out of slavery "were stupid squares. They still freaked for free with the white man. They wasn't hip to the scratch in their hot black asses." The pimp existed as a necessary evil, Bell proclaimed, because he helped black women fleece the white man. "Those first nigger pimps started hipping the dumb bitches to the gold mines between their legs. They hipped them to stick out their mitts for the white man's scratch. The first Nigger pimps and sure-shot gamblers was the only Nigger big shots in the country."[61]

At best, Bell's origin story of the black pimp is a self-serving delusion; at worst, it is an outright lie used to justify the exploitation of black women. In reality, black women had been driven into the sexual labor market almost as soon as they arrived in Chicago after emancipation. As Chicago's black population grew steadily after 1880, black women were concentrated largely in low-paying personal and domestic service work. They toiled in physically demanding jobs, which were often seasonal and therefore highly unstable. In order to earn a living wage, black women in Chicago frequently turned to sex work as a viable, though dangerous, alternative to domestic work. In the early years of Chicago's sex trade, black women worked in brothels clustered around Twelfth Street near the origin point of the Black Belt. Sometimes they owned these brothels, which catered to black and white workers commuting back and forth to their jobs. Sex workers charged a dollar for their services, and even with the madam's take of half their wages, black sex workers often made double what domestic servants did. As many brothels closed following the Chicago Vice District–led crackdown of the red-light district in 1912, prostitutes took to the streets and saloons in larger numbers. By the 1920s, black pimps took greater control of the sex trade, frequenting the saloon, the speakeasy, and the street in order to enlist black sex workers who were more exposed in Chicago's dangerous streets and bars.[62]

Bell modeled his organization on the industrial factories of Chicago, and he treated his women like an exploitable labor force. "Whores in a stable are like working chumps in the white man's factory," Bell told Beck; "they know in their sucker tickers they're chumping."[63] Since the women might at any time organize, quit, or even rise up against the boss's authority, the pimp's challenge was to devise methods to keep the workers divided. As Bell explained, "A good pimp is like a slick white boss. He don't ever pair two of a kind for long. He don't ever pair two new bitches. He ain't stuck 'em for no long scratch. A pair of new bitches got too much in common. They'll beef to each other and pool their skulls, plot, and split to the wind together."[64] The pimp should create a false competition between teams of prostitutes, because "a stable is sets of teams playing against each other to stuff the pimp's pockets with scratch."[65] The most important aspect of controlling a stable was controlling the bottom woman. She was the manager and recruiter, and it was a common wisdom in the pimp book that scorning a bottom woman was the fastest way for the pimp to find himself in prison. "A good pimp has gotta have like a farm system for bottom women. He's gotta know what bitch in the family could be the bottom bitch when mama bitch goes sour. He's gotta keep his game tighter on his bottom bitch than on any bitch in the stable. He's gotta peep around her ass while she's taking a crap. He's gotta know if it's got the same stink and color it had yesterday."[66]

Bell's form of pimping was more violent and manipulative than anything Beck had ever seen in prison or in the taverns of Milwaukee. His main philosophy was "One whore ain't got but one pussy and one jib. You got to get what there is in her fast as you can. You gotta get sixteen hours a day outta her. There ain't no guarantee you going to keep any bitch for long. The name of the pimp game is 'Cop and Blow.' "[67] Bell encouraged Beck to use a wire hanger to beat his women into submission if they resisted. It was efficient, he said, because, "ain't no bitch, freak or not, can stand up to that hanger."[68] He also emphasized that psychological manipulation proved an even more effective tool in motivating a prostitute than physical violence. For instance, he instructed Beck to drive to Terre Haute, a city a few hours from Chicago, and send money back to himself using Western Union under the name of a false female rival. "That lazy bitch will think she's got competition," Bell would say. "Watch the sparks fly out of her ass. She'll try to top that bitch that doesn't exist."[69] The ultimate key to pimping, Bell said, was to be mysterious and aloof. "Never get friendly and confide in your whores. You got twenty whores, don't forget your thoughts are secret. A good pimp is always really alone. You gotta always be a puzzle and a mystery to them. That's how you hold a whore. Don't get sour. Tell them something new and confusing every day. You can hold 'em as long as you can do it."[70] Pimping was not about charm or sexuality or even outright brutality. Pimping was a thinking man's game, like chess. Bell liked to say, "A good pimp could cut off his swipe and still pimp his ass off. Pimping ain't no sex game. It's a skull game."[71]

Through his relationship with Bell, Beck realized he had a number of limitations. He simply wasn't as merciless as Bell, and he smiled too much. Bell used to tell him, "Green-ass Nigger, to be a good pimp, you gotta be icy, cold like the inside of a dead-whore's pussy. Now if you a bitch, a sissy, or something let me know. I'll put you in drag and you can whore for me. Stay outta my face Nigger, until you freeze up and stop that sucker grinning."[72] Although Beck thought of himself as hardened from his two bits in prison, Bell showed him just how weak and emotional he really was. Beck's hatred of women simply didn't go as deep as that of some of the other pimps, who believed that "a ho ain't worth a thimble of poo-poo."[73] Beck's feelings toward his own mother were deeply ambiv-

alent, so it was difficult to be so inhumanly merciless toward all
women. As Beck admitted years later in a number of interviews, "I
had a very good mother. Most of the successful pimps back in those
days had been dumped into garbage cans, had been abandoned and
had never known maternal love. They were the cold-blooded ones.
You see because if you never have a mother who gives you affection,
and tenderness, and concern, and warmth, when you get to be an
adult, you can't give it. But I always had that sucker streak in me.
I don't mean that it compromised my pimping, but it was always
there. There is just a certain distance I would go with the brutality.
Most of it was all show."[74]

To add to his concerns, Beck suddenly found himself competing
with some of the most talented pimps in America. They were far
more hip and well-spoken than any of the players Beck knew in Wisconsin. These pimps drove Duesenbergs. They kept panthers and
ocelots as pets. They had a command of a secret street language that
bewildered and intrigued him. In *Pimp*, he recounted the first time
he ever heard a group of pimps performing a toast:

> *Before I'd touch a bitch's slit,*
> *I'd suck a thousand clappy pricks and swim through liquid*
> *shit.*
> *They got green puke between their rotten toes and snot runs*
> *from their funky noses.*
> *I hope all square bitches become syphilitic wrecks.*
> *I hope they fall through their own ass-holes and break their*
> *motherfucking necks.*[75]

Although he couldn't know it at the time, Beck was witnessing one of the origins of gangsta rap and hip-hop in these toasts.
A pimp toast was a long, profane poem that was performed orally
and emphasized exaggerated sexual humor. It was composed of creatively rhymed couplets (often improvised), and featured punning,
wordplay, and aggressive boasting. Although no one is exactly sure
of the toast's origins, it most likely had its roots in black urban street
culture at the turn of the twentieth century.[76] Toasts were probably

first performed in barbershops, in bars, and on street corners where working-class black men congregated. The most well-known toasts included "The Signifying Monkey," "Stackolee," and "Shine." In each toast, the speaker creatively bragged about a folk hero's cleverness or "badness." Like the dozens and the pimp book, these toasts grew out of African American oral expressions, and they became the direct forerunners of the comedy of Rudy Ray Moore and the gangsta rap of N.W.A, Ice-T, and Snoop Dogg.[77]

Witnessing the pimp toast for the first time made Beck realize how much he had to improve his game. These men were not criminals because they lacked the skills or smarts to make it in the straight world. These men were criminals of the highest order precisely because they were so brilliant at their craft. As Beck remarked many decades later about this community of pimps, "We are talking about class and intellection. You know, a lot of people think that top pimps are dummies. That's not true. They're just perverted. I've never known a top pimp who didn't have a high IQ. He's all screwed up in the head. That's his problem. If he had an opportunity, believe me, he could have been anything."[78] After learning from Bell's pimp book and hanging out with some of Bronzeville's top players, Beck saw that he would have to learn how to "rap transcendentally" if he was going to make it on the fast track. He soaked up everything he could from these master players. "My ears flapped to the super-slick dialogue. I was excited by the fast-paced, smooth byplay between these wizards of pimpdom."[79]

Beck started recruiting women and building up his stable. He instructed Phyllis to take in other women from the street. He told her, "You see a young girl out there, square or whore, pull her. Be friendly to her. Build me up. You know, tell her how smart and sweet I am. Don't let no bitch pull you. This family needs some whores. Don't bring no junkie bitch to me."[80] When Beck met a girl he wanted to bring into his stable, he often used cocaine to draw her in. He would tell her, "Banging cocaine will spin a magic web of music and bells inside your skull. Every pore in your body will feel like Daddy's jugging his swipe in all over you. It will torch off a racy secret fire of life inside you. It's a miracle. You get all that thrill and no habit. I know you ain't chickenshit. Are you game to try?"[81] Once he got them high, he would entice them into a life of prostitution by making impossible promises of a luxurious life. He would say, "You have wanted since you were a little girl to live an exciting, glamorous life. Well, Sugar, you're on [Slim's] magic carpet. I'm gonna make your life with me out-shine your flashiest day dreams. I'm a pimp. You gotta be a whore."[82] As many of the women Beck encountered were victims of abuse, he also lured them in by promising to guard them from the dangers in the world. "My little baby, I'll protect you with my last drop of blood. If any mother-fucker in those streets out there, stud or bitch, hurts you, or threatens you, come to me . . . I take an oath to protect you for as long as you are my woman."[83] Once Beck had hooked them, he made them take an oath. It went as follows: "From this moment I belong to Slim. I am his whore. I will do everything he tells me. I won't ever fuck with his scratch. I will hump my heart out every night. I gotta make a bill a night."[84]

At first, Beck had a difficult time adjusting to the brutality and complexity of the pimp game. He was still emotional, and he still smiled too much. Then he came upon a solution he had learned back in Milwaukee: cocaine. As it helped him suppress his nightmares, it enabled him to keep his emotions in check. Beck remembered later, "The drugs keep you in a trance. All you know is that you've got to pimp. When you are a pimp, because of the nature of the prey, the enemy, it takes all of your thoughts. You can't think of anything. And it takes so much effort to control yourself, to control your emotions, because . . . you have got to be in refrigeration. You can't be a normal person, not and succeed in that life. And you have got to be absolutely unflappable. What you do literally, is play God."[85] Beck followed a strict regimen of using cocaine while pimping, followed by ample rest. He lived in a room by himself in a midtown hotel, and often stayed there while others went out all night. "I was never the best looking nor the best pimp. Among my contemporaries, there were fabulous people . . . young, black pimps, well, hybrids really, racial hybrids, who were beautiful. And I had to have an edge. My edge was always class. Even though I used drugs, I would never stay out with the pimps 'till 6 or 7 in the morning. I'd drink a quart of milk, no cocaine . . . you see, I was about to go to sleep."[86]

Beck practiced his pimp soliloquies and come-ons he had picked up from Bell and other pimps in front of a mirror. He was always armed with lines like "It's you and me against the world. I'm gonna' make a star out of you. We are going to get rich as cream. You gotta hump your ass off in those streets, Baby."[87] Or he might say, "You met me in your first hot dreams, remember? You know that pretty joker in your little girl dreams that always faded when you woke up wet between the legs. You waited and wished. You lucky bitch, I've stepped out of your dreams."[88] Beck eventually took his speeches to street corners, where he picked up women and impressed crowds of onlookers. One of Beck's literary contemporaries, Odie Hawkins, remembered, "There was an area on the South Side of Chicago known as 39th and Cottage Grove. And basically it was a red-light district. Iceberg Slim was one of the neighborhood role models. When I first heard Iceberg Slim, my impression of him was of a towering intellect. He was talking about the economics of sexual intercourse, and how he looked upon what he was doing as a broker."[89]

Over the next two years, Beck emerged as one of the South Side of Chicago's new top pimps, and for the first time in his life, he felt free. "I felt the birth stirrings of that poisonous pimp's rapture. I felt powerful and beautiful. I was still black in the white man's world. My hope to be important and admired could be realized even behind this black stockade. It was simple, just pimp my ass off and get a ton of scratch. Everybody in both worlds kissed your ass black and blue if you had flash and front."[90] With his stable of women and growing command over the book, he was emerging as a major player in Chicago. He spent more money and snorted more coke, and he was living a life of luxury. "My name was ringing . . . I pimped strictly by the book for the next [two] years. I traded in a Hog each year. I never had less than five girls in the family . . . I took a suite in a swank midtown hotel. I had the privacy, the jewelry, and all the flash and glamour of a successful pimp. I had managed to solve the fast track. I was fast becoming one of its legends."[91]

During these few years, Beck estimated that he copped and lost sixty to seventy women, and he kept between five and ten girls in his stable at any one time. "The turn-over in turnouts was big. Some of them would hump for a month and split. Some a week. Others a couple hours before they cut out. [Bell] had been so right years ago. The pimp game was sure 'cop and blow.'"[92] By mastering the rules of the pimp book, Beck created for himself a pimp's paradise. He had the money, the women, and the glamour that the game had promised. But perhaps most importantly, pimping provided him with his first buffer from the racist white world. Hidden away in his apartment, Beck had the luxury to avoid white racism in all its forms. He later reflected, "The greater society was so repressive that one's ego needed at least in his own particular milieu to be thought of as great and grand. This was the way to do it, to have your own little kingdom and to be apart from racism. You see, only your own racism . . . The census takers don't even count people in the underworld. That's what I liked about it . . . I didn't have to be bruised and wounded in my efforts to make a living by coming into contact with white society. I was never reminded I was a nigger. My environment didn't include that. The only white men I saw were white men riding in cars looking for black pussy."[93]

CHAPTER 5

LEAVENWORTH FEDERAL PENITENTIARY (1944–1946)

In the spring of 1944, Robert Beck was living the pimp's dream. He had the Hog (his Cadillac), the vines (his fine clothes), and the scratch (his cash money) of a well-heeled pimp. Although it was the height of World War II, he avoided being called up for service by refusing to reveal his address to the armed services. He hadn't visited his mother in over a year, though he spoke to her sometimes on the phone. He tried not to worry about it too much; she had remarried by this point, to a man named Ural Beck who worked for the railroad. Born August 16, 1876, in Winston-Salem, North Carolina, Ural wedded Mary sometime in the early 1940s, and they moved into a modest house in a mixed-race Milwaukee neighborhood east of the Black Belt, called Brewer's Hill.

Perhaps it was Beck's success that made him overconfident. Or perhaps it was his vanity that prevented him from "tightening his game," as the other pimps called it. Whatever the case, his control over his stable was starting to deteriorate, and he didn't realize he was heading for the penitentiary again until it was too late. By his own accounts, he had been sending some of his girls, including his bottom woman, Phyllis, across state lines to Wisconsin to work at the military camps. He was most likely dispatching them to Fort McCoy, which hosted the largest concentration of American troops in the Midwest since World War I. For Phyllis, selling herself to an endless line of servicemen was the final insult. When she returned home from one of these trips, she confronted Beck directly, telling him: "Nigger, you were a raggedy nowhere scarecrow until you got me. You didn't have no wheels. You muscled me for mine. Nigger,

I'm the bitch that made you great. Without me right now, you'd go to the bottom fast as shit through a greasy funnel."[1] Phyllis challenged her pimp in front of all the other girls, and still being relatively inexperienced, Beck reacted with violence and brute force. He punched her in the face as hard as he could, breaking her jaw. As the other girls took Phyllis to the hospital, Beck realized that his days as a Chicago player were numbered. "I had made a pimp's classic blunder," he remarked later. "I had blown a tired bottom bitch."[2]

Tricked or intimidated into sex work with false promises of an easy life at the end of her career, the bottom woman—the key to the pimp's whole operation—eventually became disillusioned with the pimp's lies. Some left for another pimp. Others squared up or went straight. Many took revenge. As one of Beck's pimp rivals told him, "A bitch like that is a ticking bomb. Every day, her value to the pimp drops to the zero line. She's old, tired, and dangerous. She can rattle a pimp into goofing his whole game. If the pimp is a sucker he'll try to drive her away with a foot in the ass. She's almost a cinch to croak him or cross him into the joint."[3] The most merciless pimps did not use violence to drive embittered bottom women away; instead, they tried to drive them mad. They pumped them full of heroin or cocaine. They covered them with chicken blood while they slept and told them they found them sleepwalking in the streets. As one pimp in Beck's inner circle bragged, "I got a thousand ways to drive 'em goofy. That last broad I flipped, I hung her out a fifth floor window. I had given her a pure jolt of cocaine so she'd wake outside that window. I was holding her by both wrists. Her feet were dangling in the air. She opened her eyes. When she looked down she screamed like a scared baby. She was screaming when they came to get her."[4]

Beck simply didn't have this kind of calculated brutality in him, no matter how much cocaine he snorted. His violence toward women was a panicked type of violence, an emotional response that Bell tried to coach out of him. After Beck's confrontation with Phyllis, she and one other woman went to the police to testify against him. The FBI picked up the case and issued a federal arrest warrant for his violation of the Mann Act. Also known as the White-Slave Traffic Act, the statute was created in 1910 to combat the trafficking of young women across state lines. Beck could get ten years in Leavenworth Federal Penitentiary for his crimes, so he abandoned his apartment and went into hiding in one of the derelict buildings in Chicago's South Side. "I was now trapped in my dingy one-room kitchenette. It was in a very old two-story building. I was on the first floor in the rear in number ten. Down the hall at night, rats would come scampering and squealing from the alley. They came under the back door which hung crookedly on its hinges."[5]

While he was on the lam, Beck called his remaining prostitutes weekly, pretending to be on the East Coast running a range of cons. He made up wild stories of scams he was devising to make them all rich. He told them that he had gotten into the business of counterfeiting money. "You are the luckiest whores alive," he said. "Your man's got a genius white engraver for his pal. He used to be an engraver for the government. We've got some plates he's just finished. We've turned out three hundred of the prettiest hundred-slat bills the human eye has ever seen."[6] Every time he called them, he stalled by telling them that he and the engraver were looking for special paper or ink, or some other item necessary for printing cash. In the meantime, Beck encouraged them to keep on working in the streets to support the stable. One day, he promised, "I'm gonna breeze back into town the only millionaire pimp in the world. I'm gonna buy a beach and a mansion in Hawaii for my stable. If we run outta scratch, we'll just run off another bale. So stay cool and keep humping."[7]

For months, Beck evaded the police and kept his prostitution operation running. His nightmares got worse during this time; he still dreamed about brutally whipping his mother, and the drugs no longer helped. "It was getting almost impossible to sleep . . . When I did fall off into fitful sleep I'd have nightmares. Those dreams about Mama would hog-tie me on a sweaty rack of misery. I had an awful fear of another jolt in the joint. The guilty daydreams on the heels of the nightmares were torturing my skull."[8] Beck quit using cocaine altogether, as the drug "only magnified [his] terror and worry."[9] However, on August 25, 1944, he left the apartment to buy a small dose of heroin, as he hoped a bump of "horse" would calm his nerves. The police spotted him on the street and arrested him. They delivered him to Cook County Jail, an overcrowded facility full of drug addicts and homeless men serving short-term sentences. Locked up in one of the tiny six-by-ten-foot cells, Beck hadn't seen conditions that revolting since Wisconsin State Reformatory. "The tiny cell was too small for two men. Eight of us were in it. I was lying on the concrete floor. My cellmates were bums and junkies. Two of them were getting sick. They were puking all over. The bums were stinking almost as bad as the junkies. A drunk lying beside me dug his fingernails into his scalp and crotch over and over again."[10]

Beck faced criminal prosecution from all sides. On August 30, 1944, he was remanded to the custody of the United States Marshal to face charges of failure to update his address for the draft, "[a] delinquency due largely to his activities with prostitutes."[11] The Wisconsin assistant attorney general made a deal with Beck. He promised to drop the draft evasion charges and only pursue a light sentence on the white-slavery charges if Beck pleaded guilty. As he said later in his official inmate statement, Beck felt pressured into pleading guilty, even though he wanted to fight the indictment. "I was charged with transporting two young women, but there was certain aspects in the case that caused me to plead guilty, although I was not guilty to all the charges. There was an indictment against me for draft evasion, so I [pled] guilty to this charge."[12] Beck borrowed $750 from his mother's new husband, Ural,[13] and posted the $2,500 bail.[14] He returned to the streets briefly to scare up what cash he could, but this was difficult, as everyone knew about his impending imprisonment. "I stayed out on bail four months. I had two turnouts and three seasoned whores during that time. None stayed longer than a month. Everybody in the street knew about that rap over my head. I guess the whores didn't want to fatten a frog for snakes."[15]

On May 24, 1945, Beck went to court to face his charges. He was defended by George Brawley, a brilliant Milwaukee lawyer who was also the chairman of the Negro Citizens Welfare Committee, which advocated on behalf of black youth. With Brawley at his side, Beck pleaded guilty to the charge that he "unlawfully did knowingly transport in interstate commerce certain women for the purpose of prostitution and other immoral purposes."[16] Judge F. Ryan

Duffy—who handwrote "Negro" in the margins of Beck's case file—sentenced him to Leavenworth Federal Penitentiary for eighteen months. Beck was relieved. He could have gotten five to ten years in prison for his white-slavery charges. On May 31, 1945, the United States Attorney of the city of Milwaukee signed off on the judgment, stating that Beck was officially considered a "menace to society—a confirmed pimp."[17] A week later, he boarded a train to make the five-hundred-mile trip to Kansas.

Leavenworth Federal Penitentiary was the first federal penitentiary built in the United States, and the largest maximum-security prison of the twentieth century. It was commissioned in 1891 as part of the Three Prisons Act created by Congress, and built fifteen miles north of Kansas City in the middle of rolling farmland. Leavenworth has gone by many names—the Hot House, the Big House, the Wall—and is, as one prisoner described it, "a grand mausoleum adrift in a great sea of nothingness."[18] It was the product of the Progressive Era—a moment that witnessed the end of westward expansion and the rise of urban modernity—and the complex was imbued with a vision of grand reform. The architect William S. Eames, wishing the structure to inspire people as much as the national monuments in Washington, D.C., created the prison to be an exact replica of the nation's Capitol building. Following the model of the Capitol, the central administration building was constructed of white limestone, and when it was completed, the dome was 150 feet high, second only to the actual Capitol in size. The two cellblocks emanating like wings from the central administration building were fashioned after the separate chambers of government. Cellblock A was modeled after the House of Representatives, and it held eight to twelve people per cell, while cellblock B was modeled on the Senate and held two inmates per cell. They are each two-and-a-half city blocks long and five stories high. When seen from the front, there is not a more breathtaking prison in America than Leavenworth.

The prison complex itself was created to be like a small city.

The twenty-two-acre campus could hold 2,500 prisoners when Beck arrived, and it contained a shoe and brush factory, a powerhouse, a barbershop, a laundry, a dry cleaner's, a machine shop, a warehouse, a garage, a four-story hospital, a farm, and the very first school to be built inside a penitentiary. There was a regular paper called the *New Era*, which eventually became the longest-running prison newspaper in history. Inmates attended church services and movies, and they could spend their free time reading in the massive library. The prison even had a regulation baseball field, complete with bleachers and teams divided along racial lines. The African American team was known as the Booker T. Washingtons, the whites formed a squad called the Brown Sox, and Native Americans went by the name Red Men. Some of the most famous criminals in American history were incarcerated here, including boxer Jack Johnson, Bugs Moran, George "Machine Gun" Kelly, Waxey Gordon, and Robert "Birdman of Alcatraz" Stroud.

Although Leavenworth's outward facade reflected the democratic ideals of America's bicameral legislature, the prison itself was a tightly controlled space of surveillance and discipline. The walls extend forty feet high and forty feet below the surface of the ground, in order to prevent escape. From inside the yard, there is no vantage point from where inmates can see the outside world. They can only look up and see endless Kansas sky. There are no exits in any of the buildings, and all of the windows are barred.[19] Leavenworth followed a strict silent rule while prisoners were marched in lockstep to and from their cells. At mealtimes, inmates sat front-to-back, all facing one direction. They ate in silence, served by waiters; as at Waupun, prisoners used a complex system of hand signals to request more food and water. Like the other prisons where Beck had been incarcerated, the cellblocks were designed following the Auburn model, with long rows of cells stacked five stories tall and facing the interior walls of the building. Most of the cells themselves were four and a half by seven feet wide, and roving guards constantly patrolled the narrow corridors between the cells and the walls. There was no air circulation in the cellblocks, and as the sun cast light through the

cathedral windows, it created a greenhouse effect. It was for this reason that the prison earned its most famous name, the Hot House.[20]

When Beck arrived at Leavenworth on June 6, 1945, he realized
immediately that Leavenworth was a tougher prison than anyplace
he had previously been incarcerated. It wasn't the cruelty or unsanitary prison conditions that worried him. It was the psychological
pressure that the institution imposed. "Leavenworth was what the
government called a class-A joint. It was big and escape proof. It was
run by master psychologists. There was no screw [guard] brutality.
It wasn't necessary. The invisible mental shackles were subtle but
harder than the steel bars."[21] Beck got his first glimpse of this discipline when he was processed into the institution. During his first
month in quarantine, he was questioned endlessly by psychologists,
chaplains, doctors, and prison officials. Three days after his arrival,
he received his Initial Medical Examination, which showed that with
the exception of his continued dental problems, he was healthy overall. He was diagnosed as "an erect Negro male" with normal blood
pressure, healthy skin, and firm muscles. He had no needle scarring
from drug use, and he tested negative for both gonorrhea and syphi-
lis.[22] A week later, he was given a Stanford Achievement Test, and
he qualified as the educational equivalent of a sixteen-year-old with
the schooling of an eleventh-grader.[23] Beck also scored a 105 on the
intelligence test, which was consistent with the other IQ tests he
had taken over the course of his life. In the eyes of the institution,
Beck was considered a man with only "Average Intelligence," and as
a result, he was assigned the job of "Truck detail."[24]

In his interviews with prison officials, Beck faced even more
rigorous interrogation. In his entrance interview with the psychiatrist, he tried to minimize his past as a pimp. He lied outright in
some cases, claiming that he graduated from both grade school and
high school, though every existing record suggests otherwise. He
bent the truth in other cases. He told the psychiatrist, Dr. Stanley
Krumbiegel, that he'd studied agriculture at Tuskegee, and had fully
intended to switch his major to photography before he was expelled.
Beck proclaimed that, following college, he'd worked as a salesman

of real silk hosiery, a hotel clerk, an entertainer, a singer, a nightclub dancer, and even a magician. However, the psychiatrist saw through these lies. In Beck's official entrance report, Krumbiegel wrote: "He early came in contact with prostitution and has apparently been concerned directly and indirectly with earning money by prostitution for several years. He does not like to admit that he has been a procurer, all he will say is that he accepted favors from prostitutes. It seems evident, however, that he has very definitely made money off prostitutes and that he was guilty of the instant offenses, the telling of which he is very vague and which he tries to minimize. His moral standards are of the lowest, but he is likely to make an excellent adjustment in the institution. He has no preference regarding work, seems suitable for common labor."[25] In the final result, prison officials viewed Beck as a rather average prisoner, perhaps with an inflated view of himself. The associate warden concluded in his own initial report, "During the interview was quite talkative and somewhat of a 'big shot' complex. May have minor disciplinary violations, however do not anticipate any serious problems."[26]

Beck's attempts to deceive prison officials quickly backfired on him. When he arrived at Leavenworth, he had only $5.91 to his name. He owned only a few possessions, and still owed his stepfather for the money he had borrowed to make bail. Beck still had two women prostituting for him, and he hoped to keep them working and sending him a steady stream of money while passing them off as relatives. On his List of Correspondents sheet, he recorded that his mother and stepfather were living at 101 West Vine Street in Brewer's Hill, Milwaukee. He also listed Mrs. Robert Maupin (whose real name was Eloise Jones) as his wife, living at the same address. Little is known about Jones. She was born in 1921 in Arkansas and then migrated to Chicago with her mother and father to 4804 Forrestville Avenue, an old brownstone near Forty-Seventh Street. She attended three years of high school before she met Beck and began prostituting herself for him. On his List of Correspondents, Beck also put down a Miss Mary Smith as a cousin living at 707 West Walnut Street, Milwaukee.[27] However, prison officials did not believe Beck's flimsy story. On June 23, parole officer A. T. Miller discovered his deception, and he charged Beck with deliberate misrepresentation. According to Miller: "This inmate when interviewed in quarantine informed the parole officer he was married in Chicago, Ill., April 1944. Questionnaire returned from supposed wife—stated she is not married. He was again interviewed and admitted he never has been married. He further listed a cousin—has now admitted she is no relative. We feel he has deliberately misrepresented his marital status."[28]

A week after these charges were filed, Beck was brought before the good-time board to answer for his dishonesty. The board consisted of Associate Warden C. H. Looney, Captain N. F. Stucker, and the prison psychiatrist, Dr. Krumbiegel. The transcript of the interrogation is one of the few surviving documents to quote Beck directly during this early period in his life, and it provides interesting insights into his method of deception. In his opening statement, Beck admitted right away that he was guilty of lying, but he defended himself by explaining, "I made the statement to protect the lady. She is living [at] home with my mother and my mother was under the impression we were married."[29] The associate warden then asked him about Mary Smith, the woman he listed as his cousin. "You listed her as a cousin, in reality she is only an acquaintance, because you knew after you listed the first woman as your wife you would not be able to write to a single woman." Beck admitted that indeed, "The first one influenced the second one," but he explained that prison officials did not warn him about the consequences of misrepresentation until after he had filled out the questionnaire, stating, "I received the questionnaire the same evening in quarantine."[30]

Throughout the interview, Beck tried to portray himself as a dedicated fiancé and a hapless victim of rules he did not fully understand. He told the board that he had lived with Eloise for fifteen months and that he loved her. When the associate warden asked him if he was "devoted to her" and "ever [intended] to marry her?" Beck replied, "Yes Sir, in fact I was planning on it when I was apprehended, but I had been a fugitive for at least 10 months and that is why I was waiting." This response seemed suspicious to the associate warden, and he continued to press Beck about having two single women on his List of Correspondents. "If you intended to marry this person why did you attempt arrangements to have the name of another girl friend placed on your correspondence list?" he inquired. Beck feigned innocence by claiming that "Mary Smith and I had several things in common and she was just a friend of mine and we had some dealings on a platonic basis."[31] Beck then tried to convince the board that he was really a romantic at heart. The reason that he developed a relationship with Mary Smith was so she could help him with his marriage proposal to Eloise. "My prime interest contacting her was to arrange for the acquisition of a ring, that was my prime motive for contacting her in the first place." At the conclusion of the interview, Beck defended his actions one last time by claiming he was just ignorant of the rules of the prison. "I was not fully aware, I can read, but I mean I did not quite understand the severity of the offense at the time and certainly would not have attempted it if I had known the severity of it."[32] The board did not believe him at all, and they revoked his early release privileges before he was even out of quarantine. As they stated in their summary: "The man admits to falsifying the correspondence records, both as to his purported marriage to Eloise Jones and as to his relationship to Mary Smith whom he reported as his cousin and the Board recommends the forfeiture of 30 Days Statutory Good Time"[33] ("good time" meaning time served in prison that is deducted from the duration of the sentence).

On July 5, 1945, Beck was taken out of quarantine and placed in the general prison population. He was issued standard prison equipment: a Bible, cup, mirror, towel, a piece of hard soap, comb, brush, nightshirt, sheet, blanket, and water jar with cover.[34] Like the other black men in the prison, he was held in the segregated D-block, "in a cell house with mostly pimps, dope dealers, and stick-up men."[35] The prison population as a whole was organized along racial lines, and it made for a dangerous environment. "It was a joint of con cliques," Beck remembered. The most dangerous clique was the Southern cons. They hated Negroes!"[36] He witnessed countless acts of racial violence, particularly white on black violence. Sometimes these conflicts were rivalries over sexual partners. After one of Beck's friends known as Doll Baby stole a "lanky white boy with watery blue eyes and bleached corn-silk hair" from a jealous white con from Mississippi, he was stabbed nearly to death by a pack of "shiv men." "Hundreds of cons were pressed together filing from the bleachers and playing the field. I saw 'Doll' throw up his hands and scream. He disappeared. The gray tide moved on. Three screws were standing over him. He was on his back. Blood was gushing from his open mouth. Blood seeped from holes in his jacket. He lived, but he had a bitch of a time making it."[37] At other times, the violence seemed absolutely random. "I was filing out to sick call one morning. A group of cons on the other side of the road was filing to work. I saw a con marching behind a dark-complexioned con raise something that glinted in the sun. It was a shiv. He was chopping away at the con. Finally the con folded dead. Screws rushed up and took the hatchet man away."[38]

After witnessing these incidents of violence, Beck tried to keep his head down and do his time without conflict. He exchanged letters with his mother once a week, and he continued to keep in contact with Eloise Jones. He was lonely, and he considered having sex with one of the young homosexuals in his cellblock. "There were a half-dozen cells where two packs of butts could summon a pink puckered anus to press eagerly against the bars for a guy's blood-swollen organ to rip off." Beck repressed these urges, and instead "would go lie in the quiet gloom of my cell with the terrible convict hunger for the presence and odor of a female. I'd close my eyes, flog my monster."[39] Beck also redirected his sexual frustration toward studying. He took a class titled Human Problems, and he pursued independent courses from his cell. However, it was in his weekly therapy sessions with the prison psychiatrist, Stanley Krumbiegel, that Beck had an experience that would transform his pimping and, later, his writing career. Krumbiegel was a Freudian psychoanalyst, and he firmly believed that pimps, especially black pimps, had unresolved issues with their mothers. "In the late forties," Beck wrote decades later, "a headshrinker in the Federal penitentiary at Leavenworth, Kansas, told me that I had possibly become a pimp because of a savage and unconscious hatred for Mama, who was the perfect loving mother, except for that one mistake when she fell in love with a snake and tore me away from my stepfather—my only and beloved father image."[40] At first, Beck regarded Krumbiegel as little more than a "slick joker." All this talk of unconscious drives and feelings of unresolved guilt seemed ridiculous to him. Then Krumbiegel gave him a copy of Karl Menninger's *The Human Mind* (1930), and that book changed everything. The first popular book of psychoanalysis written for a mass audience, *The Human Mind* posited that criminals were only slightly different from "normal" people, due to traumatic experiences from their past. Particularly important to Beck was Menninger's idea that the absence of parental affection accounted for much criminal behavior. Menninger argued that treatment, not punishment, was the only effective way to help prisoners, the emotionally disturbed, and the mentally ill.

Menninger's work inspired Beck to read things he had never read before. He had read plenty of fiction while incarcerated in Wisconsin, but now he wanted to understand psychoanalytic theory. Leavenworth at that time held over 100,000 books, and Beck set out to read as many of them as he could.[41] This partly served a practical purpose, as psychoanalysis provided him with the skills to endure a long-term prison sentence, now and in the future. "During my bit I had read the second cell house full of books. I had read mountains of books on psychiatry, psychology, and psychoneurosis. I couldn't have done a smarter thing. I'd have to be my own head shrinker when the white folks entombed me in that steel casket in the future."[42] From *The Human Mind*, Beck went back to the origins of Menninger's theories, reading Sigmund Freud and his most famous student, Carl Jung. He read whenever he could find a spare moment: in the yard during recreation time and late into the night using the ambient light that bounced off the prison walls. He knew that the pimp clique would never understand his fascination with reading, so he kept his habit to himself. As he recounted later, "Well, I always read books that I would never even let my friends even know I read. You know, I was a closet pursuer of knowledge. I mean, because look: on several occasions they would see certain things, you know, like Jung and Freud and all and they'd say: 'You square-ass motherfucker. There ain't nothing in there motherfucker, that's gonna help you pimp.' They would, you know, they would rib me, so I'd hide the fact that

I was a seeker of knowledge—above and beyond pimp knowledge, you dig?"[43]

This reading transformed Beck's concept of pimping entirely, though not in the ways that the prison psychiatrist intended. Years later, Beck expressed his understanding about the significance of the pimp/mother relationship in a range of writings. In his collection of essays titled *The Naked Soul of Iceberg Slim*—a book modeled on James Baldwin's *The Fire Next Time*—Beck philosophized, "I am convinced that most pimps require the secretly buried fuel of Mother hatred to stoke their fiery vendetta of cruelty and merciless exploitation against whores primarily and ultimately all women. Throughout most of my life my unconscious hatred for my mother leapt painfully from the depths like bitter bile from the guts of a poison victim."[44] Beck repeated this essential proposition in essays, interviews, and literary representations alike. In his autobiography, *Pimp*, and in the first two major fictional works, *Trick Baby* and *Mama Black Widow*, he represented the mother as the source of the main character's downward spiral into a life of crime or marginal social status. In his 1976 spoken word album, *Reflections*—one of the unacknowledged precursors to rap that influenced artists such as Ice-T—Beck's toast "Mama Debt" identified his troubled and unresolved relationship with his mother as the reason for his imprisonment. It begins:

> *Since I was just a boy*
> *I punished hos with sick joy.*
> *For pimping, I've been to the joint*
> *And that ain't ha ha.*
> *Up that way*
> *I heard a shrink say,*
> *"Son, it appears to me you hate your mama."*
> *"Doc," I pleaded, "I want to be fair.*
> *Can't I make it up somewhere?"*
> *"From the start," he sighed,*
> *"You've mugged her heart.*
> *You've lived like Satan's pet.*
> *I bet nobody can pay a mama debt."*[45]

There was no more important figure in Beck's development as a criminal and as a writer than his mother, and as these works show, it was at Leavenworth where he gained the tools to understand and articulate that relationship.

Even though psychoanalysis provided Beck with insight into the forces that influenced his behavior as a criminal, it did not mean he planned to use this knowledge to go straight. In fact, armed now with these intellectual methodologies, he set out to create new, more creative rundowns designed to snatch up unsuspecting victims. In one such pitch, which he called the "Mama Rundown," he used the story of his father's early abandonment of his mother to gain the sympathy of a potential prostitute. The effect of this rundown was particularly powerful, as it was a story that Beck retrieved "from the bitter roots of my own pain and poisonous ambivalence for Mama."[46] He would say to an unsuspecting victim: "He [Robert Sr.] and Mama fought like pit bulldogs one early bright. He pranced home stone broke with his fly fouled with 'come' . . . his mustache starched with cunt juice . . . He beat the puking, living crap out of Mama . . . He bounced me off a tenement wall to close his act . . . He split with a cardboard suitcase and his pearl grey spats flashing in the zero wind."[47] After recounting how his mother kept them alive through the winter with her door-to-door hairdressing business, and then relating his happy childhood in Rockford, he finished the narrative with the tragedy of Steve taking them to Milwaukee. "I cried until my guts dry locked . . . The pretty bastard was so cruel to us! Tried to turn her out. Mama cut him loose finally. But it was too late for me . . . I was already street poisoned."[48] Beck told and retold this story to countless prostitutes after his release from Leavenworth, and much later used it as the cornerstone of his autobiography. Starting in Leavenworth, he came to understand a deep and intimate relationship between pimping and storytelling. In both conning young women and writing narratives, he revealed just enough of his emotional vulnerability to enlist the sympathies of his audience. As he once said in response to a fan letter about how to write a book: "Be brief with pre adult bio segments unless you have determined that certain of these experiences (parental failure) are causal in the later traumas of your life. Keep your sentences crisp and release as many ego restraints and inhibitions as you can when you start your journey. In a biographical work, to confess imperfection and vulnerability on the page is to charm and win the empathy of readers."[49]

One powerful example of Beck's strategic form of storytelling is his representation of his father. According to his memoir and other sources, Beck repeatedly claimed to have been physically abused by his father as a baby, and then abandoned. He reported that he saw him briefly as an adolescent when he worked on "Big Bill" Thompson's yacht, and that they did not meet again until 1944 in Chicago outside of a barbershop, just before Beck went to Leavenworth. He described the meeting there as short, and Robert Sr. as little more than a pathetic and desperate figure: "A tall skinny stud in a barber's apron was on the sidewalk. His white spats flashed on his feet. He was screaming and flailing his arms like a minstrel clown singing Mammy. He was loping down the sidewalk. The out-of-fashion bastard was yelping, 'Son! Son!' "[50]

There are at least a couple pieces of evidence from Beck's prison records that contradict this story. While he was incarcerated at Wisconsin State Reformatory in 1938–1939, for instance, he listed his father as living at 9601 Saginaw Avenue on the South Side of Chicago, occupation "chef." On this same record, he also listed two half-sisters from his father's second marriage, one whose name he did not know and the other named Maggie Maupins. Furthermore, upon his entrance to Leavenworth, he told prison officials he believed his father was dead, even though his mother recorded his address as 3448 Wabash Ave., apt. B, in Chicago.[51] Finally, and perhaps most importantly, in 1946 Robert Sr. wrote Leavenworth a number of times in an attempt to help secure his son's parole. He offered a room in his home and aid in locating a job.[52] According to official records: "In June 1946 the inmate's father, Mr. R. L. Maupin, Chicago, Illinois, wrote us that the inmate would be welcome in the home. Parole adviser and Employers forms were forwarded to the father in hopes that he might be in a position to develop a release plan for the inmate in Chicago, where he would have the benefit of his father's home."[53] Even if Beck did have a troubled and limited relationship with his father, as he says in his memoir—a story that evokes compassion from the audience—these prison records suggest that he had a more extensive and complex relationship with him than he cared to admit in print. Beck once famously wrote at the opening of *The Naked Soul of Iceberg Slim*, "I learned also that sympathy is a counterfeit emotion for suckers which is usually offered with a crooked con grin of amused contempt."[54] It appears that, as both a pimp and a writer, Beck used the story of his abusive father as a sympathy con to win the compassion of prostitutes and audiences alike.

In July 1946, about a year into his sentence, Beck requested a restoration of the thirty days of good time he had lost during his first month at Leavenworth. Whether he did this in response to his father's offer of his home, or because he'd kept a clean record throughout the year, is unclear. He asked to be returned to Chicago, as he was worried about the police in Milwaukee targeting him. Dr. Krumbiegel, seeing that Beck had made little progress in his rehabilitation, did not think he was ready for the outside world. "It is believed that this man offers a good outlook for continued good institutional adjustment but that the prognosis for future rehabilitation in the community is extremely poor because of very lax moral standards and distinctly criminalistic attitude and habit. He has shown no improvement in character standards, insight or judgment."[55] Nevertheless, the Classification Committee saw that he had made a strong enough improvement that they were willing to restore his lost good time. "[H]e has maintained a clear conduct record for over a year, therefore, it was unanimously agreed that he is deserving of a full restoration at this time. It was noted that he has made an average work adjustment since his commitment and the psychiatrist is of the opinion that he will be able to continue with a highly satisfactory institutional adjustment for the remainder of his sentence but he also stated that this man's insight or judgment has not improved and because of his lax moral standards, the outlook for the future when he leaves the institution is very poor. It is believed, however, that the restoration of the 30 days would be warranted in view of his good adjustment since the good time forfeiture."[56] When Beck was released from Leavenworth on August 7, 1946, he had $18.66

and the clothes on his back. He was completely starting over. "I had no flash and glamour, no pimp front. I was just another pimp down on his luck. I was starving for a whore."[57] However, armed with the pimp book and his newfound understanding of psychoanalysis, he was ready to make a run at the fast track for the second time in his life.

CHAPTER 6

ON THE ROAD (1946–1962)

A few days after his twenty-eighth birthday, Robert Beck was released from Leavenworth Federal Penitentiary. After three tough bits in prison and years of studying the pimp profession, he was a changed man. He no longer had his youthful good looks of a decade before, but he now possessed the skills and knowledge of a seasoned player. "Drugs and the pimp game had hardened away my baby face," he later wrote. "My hair was thinning. I was turning twenty-eight but I looked forty. For seven years I had devoted myself to getting hip by that pimp's book. I had labored with the zeal of a Catholic Brother agonizing for the Priesthood. I had thought and acted like a black God."[1] Beck stopped by his mother's house for a week's obligatory visit, and then headed back to Chicago. He was starting again from nothing, and as he well knew, a pimp without the bankroll, the attire, and the car did not have the tools to catch women for his stable. "In a pimp's life, yesterday means nothing. It's how you are doing today. A pimp's fame is as fleeting as an icicle under a blow-torch. The young fine whores are wild to hump for a pimp in the chips. A pimp in bad shape can't get the time of day from them. A pimp's wardrobe has to be spectacular. His wheels must be expensive and sparkling new. I had to get the gaudy tools to start pimping again."[2] Even though Beck was down on his luck, he still had the rundowns he had learned from Baby Bell that he could use to build up a stable. "I had memorized an arsenal of howitzer motivators I'd kept on instant alert in my skull. I'd barraged them daily for three years to persuade a ten ho stable to hump my pockets obese."[3] Beck felt confident that if he could just put together a modest bankroll first, he would find his way back to the fast track.

Without the cash to start up his pimp operation again, he had limited options. "I had three choices. I could cop a piece of stuff [heroin] on consignment from a contact I had made in the joint. I could peddle it retail and get nine or ten grand in weeks. I could take a dog, a broken-down whore with trillions of mileage on her. Maybe I could keep my foot in her ass and grind up a bankroll. I decided to take the third out. Do a slick fast hustle."[4] With an accomplice, Beck attempted to pull off a series of robberies of Black Belt drug dealers. However, strong-arming wasn't really his racket, and he was arrested for armed robbery in the early spring of 1947. According to his memoir, he was sentenced to a year at the Chicago House of Correction, a prison workhouse on Twenty-Sixth Street and California Avenue on the southwest side of the city. Built the same year as the Chicago Fire of 1871, the bridewell (an English term for a prison that held inmates on a short-term basis) was created to incarcerate thieves, pickpockets, drunks, and other poor people unable to pay fines. The House of Correction was considered one of the toughest and most outdated facilities in the United States. Although there were numerous shops onsite for training inmates in the construction of shoes, brooms, mattresses, bricks, leather goods, and pottery, there were no educational or training courses open to them. The prison staff was undertrained in modern penal philosophies, and they treated inmates like indentured servants working off debts. The prison was overcrowded and lacked modern facilities; single-person cells were often crammed with two or three prisoners. In 1952, a mayoral commission on the House of Correction concluded: "In this antiquated plant with its inadequate kitchen, multiple makeshift feeding locations, poor hospital facilities, inadequate and congested quarters, where as many as 200 prisoners must be received and a like number discharged daily, insufficient fire protection, scattered random shops, crumbling walls, and at least one hidden guard tower, it is obvious that the Chicago House of Corrections 'grew like Topsy' and was built without any thought of coordinated planning and the best interests of the inmates or the citizens of Chicago."[5]

Beck found the conditions here impossible. "It was like a prison only tougher. A joint is always rough when there's graft and corruption. Only cons with scratch are treated and fed like human beings. The walls were just as high. Most of the inmates were serving short thirty and ninety-day bits. The joint was filthy. The food was unbelievable. The officials had an unfunny habit of putting pimps on the coal pile. I did a week on it. I was ready to make a blind rush at the wall. Maybe I could claw up the thirty feet before I got shot. I was really desperate."[6] He made a plan to escape; he simply couldn't handle a year in the prison, especially after just being released from Leavenworth. Working on the coal pile was backbreaking labor, and besides, he reasoned, "No con misses his freedom more than a pimp. His senses are addicted to silky living."[7] As Beck related it in his various writings, he made a daring escape from the prison on April 4, 1947, Good Friday. He set up a dummy in his cell, using a stolen pair of pants, a shirt, and a sheet for stuffing. He hid in a prison shed until nightfall, climbed up the side of an administration building, and then dropped over the eighteen-foot wall.

It is difficult to say with any real certainty whether this actually occurred, as no definitive record of the event exists anywhere. There is nothing in Beck's FBI file mentioning an incarceration at the House of Correction. A Freedom of Information Act search of the Cook County Sherriff's Office yielded no results, and an exhaustive exploration of the Records Center by the Clerk of the Circuit Court of Chicago uncovered no documents either. However, a few small clues indicate that it is likely Beck was at least incarcerated there, and perhaps did indeed escape. One of the most compelling pieces of evidence supporting Beck's claims is that his description of the layout of the prison yard almost exactly matches official reports. There was, in fact, a nine-by-twelve-foot shed built in 1909 to be used as a tin and machine shop, and it sat directly adjacent to the coal pile. Furthermore, Beck related that he climbed up the side of the mess hall, then onto the roof of the chapel, and finally onto the ridge of a cell-house roof before dropping over the side of the wall. This matches perfectly with available descriptions of the prison's design, in which the mess hall was connected to the chapel and adjacent to the cell house. Beck simply could not have so precisely described the path of his escape unless he had been incarcerated there.[8] Most illuminating of all is a *Chicago Daily Tribune* article from 1961, which reported on Beck's recapture by the Chicago police. According to the brief article, entitled "Denies Escape from City Jail 14 Years Ago," Beck had in fact served time at the bridewell in 1947 for larceny. Although he claimed in the article that he had served out his sentence of one year for the crime, the FBI strongly suspected that he had busted out of prison. The police ended up siding with the FBI and holding him for ten months, the unserved time he owed. The criminal justice system did not believe Beck's story that he was a "victim of mistaken identity."[9]

What happened after Beck's apparent escape is one of the few instances in which recently uncovered records actually contradict his own account of his journey in his memoir. As he repeatedly bragged in his writings, he broke out of the House of Correction in the spring of 1947 and then lived as a fugitive until 1961. "I did a black Houdini to Indiana on Good Friday. For the next thirteen years, I yo-yoed up and down the pimp string in a dozen states."[10] The truth is a little more complicated. In the summer of 1947, Beck met the woman who would become his first common-law wife, Mattie Cooper, aka No Thumbs Helen—perhaps so named for her inimitable skills as a pickpocket. After a brief courtship, they married in Chicago and then moved back to Beck's mother's house in Milwaukee, where they would live off and on for about the next four years. Although he mentioned Mattie only briefly in his autobiography, she had a significant influence on his life in the years following his release from Leavenworth. Mattie was born in Galveston, Texas, on November 4, 1913, to Robert and Eldora Cooper. Robert was a longshoreman, and when Mattie was fourteen he moved the family to New Orleans to find better work. Mattie only made it through the sixth grade at a Lutheran school before she dropped out. She got into a life of crime as early as 1928, a year after the family arrived in the Big Easy. Her range of crimes included assault and robbery, possession and sale of narcotics, disorderly conduct, highway robbery, and disturbing the peace. To escape detection by the police, she took on various aliases during her teens and twenties, including Mattie Gray, Madeline Roach, and Mattie LaRoche.

Mattie was prone to drink and violence, and by the time she met Beck she had a lengthy rap sheet. In September 1941, she was arrested in New Orleans and charged with robbery, but then released. The day after Christmas that same year, she was charged with disturbing the peace by assault and "carrying an oversized knife." She was sentenced to pay a fine of one hundred dollars and serve sixty days in Parish Prison. A few months after she was released, she was arrested for prostitution and using profane language. She was fined ten dollars. Following this, she changed her name to Mattie Gray and moved to Alexandria, Louisiana. On November 5, 1942, she was arrested there for highway robbery, and a week later she was arrested for petty larceny. The charges were eventually dropped. In 1944, she served a short sentence at the federal prison in Alderson, West Virginia, for narcotics abuse. She moved back to New Orleans, where over the course of the next few years she was arrested for loitering, larceny, and prostitution. After this string of arrests, she fled to Chicago probably in late 1946.[11] She worked for nine months at the Bushman Company making raincoats, until she met Beck in the summer of 1947. They married on July 7. They stayed in Chicago for a few weeks, during which time Mattie was arrested for drunk and disorderly conduct, and then they moved in with Beck's mother in Milwaukee at 101 Vine Street on the edge of Bronzeville. Married life in Milwaukee did little to deter Mattie from her criminal behavior. Between September 1947 and early January 1948, she was arrested multiple times for drunk and disorderly conduct.[12]

It is perhaps because of her growing notoriety in Milwaukee that the fugitive Beck took her on the road during 1948. In his autobiography, he did write about her briefly, calling her by the moniker "No Thumbs Helen." "She was at that time one of the slickest 'from the person' thieves in the country. We got about in a 'forty-seven Hog. She was a magician. For almost a year she left a trail of empty wallets across five states."[13] Her method of robbery was to stand in an alley and pose as a desperate woman looking for quick sex. "She would lurk in some shadowy doorway or alley entrance. When the trick came by she'd go into a con act. She'd stand wide-legged and bend her knees to an almost squatting stance. She'd whip up the front bottom of her dress. She'd expose the gaping, hairy magnet to the bugging eyes of the sucker. The pull was magnified by her stroking her cat."[14] Once the mark entered the alley and started grinding himself against her, she would expertly unbutton his pants pocket with one hand, take out his wallet with the other, and rob him blind. "With both hands behind his neck, she'd remove the scratch from the hide. She'd up the sexy chatter and the strong grind against his scrotum. She'd roll up the bills into a tight suppository shape. She'd slip the wallet back into the pocket. She wouldn't forget to rebutton the pocket. She was ready to blow the sucker off, get rid of him. She'd crack that she had to 'pee.' Stooping quickly, she'd ram the rolled bills up her cat."[15] Pretending to see a vice cop driving down the street, Mattie would then tell the mark to meet her at a local hotel, and disappear down the alley to find another sucker.

Beck and Mattie were successful with this con game for at least a year. In the only known photograph of the two of them together, found among Beck's possessions, he wrote on the back: "Mattie 'No Thumbs Helen' My superstar thief. One of America's crème de la crème. A ballsy bitch who would rather die than kick back a penny of a sting to a sucker. A wizard with a top score of 27 grand from the well of a sodbuster's lumber jacket in Iowa." While the amount of the score was probably an exaggeration, the sting itself was probably not. As Beck wrote about it in his memoir: "We were in Iowa when Helen stung a rich sodbuster for seventy-two hundred. I was in bed when she threw it on the bed. Excited! Sure I was. My heart boomed like bombs going off. She didn't know it. I was icy cool."[16] For all his success with Mattie as his partner in crime, however, Beck couldn't shake the feeling that he needed to get back to pimping a stable. After all, he had learned so much from both the pimp book and from his reading in Leavenworth. Running the pickpocket con with Mattie seemed to Beck like a waste of his talents. "I didn't feel like a pimp with only one whore. I decided to steal the technique of stealing from [Mattie]. I could use it to train other whores when I cut her loose."[17] However, Mattie refused to be stabled; they were married, after all, and she didn't want to compete with other women. When Beck tried to bring his second girl into the group, she attacked them both with the oversized blade she was known for carrying. "She drew her knife. The young whore fled. I disarmed Helen and punched her around. Helen went to work. I fell asleep. I woke up fast. Helen was jabbing her knife into me. I rolled away. She had stabbed me in the forearm and the side of an elbow. I took a golf club and knocked her out."[18]

This confrontation sobered Beck, and he began looking for ways to rid himself of her without getting killed or thrown back in prison again for the Mann Act. Sometime in early 1949, they moved back to his mother's house. For a few months, they hustled up and down Walnut Street and throughout the red-light district. On March 8, 1949, Mattie was caught during her alley con routine and arrested for "larceny from the person." With her lengthy arrest record, she was sentenced to one to three years at the Wisconsin Home for Women at Taycheedah. Like Wisconsin State Prison at Waupun, the Wisconsin Home for Women focused on training and education as a method of rehabilitation. Reflecting the gendered division of labor in the late 1940s, the inmates did laundry, sewing, gardening, kitchen, and farmwork. Despite her long tenure as a street hustler, Mattie seemed to take the program of rehabilitation seriously during her stay. She had perhaps grown weary of her life with Beck and was looking for ways to escape from him as well. She gardened and made clothing, and she enrolled in a class called Home Care Management. She was considered a good worker by her supervisor, Marcia Simpson, who stated in her conduct report: "Her work habits were good, as a rule she was cooperative, willing. She had a nice sense of humor, and was fairly well liked by most of the clients. She dressed neatly, and was in fair health." In fact, Simpson wrote, Mattie had only a few problems. "One could list her liabilities as, uncontrolled temper, quarreling, and running away from unpleasant situations."[19] Mattie tried to improve her life in other ways. She joined Alcoholics Anonymous, and she took a number of other classes, including chorus, band, Bible study, two literature courses, World Today, and Travelogue. The teaching staff noted that Mattie, because of her lack of education, was "Intellectually Limited, but had a good attitude in her classes."[20] Because of her efforts at self-improvement and rehabilitation, Mattie served a year and a half of her possible three-year sentence, and then she was paroled on November 21, 1950. She moved back in with Beck, who was still living with his mother at 101 Vine Street.

Back on the streets of Milwaukee, it didn't take long for Mattie to find herself in trouble with the law again. She simply could not resist the pull of Bronzeville's streets. In the summer of 1951, she was arrested for "assault with intent to do great bodily harm" when she stabbed a man four times and nearly cut off his thumb in a fight. This might be another explanation of how she earned the moniker "No Thumbs Helen." According to court documents, she claimed she acted in self-defense. "She was in a restaurant when the man she assaulted came over to her and tried to get her to go out with two white men who were looking for a prostitute. She tried to explain that she couldn't go because she was on parole, but this man insisted and finally drew a knife. She struggled with him to get the knife, and succeeded. In the struggle, her coat was slashed in several places, but the man was cut in four places and had to be taken to the hospital."[21] The victim in the case, a former Wisconsin State Prison inmate named James Roth Jr., testified that Mattie stabbed him with her own knife during a fistfight he was having with her friend Jonas Avery at the Burns Tavern on Walnut Street. The judge believed him. Mattie was sentenced to one to three more years in prison, and she was recommitted to the Wisconsin Home for Women on June 8, 1951. It appears that after Mattie returned to prison, Beck left town. She wrote to him at his mother's house only once, on September 19, 1951, and he did not write back to her.[22] Furthermore, in the official court testimony, Mattie claimed that Beck was one of the causes of her continued illegal behavior, and she wanted to leave him entirely. "She never wants to go back to Mr. Maupins, but may want a reconciliation with her first husband. She thinks that the only way she can keep out of trouble is to stay away from Milwaukee."[23] By the spring of 1952, prison officials concluded that Beck had probably left the city, and it was unlikely they would hear from him at all. "Mrs. Maupin is vague about her so-called husband's occupation, claiming he is a traveling salesman. We have never been able to contact him, and we are under the impression that he has taken himself out of the picture."[24] Beck probably left town sometime between 1951 and 1952, no doubt fearing that the police would figure out he was a fugitive from justice.

Despite distancing herself from Beck, Mattie was unable to straighten herself out. She did not adjust to prison life as well as before. She got into fights with fellow inmates, attempting to stab a fellow prisoner with a pair of scissors in December 1951. She was also considered generally rowdy and undisciplined, and was cited for using profane and vulgar language on May 19 and July 22, 1952. Despite these problems, she was released on parole on November 7, 1952, and accepted a job doing housework at the home of Mrs. Bertha Brewster in exchange for room and board. She stuck it out for ten weeks. However, she soon started drinking on the job and then stopped showing up for work altogether. On Christmas morning of 1952, she took a joy ride with two men who had just purchased a new Cadillac. They ended up in Cleveland, where Mattie attempted to find work and a place to live. However, after her landlady found out about her parole violation, she convinced her to turn herself in to the Cleveland police. Mattie did so, and police returned her to the Wisconsin Home for Women on January 13, 1953. At her parole hearing later that year, Mattie actually requested that parole be denied, as she was not confident she could resist her violent or addictive tendencies while staying in Milwaukee. According to the record of her statement to prison administrators, "Mattie now feels that she would prefer to remain in Taycheedah until the expiration of sentence when she plans to leave Wisconsin."[25] After her release from prison on November 14, 1953, Mattie moved back to her sister's home in Galveston, Texas. She hoped that by moving away from Milwaukee and the destructive life with Beck, she might be able to go straight. However, that was not to be. The last documents that exist about her indicate that on February 7, 1956, she was incarcerated at the Texas State Penitentiary at Huntsville for murder.[26] Beck never heard from her again.

—~—

It was around 1951 or 1952 that Beck began his travels around America, pimping his way from the Midwest to the Pacific Northwest. He left Milwaukee for a number of probable reasons. His mother and her husband, Ural, sold their house at 101 Vine Street and moved to Los Angeles, and he no longer had a place to stay. Furthermore, with Mattie repeatedly incarcerated at Wisconsin Home for Women, he probably feared that she might tip the police to his location. However, there is an additional explanation for Beck's movements during the 1950s. This was an era of unprecedented transformation of black neighborhoods, and the pimp culture that he knew was quickly vanishing from the American scene. It was the age of the Second Great Migration, as five million African Americans moved to industrial urban centers between 1940 and 1960. In the late 1940s, the boundaries of the black ghetto began to expand after the Supreme Court ruled, in the landmark 1948 case *Shelley v. Kraemer*, that restrictive covenants were no longer enforceable (though they were not made illegal). Perceiving an "invasion" of black migrants from the South, white middle- and working-class Americans began moving to rapidly growing suburbs. This "white flight," coupled with discriminatory lending practices by banks, isolated the growing black population in American inner cities across the country, even as those neighborhoods expanded in size. For instance, in Levittown, New York, the first major American suburb ever built, there was not a single black resident among the original 82,000 settlers. This racial divide between suburbs and inner city was created in every American city with a sizeable black population. Additionally, "slum clearance" policies were enacted by local city planners and backed by the federal government. The vibrant black neighborhoods that had been created during the First Great Migration were written off as slums and bulldozed to make room for segregated housing projects and interstate highways. Starting in the 1950s in Milwaukee, for example, these so-called urban renewal strategies destroyed Walnut Street and large sections of Bronzeville, as 7,500 black dwellings were razed to make room for Interstate Highways 43 and 94.[27] The creation of this "second ghetto," as Chicago historian Arnold Hirsch called it, was one of the most significant structural transformations of the American city in the twentieth century, and it fundamentally altered the character of black urban America.[28]

Beck fled Milwaukee and moved to Detroit, which at the time was still America's symbol of industrial might. He didn't have much money, but his years of experience made him confident that it was a good city in which to start over. "I heard whore-catching was good in Detroit. I took my last ten-dollar bill and caught a Greyhound. Detroit was the promised land for pimps all right. The town was teeming with young fast whores. The local pimps were soft competition."[29] He most likely moved to Detroit's lower East Side in a neighborhood known as Paradise Valley. Bordered by the Black Bottom community—a neighborhood of old hotels and nineteenth-century row houses that was the destination of black migrants—Paradise Valley was the center of Detroit's black cultural and commercial life from 1914 to the 1950s. Hastings Street served as the main thoroughfare running through the district, much like Forty-Seventh Street in Chicago, Walnut Street in Milwaukee, and 125th Street in Harlem. At the height of its influence, Paradise Valley was home to numerous black churches, storefronts, barbershops, clothing stores, theaters, over 350 businesses, and even a miniature-golf course. It had saloons and cabarets, but also elegant hotels, such as the Mark Twain, the Garfield, and the most high-class of them all, the Gotham. In the Gotham's grand dining room, known as the Ebony Room, Miles Davis dined with Dizzy Gillespie, the Harlem Globetrotters ate whenever they came to town, and Sammy Davis Jr. tipped big. Paradise Valley was also home to some of the most famous jazz and blues clubs in the United States, including the Flame Show Bar, the 606 Horseshoe Lounge, The Palms, the Forest Club, Sportree's, the Ace Bar, and a dozen other venues. The clubs rivaled those in Harlem, Chicago's South Side, and Los Angeles's Central Avenue, and they featured such famous black musicians as Cab Calloway, Duke Ellington, John Lee Hooker, T-Bone Walker, and Billie Holiday.[30]

Paradise Valley and the adjacent Black Bottom were also the parts of town where prostitution, gambling, and drinking could be most readily found. Starting in the early part of the twentieth century, Detroit was a "wide open" town, particularly in the African American East Side. Hustlers set up three-card monte tables in the alleys, numbers runners collected bets for the day's lottery, and prostitutes walked the streets with relative impunity. By 1910, as many as 10 percent of African American Detroiters worked in saloons, whorehouses, and gambling parlors.[31] Given Detroit's proximity to Canada and its readily available liquor supply, it became the nation's center for "blind pigs" (speakeasies) during Prohibition. In fact, the sale of booze was the second-largest industry in Detroit after the production of automobiles. Gambling could be found everywhere in Paradise Valley, and its influence was felt even at the top levels of city government. In the late 1930s, a crackdown on policy in Paradise Valley led to the arrest of the mayor, who himself had been receiving payoffs from the Great Lakes Mutual Numbers House.[32] Prostitution was also a massive industry in the city. A thriving community of buffet flats—small houses usually run by a madam—offered customers a range of services, including erotic shows, gambling, liquor, and of course, prostitutes. Black women often left behind low-paying domestic work in order to earn higher wages in these buffet flats, or in the alleys next to Hastings Street. This led to a prostitution epidemic during the Depression, as thousands of teenage girls sold their bodies in order to help support themselves and their families. In the 1930s, three-quarters of the prostitutes in Detroit jails were African American, a harsh reminder of the few economic opportunities black women had during this era.[33] As a Detroit social worker reported, "[T]he depression has made competition so keen that girls, both black or white, can be secured for 25 cents in the Hastings Street District. On a Saturday night in an hour's time one will be approached by from 20 to 25 women. As high as 8 girls have been found working on the same corner at the same time."[34]

Hastings Street was immortalized in the crime novels of Donald Goines, Beck's most famous literary protégé. Goines was a pimp and a small-time thief in Paradise Valley during the 1950s, and after he read Beck's autobiography during a prison term in Jackson State Prison in 1970, he set out to represent Detroit's gritty underworld. He would eventually write sixteen novels before his tragic murder in 1974, and became known as Detroit's greatest African American crime writer. He titled his first book *Whoreson: The Story of a Ghetto Pimp*, as a tribute to Beck, and this fictionalized autobiography charts the rise and fall of the title character as he seeks to become Detroit's greatest pimp. The story begins along Hastings Street with a pregnant prostitute desperately looking for tricks even though she is about to give birth. The narrator says: "From what I have been told, it is easy to imagine the cold bleak day I was born into this world. It was December 10, 1940, and the snow had been falling continuously in Detroit all that day. The cars moved up and down Hastings Street, turning the white flakes into slippery slush. Whenever a car stopped in the middle of the street, a prostitute would get out of it, or a whore would dart from one of the darkened doorways and get into the car. Jessie, a tall black woman, with high, narrow cheekbones, stepped from a trick's car, holding her stomach. Her dark piercing eyes were flashing with anger. She began cursing the driver, using the vilest language imaginable about his parents and the nature of his birth."[35] With the image of a prostitute desperately trying to make a living even in the ninth month of her pregnancy, Goines's first novel provides a disturbing symbol of the desperate conditions of Detroit's underworld sex economy along Hastings Street. Whether he was writing about sex workers, heroin junkies, convicts, pimps, or black revolutionaries, Goines represented black working-class Detroiters in the 1950s as flawed but sympathetic heroes struggling against the overwhelming forces of racial and gender oppression and urban violence.

Beck arrived in Detroit just about the time Goines was getting his start as a pimp. It was also a moment when Detroit's black neighborhoods were in the middle of startling and irrevocable changes. Beginning in the late 1940s, and continuing into the '50s and '60s, city planners began leveling Hastings Street and demolishing large sections of Paradise Valley and the Black Bottom to make room for the John C. Lodge and Chrysler Freeways. Further, "urban renewal" policies were being used to destroy the businesses and dwellings of thousands of Detroit blacks. Everything from jazz clubs to the local YMCA to rooming houses was being torn down to build interstate freeways and high-rise public housing projects.[36] Beck came to Detroit at the very moment that the neighborhood was about to disappear forever, though at first its abolition did not deter him from rebuilding his pimp empire. When he arrived, he had only the clothes on his back, but he found that the fast track in Detroit wasn't nearly as difficult as it had been in Chicago. "I was walking, but I was sharp as a Harlem sissy. Anyway, these whores were a different breed than the ones back in [Chicago]. They were gullible, and a fellow didn't have to play his heart out to cop them."[37] After a few months in the city, he had captured a seventeen-year-old girl and a "huge, black dangerous jasper [lesbian]" who ran her own "fast-sheet setup," a small hotel that catered to prostitutes and their tricks.[38] With these two women serving as the foundation of his stable, Beck quickly made his way back into the pimp game. "Within eight weeks after I hit Detroit," he boasted later, "I was cruising the streets in a sparkling new forty-eight Fleetwood. I had a fat bankroll."[39]

Over the next few months, he expanded his stable to five women. He had learned self-control from his study of the pimp book and from his extensive reading of psychoanalysis. When one of his women challenged him the way that Phyllis had years earlier, he no longer reacted with physical violence. He had figured out that "the best pimps keep a steel lid on their emotions," and that the top pimp "gets his pay-off for always having the right thing to say to a whore right on lightning tap."[40] Instead of allowing himself to be baited into a fight, he responded with a "cold overlay." He responded: "Listen square-ass bitch, I never had a whore I couldn't do without. I celebrate, Bitch, when a whore leaves me. It gives some worthy bitch a chance to take her place and be a star. You scurvy Bitch, if I shit in your face, you gotta love it and open your mouth wide."[41] Reverse-psychology gimmicks like these worked better than physical abuse, and Beck successfully made his living in Detroit until urban renewal and freeway construction finally turned much of the East Side into what one Detroit scholar called a "'no man's land' of deterioration and abandonment."[42] Beck probably left Detroit sometime in the early 1950s, because, as he put it, "Detroit folded and the lid slammed down."[43]

His next destination was Cleveland. Much like Milwaukee, Chicago, and Detroit, Cleveland had developed its own distinctive black community adjacent to the downtown. During the first Great Migration, the Cleveland Real Estate Board started the widespread practice of using restrictive housing covenants to keep African Americans out of white neighborhoods.[44] Because of these restrictions, African Americans were crowded into a Black Belt that was located in the city's Central District. It was bordered on the west by the Cuyahoga River and bordered on the east by Fifty-Fifth Street; Euclid Avenue enclosed it to the north, while Woodland Avenue was the main dividing line to the south. In this small rectangular expanse of city, African Americans often slept in overcrowded kitchenette apartments, storefronts, garages, and even train boxcars that were divided up to accommodate multiple families.[45] As in other Midwest industrial cities, blacks had initially come to Cleveland for the plentiful jobs. In the early twentieth century, it was the fifth largest industrial city in America, producing metals, automobile parts, varnishes, and garments. Black men were for the most part excluded from unionized labor and skilled trades; they were employed as barbers, servants, porters, elevator operators, and laborers on construction projects. They did the rough work in railroad yards, foundries, blast furnaces, and iron works factories. Much of this work was temporary and insecure; black men were often the last to be hired and the first to be fired. Black women were typically employed in household service, laundry work, and occasionally in box-making factories, where noxious fumes and dangerous machines made for unsafe and unpleasant work.[46]

As a result of these geographical and economic conditions, Cleveland's Central District developed a thriving vice scene. Brothels, saloons, gambling houses, and speakeasies operated all over the black section. Among city leaders and police, there was an unspoken agreement to allow these vice industries to operate with impunity, as these criminal enterprises reaffirmed racist assumptions about the connection between blacks and immoral behavior. It was also a way for civil authorities to monitor closely prostitution, gambling, and drinking without allowing them to spill over into "respectable" white neighborhoods.[47] The pioneering black detective novelist Chester Himes grew up in Cleveland during the 1920s, and he was fascinated with the whorehouses and Prohibition speakeasies along the infamous Scovill Avenue, known as the "Bucket of Blood." As he wrote at the opening of his autobiography, "Scovill Avenue ran from 55th Street to 14th Street on the edge of the black ghetto and was the most degraded slum street I had ever seen. The police once estimated that there were fifteen hundred black prostitutes cruising the forty blocks of Scovill Avenue at one time. The black whores on Scovill for the most part were past their thirties, vulgar, scarred, dimwitted, in many instances without teeth, diseased and poverty-stricken. Most of the black men in the neighborhood lived on the earnings of the whores and robbed the 'hunkies' [Hungarian immigrants]. They gambled for small change, fought, drank poisonous 'white mule,' cut each other up and died in the gutters. It was nothing unusual to see a black man lying in the gutter, drunk and bleeding and dying."[48]

By the early to mid-1950s, black Cleveland was undergoing striking changes as a result of suburbanization, highway construction, and urban renewal policies. Whites were fleeing to the suburbs in ever-larger numbers, while African Americans remained segregated in some of the oldest areas in the city. One study in 1952 estimated that of the 60,000 new homes constructed in the Cleveland suburbs, only 200 were made available to African Americans.[49] City planners adopted their "urban renewal" policies with uncommon enthusiasm. Slum clearance along Scovill Avenue had begun in Cleveland as early as 1939. At the height of this practice, in the mid-1960s, more acres were earmarked for destruction in Cleveland than in any other city in America, nearly double the acreage of the next largest city, Philadelphia.[50] African Americans in massive numbers were removed from their homes by these policies. From the 1940s until the 1960s, reported one historian, "Cleveland embraced the urban renewal strategy to an extent surpassing any other city in the country. Combining urban renewal with highway construction, the city sought to contain African American residential areas, insulate downtown real estate, and protect the educational and cultural institutions."[51] Planners even used the city's entrenched prostitution industry to advance the slum clearance agenda in Cleveland. Urban renewal administrators instructed police to encourage prostitution within those areas they wished to raze; the increase of vice devalued properties and further justified arguments that such neighborhoods needed to be torn down. Once permission to bulldoze a section of the city was secured, the sex workers could be rounded up or dispersed to another black neighborhood, and the process would start all over again. As a result, by the time Beck arrived in Cleveland's Central District, it had already gained a national reputation as a "wide open" city. "Cleveland was lousy with pimps and whores and boosters from all over the country," he later recounted.[52]

Beck thrived in this environment. "Cleveland was jumping," he remembered. "I was ready for the best pimping of my career."[53] With girls working in both Cleveland and the neighboring town of Toledo, Beck was making the most money he had ever seen. He frequented the clubs throughout Cleveland's Central District, and they were constantly packed with pimps and prostitutes. "It was phantasmagoria. They wantonly danced to the funky band's erotic pound. In the red lit murk, there was the counterpoint bedlam of profane ribaldry as they loaded their skulls with cocaine and the bubbly. The mirrored globes revolving in the ceiling speckled their faces with flashing light. The meld of their perfumes was a near suffocating cloud. It was like Dante's Inferno updated."[54] On most days, Beck followed a strict regimen of going to bed early and getting up before his prostitutes. He kept clothes and appearance in order, and he never looked disheveled around his women. He even showed up at his stable's apartment early, so that when his women woke up, he would be awaiting them fresh and immaculate. He most often appeared in his bottom woman's room this way in order to illustrate his power over her. "I'd be sitting there, like a field marshal, you see, all impeccable. I might even have gone down to the barbershop and gotten myself all refurbished, everything. And there she found me, the gentleman who had gotten slightly sweaty with her during the night perhaps—but I had recouped, you see, and I was still flawless, infallible Jehovah that I was when we got in bed."[55]

But even as Beck enjoyed living the high life for the second time in his pimp career, the nightmares about his mother persisted. After one of his prostitutes died with a burst appendix, he started having new nightmares in addition to the old ones. "I used to dream that there would be puffy, green-streaked bladders," Beck said in an interview. "And they would be rushing in chaos. And, I had a subjective attachment to them, because I was fearful that they would collide. They were all tied to my own existence."[56] He went back to using cocaine, and now he mixed the coke with heroin, which put him into a trance. It was an expensive and dangerous habit, but Beck felt it was worth it to control his nightmares. "I started capping 'H' with my 'C.' I'd mix them and shoot speedballs. When I went to bed I got sound sleep. I seldom had those bad dreams. I got hooked on 'H.' It didn't worry me. I was getting long scratch."[57]

Just as quickly as the Central District gained a reputation as a wide-open neighborhood, it closed again, as the police cracked down on the widespread prostitution in the city. Urban renewal had gained a significant foothold by the early 1950s, and the sheer number of sex workers and pimps flooding Cleveland from other parts of the country prompted swift and definitive police action. "The mob of hustlers set the torch to Cleveland," Beck later wrote. "By nineteen-fifty-three the streets were so hot a whore was lucky to stand up a week between falls."[58] With the increasing instability of the sex industry in Cleveland and across the Midwest, Beck set his sights on the West Coast. From his own threadbare accounts, he spent some time with his mother in Los Angeles, and then he moved briefly to Seattle. African American prostitution had been a thriving industry there since the frontier days of the late nineteenth century. During the early period, black women who had little access to jobs other than dressmaking, domestic servitude, or cooking worked as prostitutes in small "cribs" or rooms in the red-light district along Jackson Street.[59] As Seattle's black population grew after World War II—it quadrupled between 1940 and 1950—the city increasingly gained a reputation as a wide-open town for drugs and prostitution.[60] Beck went there sometime in the mid- to late 1950s to capitalize on this burgeoning underground economy.

However, he discovered that by this time the pimp game was transforming, as cultural and political changes began to alter the everyday lives of black people. In the 1954 *Brown v. Board of Education* ruling, the Supreme Court decided that racially segregated schools were unconstitutional, and a year later, Rosa Parks refused to give up her seat on a bus to a white man, effectively launching the civil rights movement. In Seattle, blacks were encouraged by better job opportunities and higher wages than they had ever experienced before. The medium income for black Seattleites was 50 percent higher than the national average for African Americans, as they continued to work in the city's expanding defense and airplane industries, primarily Boeing. In the forties, black men and women broke the color barrier in Seattle's hospitals, public schools, and retail businesses, such as Safeway and Sears. Despite the resistance by some white labor officials and unions, black economic progress gained significant momentum in the postwar decades.[61] As Beck had learned from his mentor, Baby Bell, stable jobs and social progress spelled trouble for the pimp. When World War II broke out, Bell warned him, "The defense plants are gonna claim thousands of young potential whores. Those square bitches are gonna get those pay checks. They'll get shitty independent. A pimp can't turn them out."[62] As Bell knew, the sex industry was fueled by the desperation of black women who had few other economic opportunities, and with the rise of economic and political equality in the middle of the twentieth century, the pimp was losing his advantage. "Ain't but one real Heaven for a pimp," Bell told him once. "He's in it when there's a big pool of raggedy, hungry young bitches."[63]

The improving economy and social conditions for blacks also presented another problem for the old-school pimp. The 1950s witnessed the increasing availability of consumer goods and the rise of mass culture, both of which undermined the aura of magnetism that the pimp had enjoyed during the era of hardcore segregation. "There was a proliferation of luxury cars with the end of the war. Shoe shiners had Cadillacs," Beck contemplated long after he had quit pimping. "They might've been selling a little gangster on the side, but they still had Cadillacs. Where formerly only pimps and high powered gamblers and numbers bankers had these luxury cars, there was just a proliferation of them."[64] Popular culture also contributed to the demystification of the pimp. "With the advent of television young girls could see the opulence of the inside of stars' homes. The girl would see authentic opulence. Then the pimp would take them to these bares [empty apartments]. A pimp would buy yard goods. He'd have his bottom woman go down and get satin by the bolt. He would take sometimes tacks and cover a wall with satin so there was only a kind of sleazy opulence. So when the pimp would take these young girls, who had already seen true opulence via the boob tube, it didn't have the true impact he wanted. She was not aswoon at this synthetic splendor."[65] In this new era of popular culture and readily available commodities, pimps increasingly turned to employing heroin to hook women into a life of prostitution, a drug that would cripple black communities in the 1960s. Beck realized that the pimp book was becoming irrelevant, and he decided that he needed to change up his strategy if he was going to survive.

In 1958, Beck moved back to Chicago one last time. He didn't go back to the fast track or any of the old haunts he had frequented fifteen years earlier. He finally quit shooting heroin. The habit was turning him into a corpse, and he remembered what it had done to Weeping Shorty back in Milwaukee. He had a friend lock him in a room, and he slowly reduced the dose over a few weeks. It was the worst feeling Beck ever experienced, but he finally kicked the habit. "I tell you, if you have ever had the flu real bad, just multiply the misery, the aching torture by a thousand. That's what it's like to kick a habit."[66] He had blown down to three women, and he housed them in various bordellos, including one in Montana. Although the madam took 50 percent off the top, his girls still made him plenty of money, as places like Montana had boasted a thriving brothel culture since the late nineteenth century. With the money Beck collected every few weeks in the mail, he was living an easy life for a pimp. "At almost forty I was ancient as a pimp. I looked like a black, fat seal in my expensive threads. For the first time in many years I had rediscovered my appetite for good food. I was slowing down. I spent most of my time reading in bed. The end of my pimping career wasn't far in the future."[67]

Beck was right, though he could not have predicted the circumstances that would bring about his sudden retirement. In early 1961, Beck was arrested for the last time at 5846 South Park Avenue in Chicago on the outstanding warrant for his prison escape years earlier. He was held for two months at Cook County Jail awaiting trial. On June 13, 1961, he was sentenced to ten months in the Chicago House of Correction by Chief Justice Walker Butler.[68] Beck was placed in a tiny cell that was not meant for long-term incarceration. "It was a tight box designed to crush and torture the human spirit. I raised my arms above me. My fingertips touched the cold steel ceiling. I stretched them out to the side. I touched the steel walls. I walked seven feet or so from the barred door to the rear of the cell. I passed a steel cot. The mattress cover was stained and stinking from old puke and crap. The toilet and wash bowls were encrusted with greenish-brown crud."[69] Built just a few years after the Civil War, the cells in the House of Correction were antiquated and crumbling. The smallest cells were only seven feet long, seven feet tall, and three feet wide. They had no windows, and some of them still used slop buckets for toilets. Many were designed for prisoners to spend only one night, but prison officials sometimes used them to punish uncooperative or dangerous inmates.[70] Trapped in such a cell for nearly a year, Beck witnessed terrors that nearly drove him crazy. "A con on the row blew his top one night around midnight. He woke up the whole cell house. At first he was cursing God and his mother. The screws brought him past my cell. In my state the sight of him almost took me into madness. He was buck naked and jabbering a weird madman's language through a foamy jib. It was like the talking in tongues Holy Rollers do. He was jacking-off his stiff swipe with both hands."[71]

Beck had to draw upon all of his discipline and experience as a pimp to survive the ten months in solitary. After a few months, he started hearing voices, and so he developed exercises to keep himself sane. He remembered the lessons from his readings of psychoanalysis at Leavenworth, and he reminded himself that hearing imaginary voices was a symptom of trauma. He also recalled the screen theory that the old convict philosopher had taught him back at Wisconsin State Prison. He reminded himself that he was in control of the reality that he projected out in the world. He decided, "Every moment I'll stand guard over my thoughts until I get out of here. I can do it. I just have to train that guard. He's got to be slick enough not to let trouble by him. I'll make him shout down the phony voices."[72] Perhaps most important of all, he developed a method of creation called "writing on the ceiling" that would become the kernel of his literary production in later years. Lying on his bunk, he produced lengthy dialogues, creating stories about people he once knew in the pimp life. After months of this rigorous mental routine, Beck decided that he was going to leave the pimp life forever upon release. Word had reached him that his mother was deathly ill with diabetes in Los Angeles, and he could not risk serving this kind of prison sentence again. "Mama's condition and my guilty conscience had a lot to do with my decision," Beck later explained. "Perhaps my age and loss of youth played their parts. I had found out that pimping is for young men, the stupid kind."[73]

At the end of his term, the prison administration threatened to keep him a month longer than his legal release date. Beck composed a letter to the warden to challenge this illegal incarceration, and remarkably, it worked. The letter is the only document from Beck's incarceration in the Chicago House of Correction that has survived, and so it is printed in its entirety here.

> *Sir:*
>
> *I have requested to see you on several occasions in the recent past as to the vital importance of my legal release date. I had attributed your failure to call me for interview, to the press of a busy schedule. Now that I have by personal device managed to see you, I shall be as brief and as clear as possible. Sir: I am confused and puzzled as to what methods you employ in*

*the awarding of good time. I will be most grateful to you if you
will clarify your criterion which determines who is and who is
not entitled to good time. I am sure that you are an able man
for your position and as such you surely must be aware that
one of the vital precepts of effective penology is that good time
is always given to those whose good conduct deserves it. Sir:
in short, why in the face of my impeccable conduct has my
good time been taken? Sir: I have heard very recently a most
unpleasant rumor to the effect that good time is sometimes
unfairly given or not given on the basis of not merit, but of skin
color. This rumor, because of my faith in you as a just man, I
had discounted as utterly fantastic. Sir: another matter which
is not less important to me is the failure of your record room to
post on its ledgers 60 days to my credit which had been given to
me in court last June 13 by Judge Butler.*

*A friend of mine has researched this matter for me and the
result is that aside from Judge Butler's dictum I have yet a
stronger legal support for my 60 days claim, I refer specifically
to the fact that Mr. Churchill, an accredited and authorized
member of the (H.O.C.) official family had executed and
performed my arrest as a member of your staff. In brief my
contention is simply that if Captain Churchill had taken me
to such an unlikely location as a basement in Skokie, and
held me there for two months, instead of in County Jail as
was done, the legal effect would still be the same. My sentence
started at the instant that the Captain arrested me. Now Sir: if
I am not released on schedule the prospect of Civil Experiment
I find most attractive. In closing, I must say I realize that mine
is a tiny voice crying in the wilderness, but it is historical fact
that even a tiny voice can often bring cataclysmic change.
Thank you for your time.*[74]

Drawing on legal-sounding arguments, semi-veiled threats, and
humor, Beck quite literally wrote his way out of prison. This also
signaled the beginning of his conversion from pimp to writer. His
poetic concluding statement, "I must say I realize that mine is a tiny

voice crying in the wilderness," is a reference to John the Baptist's pronouncement to make way for the coming of the Lord. But the quote is more than just a biblical allusion; it is also a prophecy of Beck's own impending transformation into the most important literary voice in black urban America in the decades to come. Within his prison cell in Chicago, he made a startlingly accurate prediction: it was his tiny voice that would bring cataclysmic change.

Robert Beck at the age of three with Santa Claus, 1921.
Courtesy of Diane Beck

Robert Beck's seventh-grade class photo from 1931 at Theodore Roosevelt Junior High School. Beck is seated in the third row, fifth from the left. *Courtesy of Rockford Public Library*

Robert Beck's stepfather, Henry Upshaw, owner of two laundries, a leader of the African American civic and church community, and the only real father Beck ever knew. *Courtesy of Diane Beck*

(RIGHT)
Mary Beck, Robert's mother and the single most influential figure in Beck's life.
Courtesy of Diane Beck

Robert Beck at the age of fifteen. By this time, he had committed his first crimes on the streets of Milwaukee's Bronzeville.
Courtesy of Diane Beck

Robert Beck and his first partner in crime, Joe "Party Time" Evans, a mentor described by Beck as a character with a "head full of wild risky hustles."
Courtesy of Diane Beck

(RIGHT)
Pepper Ibbetts, described by Beck as an "ex-whore who had worked the jazziest houses on the Eastern Seaboard." She was his first guide in the sex industry.
Courtesy of Diane Beck

Exterior of Wisconsin State Prison, where in 1940 Beck was sentenced to two years for carnal knowledge and abuse after he tried to pimp a fifteen-year-old girl. *Courtesy of the Wisconsin Historical Society*

Albert "Baby" Bell, a pimp and enforcer for the infamous Jones Brothers, was a black Chicago icon who introduced Beck to the "pimp" book. *Courtesy of* Chicago Defender

A Wisconsin State Prison cellblock, where Beck became a "member of a clique that talked about nothing except whores and pimping." *Courtesy of the Wisconsin Historical Society*

During the 1930s and '40s, the Palm Tavern on Chicago's South Side was "the most high class Negro establishment in America." The Palm is likely the bar where Beck met Albert Bell. *Courtesy of the Chicago Historical Society*

Robert Beck's inmate photograph at Leavenworth Federal Penitentiary, where he was sentenced for violation of the Mann Act in 1945. *Courtesy of Leavenworth Federal Penitentiary*

USPLK-61956-6-6-45

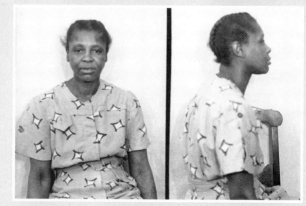

Mug shot of Mattie Maupins, a prostitute with a lengthy arrest record for robbery, who met Beck sometime in the middle of 1947. They married and then toured the Midwest robbing marks. *Courtesy of the Wisconsin Historical Society*

PIMP
the story
of
my life

by ICEBERG SLIM

Original book cover of *Pimp:
The Story of My Life*, published
in 1967 by Holloway House.
The autobiography sold millions
of copies and established Beck
as the godfather of African
American street fiction.
Courtesy of Holloway House

Based on Beck's first novel of
the same name, *Trick Baby*
(1973) established Beck
as a popular figure during
Hollywood's blaxploitation era.

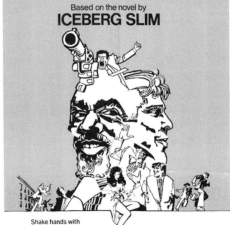

Based on the novel by
ICEBERG SLIM

Starring KIEL MARTIN • MEL STEWART

Shake hands with
"Folks"and "Blue."   And then count your fingers!

A MARSHAL BACKLAR/JAMES LEVITT PRODUCTION
Starring KIEL MARTIN • MEL STEWART
Screenplay by A. NEUBERG, T. RAEWYN and LARRY YUST • Directed by LARRY YUST
Produced by MARSHAL BACKLAR • Executive Producer JAMES LEVITT
A UNIVERSAL RELEASE • TECHNICOLOR

Robert Beck in 1977 with his Great Dane, Leana, a dog befitting a writer with enough money to buy items suited to his former pimp lifestyle.
Courtesy of Holloway House

A promotional photo of Robert Beck for his spoken-word album *Reflections*.

Betty Mae Shew, Robert Beck's common law wife. Together, they wrote seven bestselling books based on Beck's life as a pimp.
Courtesy of Misty Beck

Beck's 1967 appearance on *The Joe Pyne Show*, in this bizarre mask sewn together by Betty, resulted the next day in long lines of people outside Los Angeles bookstores looking to purchase his books.
Courtesy Iceberg Slim: Portrait of a Pimp, *from Phase 4 Films*

Mike Tyson, to Beck's left, met his literary hero and mentor in the late 1980s, after Iron Mike had become heavyweight champion.
Courtesy of Diane Beck

Robert Beck and his wife Diane Millman Beck, a fan of his work whom he married in 1982.
Courtesy of Diane Beck

CHAPTER 7

LOS ANGELES (1962–1967)

When Robert Beck was released from prison for the last time in April 1962, he vowed to leave the pimp game behind him forever. Most of the pimps he once knew had either died or become drunken bums. His pimp mentor of many years, Albert "Baby" Bell, had walked over to Chicago's Washington Park one day and shot himself in the temple, leaving a note that read: "Good-bye squares! Kiss my pimping ass!"[1] Beck did not want to suffer the same fate. He was past forty now, practically a senior citizen for a pimp. He had blown his bottom woman, and he no longer possessed the necessary finery for luring young victims. "I was caught in the nightmare bind that an older pimp faces past the age of thirty-five," Beck reflected. "He is then prone to many setbacks and disasters. Any one of them can put him on his uppers and without the basic gaudy bait, like an out-of-sight car, psychedelic wardrobe, the diamonds necessary to hook and enslave a fresh stable of humping young whores."[2]

The ten months in solitary confinement at the Chicago House of Correction—the "steel casket"—had reduced him to a shell of his former self. He had witnessed spectacles of violence and terror there that had nearly driven him mad, including convicts hurling feces at one another. Even ten years after his release, Beck remained haunted by these visions. "But that second mob of debonair demons sure butchered off a hunk of my mental ass," he later mused. "I will lay odds that until the grave the images and sounds of that violent, gibbering year will stomp and shudder my mind."[3] In a little less than a year, he had lost thirty pounds and grown a scraggly beard. When he put on his old suit upon release, he admitted, "The clothes flopped around on my skeletal frame."[4] Freed from his seven-by-three-foot cell, he decided to hoof it the entire six miles back to his old stomping grounds on the South Side of Chicago. "[I] found freedom from the box so intoxicating that I walked miles before my legs got rubbery."[5] He stopped at a barbershop on Forty-Third Street and got a shave and a mud massage. He hoped that the treatment might restore some of the youthful good looks that time and hard living had taken away. But one glance in the mirror told him the pimp dream was over. "I look like my own grandpa," he thought.[6]

There were many reasons why Beck decided to go straight. One of them, he acknowledged, was that "[his] bottom or main whore of many years had delivered [his] car, jewelry, clothes and other vital pimp flash to an obscure but younger, fresher monster than [he]."[7] However, the most important reason why he wanted to quit pimping was to make good on the promise that he had made to his mother. Mary was now bedridden with heart trouble and a severe case of diabetes, and doctors said she might die at any time. Her husband, Ural, had died in October 1956, and she had been suffering alone for years. Beck needed her to forgive him so he could be relieved from the terrible guilt that he had been carrying for decades; absolution might even end the terrible nightmares that still plagued him nightly. "Mama might die in California at any time. I had to get to her before she died. I had to convince her I loved her, that I appreciated her as a mother. That she and not whore-catching was more important to me. I had to get there as much for myself as for her."[8] Perhaps even to his own surprise, Beck was finally ready to exit the pimp game. Certainly, his age and time in prison were significant factors, but more important was his love for Mary, which had resurfaced now that she was on her deathbed. As Beck later confessed in an interview, "I was never the best pimp. To be a great pimp, you've really got to hate your mother. I always had that sucker residual. That is why I [could] transfer from pimping."[9] After spending nearly his entire adult life in prison cells and pimp palaces in the Midwest, Beck was ready to make a fresh start. Mary's friends all pitched in and bought him a one-way ticket to Los Angeles, the city of dreams.

As he left Chicago, he felt divided about his choice to abandon the career that had defined him for a quarter century. As he said goodbye to the last woman who had worked for him, he said, "I felt a stab of regret that I was leaving her forever back there. But then the pain was gone in the great relief of my smooth exit from her and the terrible emptiness of the pimp game. And it was good to realize that I would no longer brutalize and exploit black women."[10]

~

For African Americans, Los Angeles had always been a city of radical paradoxes. It had long been considered a destination of opportunity for blacks leaving the oppressive regime of the South during the Great Migration. As early as 1913, African American philosopher and race leader W. E. B. Du Bois wrote of the city, "Nowhere in the United States is the Negro so well and beautifully housed, nor the average efficiency and intelligence in the colored population so high. Here is an aggressive, hopeful group—with some wealth, large industrial opportunity and a buoyant spirit."[11] At the same time, Los Angeles followed a pattern of segregation that characterized other divided metropolises such as Chicago and New York. Starting in the 1920s, whites employed restrictive covenants to create a "white wall"—a firm geographical boundary segregating African Americans—along Central Avenue. As a result, 95 percent of Los Angeles housing was put off-limits to black Angelenos during the First Great Migration. White homeowner associations, such as the Anti-African Housing Association, were created to defend white neighborhoods from "Negro invasions." These associations often overlapped with the Los Angeles chapter of the Ku Klux Klan, which used violence and intimidation to chase blacks out of beach communities and the more prosperous Westside.[12] Such measures created a concentrated black ghetto in South Central Los Angeles. However, at the same time, an energetic cultural and musical scene emerged along the Central Avenue corridor between 1920 and the mid-1950s. After-hours spots like Club Alabam, Paradise Club, Downbeat Nightclub, and Jack's Basket Room—owned by heavyweight boxing champion Jack Johnson—featured some of the greatest black musicians in the country. Charles Mingus, Dexter Gordon, Billie Holiday, Charlie Parker, and Lena Horne could be seen performing at these venues late into the night, sometimes until daybreak. The Lincoln Theater on South Central was considered the Apollo of the West Coast, seating over two thousand people and regularly hosting musical greats Duke Ellington, Nat King Cole, and B.B. King, while the elegant Dunbar Hotel catered to black America's elite musicians, actors, and intellectuals.

These paradoxes intensified in the years preceding Beck's arrival in the city. During World War II, African Americans made significant gains in the labor market due to a deepening worker shortage and Los Angeles's growth into one of the world's largest manufacturing hubs. In the two decades following President Roosevelt's Executive Order 8802 integrating wartime industries, Los Angeles blacks increasingly left service and domestic work for better-paying blue-collar manufacturing jobs. They joined unions, and they bought homes in Los Angeles in unprecedented numbers compared to in any other American city.[13] On the other hand, starting in the 1960s, manufacturing work in Los Angeles began to disappear, neutralizing and even reversing many of the economic gains African Americans had made. Factories moved to the suburbs, while the growing aerospace and aircraft industries employed few black workers. African Americans who attempted to move out of South Central into white neighborhoods met violent resistance. Whites dynamited black homes, they set fire to crosses on their lawns, and in one instance they burned a home to the ground, killing the father, mother, and two small children inside.[14] In the era between the end of World War II and Beck's arrival in Los Angeles, whites set out to create a racially homogeneous utopia of single-family homes in the suburbs outside of Los Angeles, while leaving the African American population behind in the deteriorating inner city. It was these conditions that set the stage for the Watts Riots that would explode in the mid-1960s.

When Beck arrived, he immediately set out to show his mother that he was done with the pimp life. He moved into a small two-bedroom apartment with her in South Central. Beck's homecoming was exactly the motivation that Mary needed to cling to life a while longer. He stayed by her bedside, and they reminisced about their past life together in Rockford and Milwaukee. They also discussed plans for his future, about which Mary had specific opinions. A few years after her death, Beck remembered, "My coming to her had been like a miracle. It was the magic that gave her strength. She clutched to life for an added six months. I never left the house for those six months. We would lie side by side on twin beds and talk far into the night. She made me promise that I would use the rest of my life in a good way. She told me that I should get married and have children."[15] Beck was eager to show his mother that he was a changed man. As the first symbolic gesture of his transformation, he took her last name of Beck and shed the name Maupins. It was an important step toward showing her that he was leaving his old life behind forever.

Beck felt that finding a wife and starting a family would be a more difficult task, as he had abused, exploited, and degraded practically every woman he had ever met. He was charming to be sure, but he really knew only how to stalk women. He decided to find a wife by transferring some of the skills he had developed as a pimp to dating. He dressed in his nicest suit and, borrowing his mother's Chrysler, cruised hash houses, diners, and food stands in search of a pretty young waitress or other working girl who might make a suitable bride. Sometime in late 1962 or early 1963, he met a twenty-six-year-old white woman from Austin named Betty Mae Shew. Born February 25, 1936, in Virginia, Betty had moved out to Los Angeles by way of Texas, because she had had a falling-out with her mother. She had come to Los Angeles like many young people before her, seeking the adventure and excitement of the big city. It was a difficult start. She tracked down her father, who lived in Ventura, California. He was an alcoholic and tried to rape her during their first meeting. Betty was homeless for a while until she got a job as a waitress at a hamburger stand at the corner of Forty-Second Street and Budlong Avenue in South Central. An older black couple named Jean and Ernie owned the stand, and they immediately liked the spirited young woman from the South. Betty wasn't much of a cook, but she was charming and good at math; they hired her to take orders while they made the food. When they found out that she was homeless, they invited her to share a room with their twelve-year-old daughter, Jeanette. Betty took one twin bed, Jeanette took the other, and soon they all were as close as any conventional family.

Beck approached Betty the way that he had hit on dozens, if not hundreds, of waitresses before. Even in the 100-degree Los Angeles heat, he dressed up in his pimp uniform: a dress shirt, a jacket, a hat, and a pair of slacks with a crease ironed down the front. He drove up to the hamburger stand in the Chrysler, which he had polished as shiny as his shoes. He made a powerful impression on Betty, who told Jean in confidence: "He looks like a professional to me. Either a doctor or a lawyer or the president of some bank or some loan officer. I mean I have no idea what this man is. I mean, impeccably dressed. Shoes shined. Car spotless. Just unbelievable."[16] He ordered a hamburger, fries, and 7UP, and sat eating his meal and staring at her intensely. Whenever other men tried to pick her up, he scared them away with one of his tongue-lashings. "Jim, why don't you just make your order and leave the woman alone?" he told them. If they protested, he repeated the command: "Just give her the order. Don't you see she's working for a living?"[17] He didn't say much to Betty directly. He just handed her his basket at the end of the meal and said, "See you tomorrow, my dear." The entire performance was designed to put her off-guard. He did this four days in a row. On the fourth day, he asked her, "Could I take you someplace where you could eat something besides a hamburger?" "Like what?" she wanted to know. "Like soul food," Beck responded. She had always been drawn to black music, black food, and socializing with black people, so she said, "What the hell."[18]

Beck hadn't ever been on any real dates before, and so again he approached the situation with the same intensity of a pimp stalking his prey. When he arrived to pick Betty up, he surprised her with a large box. "I brought you something," he said coyly. "Just look at it and maybe you'll consider wearing it." She eyed him with suspicion, and then opened the box. Inside was a black and gold dress. She was a little embarrassed, but also a little excited, because no man had ever bought her a dress before. "I don't want to wear this," she protested. But Jean and Ernie encouraged her to put it on, so she went into the restroom in the back and changed into it. It was a perfect fit. This only added to the mystery of this stranger. Betty recalled later, "So I put it on and Ernie and Jean and Jeanette—everybody agreed that I looked *terrific* in that dress. And I'm looking at [him]— how in the hell does this man know what size dress to go out and buy me?" Beck drove them on their date in his mother's Chrysler, which had a record player that he had had installed in the backseat. Betty wanted to hear the blues or jazz: Duke Ellington, Count Basie, Jimmy Witherspoon, Howlin' Wolf, Big Mama Thornton, or Muddy Waters. Beck didn't have any of those artists, but he promised to have them for their next date. He took her to a nightclub in the West Adams district so she could play blues songs on the jukebox. They sat at a booth, and he gave her a nickel every time she wanted to play a song. After her fourth trip to the jukebox, she got irritated. She demanded to know, "Why in the hell don't you just go ahead and give me the quarter and let me play them all at one time and get this over with?" He responded, "Because I like the way everybody in here turns around and looks at you every time you walk to the jukebox." She smiled inwardly and held out her hand for another nickel. "OK," she said.[19]

They sat at the nightclub late into the night, listening to music. Beck drank 7UP because he didn't drink alcohol or use drugs anymore, and Betty drank whiskey. It was developing into a relatively normal date, and then something happened that would change the direction of their lives together forever. As Betty recounted the incident:

> I drank my whiskey and anybody else's whiskey I could get my hands on. It was about 1:30, 2:00 in the morning, and I said, "You know I gotta go, because I have to get up and go to work in the morning."
>
> We got in the car, and I got sick like I have never been sick before in my life. He took me to the emergency room. I threw up. I threw up. And the doctor came in and told me I

was about four months pregnant, and I was aborting, trying to abort the child. Looking at me, you'd never know I was pregnant. I never stopped having my period, so there was no way for me to know I was pregnant.

I said, "You have got to be lying."

He said, "No."

I started crying, and Bob came in and said, "What's the matter?"

I said, "Didn't they tell you what was wrong with me?"

And he said, "Yeah."

And I said, "I don't know what I am going to do, because I can't do this. I just can't do this. I think I'll just slit my goddamn throat, because I just can't do this."

He said "Do what? You are going to have a baby."

I said, "Who's going to help take care of me? What am I going to do? This man is telling me I have to have almost constant bed rest. Who is going to do this, Bob?"

And he said, "I am."

And I said, "You're set up where you can do something like this?"

He said, "I can do it."

So he took me over to the apartment where he was living with his mother. It was two bedrooms. She was in one bedroom. He was in the other bedroom across the hall.

He said, "I'll put you right here. I can take care of you, and I can take care of Mama too."

And that's what he did.[20]

Beck moved Betty into the apartment with his mother the next morning. In some ways, it was an unprecedented and totally unexpected act of kindness, considering Beck's past with women. Even Mary was suspicious. She thought that her son was setting up the beautiful young girl for a life in the streets. She told Betty in private, "Baby, you get away. Bobby's no good. He's my son. I love him, but he's no good."[21] After a few weeks of this, Betty finally asked Beck what his mother meant. He still hadn't told her what he used to do for a living; he kept the details of his past private. "I'll tell you one day," he replied. "But now is not the time." In other ways, it made perfect sense for Beck to bring Betty into his life. Mary was going to die soon, and he wanted to make good on his promise to find a wife. Furthermore, he knew that his mother's death would leave an emotional hole in his life that he needed to fill with something other than pimping. Many years after Mary died, Beck admitted in an interview, "I got married [to Betty] because there was a vacuum there. Mama had died, and I needed that kind of care—that kind of understanding. I also had a selfish reason for getting married. I had to do some dramatic personal act, which would afford some sort of insulation between my still sick brain and the streets and pimping. And I knew that marriage and responsibility—the prospect of children—would help me."[22]

About two months after Betty moved into the apartment, Mary finally did pass away. Beck was devastated. He sobbed uncontrollably, and he was an emotional wreck for days. As Betty remembered it, "She died. And that was the most devastating. I have never in my life seen anybody suffer the way he did the day his mama died [b]ecause I never saw such love of a parent as he had for his mother. And I never saw such guilt in a child for what he had done to his mother . . . It was really awful."

Even though Mary was gone, his new partnership with Betty offered him a chance at redemption and a way to stay away from the pimp game. It was a difficult start; Beck didn't really know how to do anything besides pimp, and the couple was almost completely out of money. Betty was healthier now after the constant bed rest, but she was just months away from giving birth. The unborn child was the result of a previous relationship, but Beck promised to help her raise it like his own. They moved out of the two-bedroom apartment and into a cheaper studio on Grand Street and Thirty-Seventh Avenue. The tiny room had a Murphy bed that unfolded out of the wall and just two windows. One overlooked the Harbor Freeway, and the other overlooked the Department of Motor Vehicles. Beck cleaned it from top to bottom with bleach and disinfectant, and then brought his new wife to stay there. He kept her in bed, so that she could rest, and he fed her meals prepared by a friend of Mary's named Cookie. They managed to stick it out for a few months in the studio, but Betty finally admitted to him that the place was just too depressing. She told him, "I come from wide open spaces where grass is green and horses run and cows moo. I can't stay here. I just can't."[23]

Beck understood Betty's frustration, so he moved them to a one-bedroom on Vermont Avenue. He also decided on exterminating as a way to make some money, and to keep away from pimping. He started working for the Western Extermination Company, but the commission was so small that he decided to create his own business. True to his impulses as a hustler, he first figured out what chemicals to use and where to buy them. He then created business cards for a fake extermination company called Inch by Inch. It listed Beck as the manager, his friend Julius Gray as sales representative, and a fictitious Marius Black as owner. The motto of the company was "We Murder Roaches." Beck bought a .25-caliber pistol and carried it with him for protection. Every day he dressed up in one of his best suits and lugged his canister of pesticides throughout South Central looking for new customers. He went door-to-door convincing people that they needed his services, whether they had a roach infestation or not. Working for the dummy company, Beck was able to keep the entire fee for his services, instead of just the commission. For a while, he was able to support himself and Betty this way.

However, even with his extermination con, Beck could barely make ends meet, and the baby was arriving soon. He desperately searched for alternative solutions. One night while he was out canvassing for new customers, he met a woman named Rosa Johnson, a former Los Angeles socialite who had reputedly worked for bandleader Louis Jordan back in the 1940s. She was partly paralyzed and needed help with eating and bathing. She had a spare room, and Beck proposed that he and Betty take the room in exchange for Betty's help with domestic tasks. Betty didn't like the idea, but they were destitute, so she agreed. From the beginning, the arrangement was a disaster. Johnson was an alcoholic, and she drank from the moment she woke up until she went to bed at night. She constantly invited her drinking buddies to come by and bring her liquor all day long. She even tried to get Betty to drink with her, and the expectant mother had to remind her that she was pregnant and could not drink. After a few weeks of this, Betty finally told Beck that they had to leave. "I could not clean that woman's rear end again. I could not bathe her again. I could not do any of these things again, because I will kill her and then I will kill myself, because I'd rather be dead than be doing this . . . When you leave here I'm sitting in that goddamn room and when you come back I'm sitting in that goddamn room listening to this drunk old bitch telling me her stories."[24] On Mother's Day in 1963, Beck packed up the car with the few possessions that they owned and drove Betty to another apartment on Vermont Street. He wasn't sure how they were going to support themselves, but he knew he couldn't let his wife spend one more day in that house.

By the early summer of 1963, Beck was desperate to find another job. The baby was due in less than a month, and Beck knew that he couldn't support a family as an exterminator forever. The problem was that he wasn't qualified to do much except pimp women. He certainly wasn't fit for manual labor of any kind. "He didn't know how to do anything," Betty remembered. "You would never give that man a hammer and a nail. He would bust the wall in. He was all thumbs." As Beck himself had realized during his last bit in prison, he had made a terrible choice by not staying at Tuskegee: "I had spent more than half a lifetime in a worthless, dangerous profession. If I had stayed in school in eight years of study I could have been an M.D. or lawyer. Now here I was, slick but not smart, in a cell. I was past forty with counterfeit glory in my past, and no marketable training, no future. I had been a bigger sucker than a square mark. All he loses is scratch. I had joined a club that suckered me behind bars five times."[25] With decades developing the gift of gab in the pimp game, he hoped he might translate his verbal skills into a job as a salesman. He applied for jobs at a number of white-owned businesses, but they all turned him down. "I knew I was a stellar salesman," he wrote in his memoir. "After all, hadn't I proven my gift for thirty years? The principles of selling are the same in both worlds. The white interviewers were impressed with my bearing and apparent facility with words. They sensed my knowledge of human nature. But they couldn't risk the possible effect that a Negro's presence would have on the firm's all white personnel."[26] Despite the fact that Los Angeles blacks had made significant inroads into white-collar professions in the 1960s, most of them came from middle-class backgrounds and lived in affluent African American neighborhoods like Baldwin Hills and West Adams. As an ex-con coming from the streets and living in the heart of South Central, Beck was not considered qualified for professional work, such as sales. After repeated failures to cross over into the white job world, he gave up and went back to exterminating. He felt defeated, and he told Betty, "I ain't never, ever, going to be accepted in the white world. And you also have to realize that you will never, ever be accepted in the black world. But you stand a better chance than I do. Because white men hate the fact that a black man is fucking one of their women. They just don't do that. So we will never be able to live anywhere except on the outskirts of the ghetto where there's a mixture of people."[27]

On June 24, 1963, Betty gave birth to a son, Robin Bell, named after Beck's pimp mentor Albert "Baby" Bell. Beck had no money to take Betty to the hospital, so he decided to sell the last thing that had belonged to his mother. "He gave me his mother's ring," Betty recalled. "She had a diamond ring with four one-carat stones in it. He gave that to me and told me that I was the only woman besides his mother that had ever worn that ring. He wanted me to have it. When I went into labor with Robin, he took that ring down and sold it so he could pay for me to go to the hospital. That was the kind of man we're talking about." Over the next few years, Betty and Beck's family grew. Fifteen months after the birth of Robin, Betty gave birth to their first daughter, Camille, on September 10, 1964. On the one hand, Beck was absolutely delighted in his new role as a father. As he told an interviewer later after the success of his books, "What other bastard has been able to get the thrills of pimping and then get all the thrills and excitement of a family—all within one lifetime. Pimping. Family. All within one lifetime! See my kids? You see me, I'm Papa! What the hell! I'm right here with it!"[28]

On the other hand, his life as a pimp had not prepared him for fatherhood, and he awkwardly stumbled through it at times. He had a morbid fear of being kissed by his children, and he always picked them up with their backs to him. As he explained it, "When you're a pimp, you're only as sweet as the money. They were like little whores and I'd say, 'Now get out of here.'" Beck was also afraid for their safety in South Central; he had a white wife and son, and his daughter was mixed complexion. Los Angeles in the mid-1960s was a racially divided city, and he sensed a brewing catastrophe. Betty recounted the last time her husband took Robin, who was white, out in public: "I remember one time he took Robin up to the Laundromat to do some clothes for me, and he came back and he said, 'I cannot take him anymore,' because Robin would fall down on the floor [and yell]: 'Please, please, please, let me go for a ride [on the coin-operated kiddie ride]!' And he said, 'I can't take him anymore, because of the looks some of those whores are giving me. I can't do it. If I turned away from him and somebody grabs him, I don't know what I'd do with you, and I don't know what I would do.'"[29] Beck had always had a violent temper that he fought to keep under control, and he was honestly afraid that he would kill someone if he or she did something to one of his kids. Sometimes he and Betty drove the kids to the park or the beach, but Beck would sit in the car and watch them play from a distance. It just seemed safer that way.

Beck's fears of violent racial conflict came true in August 1965, when Watts exploded in the worst race riots in American history. The riots, which lasted six days, caused $40 million in property damage and resulted in thirty-four deaths. Although a number of factors contributed to the racial conflict—including white suburbanization and a declining manufacturing base in South Central—it was a long history of police harassment that set the riots in motion. Chief William Parker's notorious police force was run like a quasi-military organization, independent from government control, and black Angelenos faced ongoing harassment from white officers. Beginning in the early 1960s, African Americans increasingly fought back against these daily acts of violent discrimination, and small-scale riots ultimately led to the full-blown insurrection in 1965. In an eerie prelude to the 1992 riots on the eve of Beck's passing, looters pulled motorists from their cars and assaulted them, they robbed businesses, and they set buildings on fire. Beck was terrified for his family as people walked through his neighborhood with openly brandished weapons and arms full of plunder. They lived at 220½ West Seventy-Eighth Street, right in the heart of South Central, Los Angeles. Beck put blankets over all the windows, and he stood watch at the front door with his pistol in hand. Betty remembered, "He told me to keep Robin in the bedroom, and he kept the bedroom locked, and I wasn't to come out of the bedroom until I heard his voice, and Robin and I had to stay in the house. I mean we didn't get out of that apartment for almost three weeks before he would take us back out on the street, because he was scared to death something was going to happen."[30]

—✑—

One of the effects of the Watts Riots was the emergence of a multifaceted black arts movement in Los Angeles in the late 1960s. The Watts Writers Workshop provided dozens of black writers with a creative outlet; it ultimately produced such important artists as Wanda Coleman, Herbert Simmons, and Odie Hawkins. The Watts Prophets laid down poetry tracks that would become one of the foundations for hip-hop, while Melvin Van Peebles pioneered the blaxploitation genre with his avant-garde film *Sweet Sweetback's Baadasssss Song.* On the anniversary of the riots, the Watts Summer Festival brought together antipoverty groups, Black Nationalist organizations, and everyday black citizens to celebrate African American heritage.[31] However, it was the rise of the third-tier paperback press Holloway House Publishing Company that represented one of the most unexpected artistic responses to Los Angeles's racial insurrections. The company was started by two Jewish copywriters, Bentley Morriss and Ralph Weinstock. Morriss was born on the West Side of Chicago in 1923 and lived there at the same time Beck was learning the pimp book from Baby Bell. He moved to Los Angeles in the 1950s to pursue acting, but was unsuccessful. He took journalism at Los Angeles City College and UCLA, worked as a broadcaster at KMX radio, and then as a publicist at Warner Brothers. Morriss teamed up with Weinstock in the late 1950s to helm the pornographic magazines *Adam* and *Knight*. In 1959, they formed Holloway House Publishing Company and began to supplement their nudie materials with paperback books that they had commissioned. Some of their earliest efforts included *The Trial of Adolf Eichmann, Hemingway: Life and Death of a Giant, An Uncensored History of Pornography*, and *Jayne Mansfield's Wild, Wild World*.[32]

The company shifted to publishing black-themed materials following the Watts Riots. According to Bentley Morriss, "These were the early sixties. We really hadn't been involved in the Civil Rights Movement, although both Ralph and myself and other people in the company had certain social inclinations and social responsibilities to the rest of the world. We felt it would be kind of cool to do books, black literature of which there was really very little. And so we felt that it would be kind of personally rewarding and let's see if we can make some money at it."[33] The company already published some sex worker confessionals, including such titles as *Point Your Tail in the Right Direction; Prostitution, U.S.A.: Call Girls, Gays and Junkies*; and *The Nine Holes of Jade*. After the Watts Riots, Holloway House saw an opportunity to expand into new African American markets previously overlooked by other publishing houses. Morriss and Weinstock put ads in the black Los Angeles newspaper the *Sentinel*, and they sent editors down to the Watts Writers Workshop to find potential novelists. Over the next forty years, they would sell hundreds of novels by many dozens of black authors to millions upon millions of readers. According to African American editor Emory Holmes, who worked on and off for Holloway House for years, "[Morriss] knew that there was a market for the writers he was publishing, and many of these writers would not have been published had it not been for Bentley Morriss and Ralph Weinstock. Even though they are, in my opinion, exploiters and in many ways terrible, terrible people. But there was a kind of generosity in their vulgarity, in their contempt for human beings. They didn't hate you because you were black, or because you were white, or because you were Chicano, or because you were a Jew—although they hated you for those things, for being those things—that wasn't their point. Their point was if they could find a way for you to make money for them, they didn't care who you were. That's an American idea, I think. They were willing to exploit anyone who can make money for them."[34]

After the riots, Beck and Betty developed a comfortable domestic rhythm. Beck still exterminated rats and roaches during the day, and at night he came home filthy and exhausted. After he changed out of his clothes and Betty put the children to bed, he regaled her with stories of his former life as a pimp. It helped him relax, confessing to her all that he had done and seen, exorcising the demons of his past. With his photographic memory, he could recall the stories of his early transgressions with Pepper Ibbetts and Party Time. He told her of the years he had served in Wisconsin State Prison and Leavenworth Federal Penitentiary. He remembered the rundowns of broken-down hustlers on Milwaukee's Walnut Avenue, and reminisced about the mentorship of the infamous Albert "Baby" Bell. Night after night, he constructed little vignettes of his days as a hardened pimp; it was theatrical, like a Shakespearean play. Initially, Betty was just horrified; she had never been exposed to anything like this. "He would tell me these outrageous things. I said, 'A woman would go out and sell herself and give the money to a man. You must be out of your goddamn mind.' I'm from Texas. You don't have pimps. Well, you probably have pimps and whores in Texas now, but where I came from you didn't have pimps and whores."[35]

These tales also enthralled Betty, and that gave her an idea. They should publish them as a book. "His stories. They were so fascinating to me. If they were that fascinating to me, they obviously would be fascinating to more than a million people."[36] One day while Beck was telling her one of his stories, Betty grabbed a notebook and started writing down everything that she could. At the end of the story, she showed it to her husband. He was suspicious. After all, how could a bunch of scrawl be turned into a book? Betty told him, "If we had a typewriter, and I am a very good typist, and I put it in book form, somebody will buy this." Beck started to feel a hope. "You really think you could do this?" he asked. "I really think that I could," she told him confidently. "I am telling you I can turn this stuff into a book."[37] What did they have to lose? There was hardly any money to buy food to feed the kids. They couldn't afford milk or cigarettes much of the time. And they now had a third child; Melody was born on September 10, 1965. Besides, Beck needed something to fill the emotional gap left by pimping, for as he put it, "There's no worse torture than that of a pimp who suddenly finds himself bereft of a stable."[38] At night, they started working on their "pimp" book. Beck told stories and performed the dialogue of the different characters, while Betty wrote it all down. Beck was a natural performer, and he would utterly lose himself in the various parts. Betty remembered, "We'd be writing, and he would be telling me what to write down, and I'm sitting in the chair, and I'm writing, and he's standing. All up in my face! [I had to say] 'Back off a bit!'"[39] Little by little, they started piecing together something that looked like the beginning of a manuscript. The book was gritty, even pornographic, but it was truly an original portrait of the underworld from which Beck had come. There was nothing like it in American literature, and if they could find a publisher, it just might capture the imagination of millions, as they hoped.

Somewhat unexpectedly, they first attempted to publish the book as an academic work. Beck was out canvassing for new customers for his extermination business one day, when he met Dr. Walter C. Bailey, a professor of sociology and one of the directors of the California Counseling Service. This was a nonprofit social welfare organization staffed by psychiatrists and psychologists who provided counseling to the community. Bailey's research focused on crime and drug prevention among teens, and he was a proponent of community outreach. At a recent Men's Day celebration, held by the Men's Federation of the People's Independent Church, for instance, he had conducted a public forum titled "Narcotic Addiction: A Major Problem for Religion and Mental Hygiene."[40] In it, he advocated that a more substantial focus on teen narcotic addiction could prevent crime. A few years after he met Beck, Bailey would move to Manhattan and become a sociology professor at the College of the City of New York and a senior research scientist with the Narcotic Addiction Control Commission. Throughout his career, he focused on community health and drug addiction prevention and rehabilitation.[41]

When Beck met Bailey in 1966, the professor was immediately interested in the well-dressed man who came to his door dragging a canister of roach poison. After asking Beck some questions about his life, he proposed that they write a book together. Bailey's credentials were impressive and he seemed to have access to publishers, so Beck agreed. "He got the obsession to write my life story and during the next several weeks I recounted on his tape recorder the material to be used in the projected 'pimp' book. I grew to like him and admire his superior intellectual gifts and writing experience."[42] As their relationship deepened, Beck started to see warning signs about Bailey that put him on his guard. "There were many things about him that showed he was dangerously flawed; like he lived his life as much as possible among white people and in white prestige bistros like the Polo Lounge. And for a professor of psychology, he had some unique hang-ups, like the cute, intelligent black girl who spent every free moment in his bed. He admitted that he loved it, but he was ashamed to be seen with her in public."[43]

Nevertheless, Beck and Bailey continued their work on the book. They decided to split the royalties fifty-fifty, and the professor had his lawyer write up a formal contract. When Beck read the contract closely, he suspected that Bailey and his lawyer were trying to con him out of his share. "The goddamn thing was eerie in its burglarious perfection. The fifty-fifty split, all of it was there. But one clause of only several words nullified the whole document and raped me of my rights. As I said before, I was just free from the steel casket and I was a very edgy citizen, so my first impulse was to slay them both with bullets in the head from a .25 automatic (carried because the Professor was suspect as an enemy) dangling from a length of elastic inside my right coat sleeve."[44] Instead of murdering Bailey, Beck decided to write the book himself with Betty as he'd originally planned; "and because I had once really liked the guy," he remembered later, "I told him to go fuck himself in the coolest, kindest voice I could muster."[45] Bailey pursued the matter further, using his lawyer to try to pressure

Beck into a contract. His lawyer sent him a variety of letters, including this final one on October 5, 1966:

> I am advised that there are several people working on the
> same subject matter as this proposed biography. I think that it
> is safe to say that he who publishes first will probably corner
> most of the market for this subject matter; therefore, I think
> that it is in both parties best interest to get the assembling of
> material and rough copy of the book and etc. ready as soon as
> possible.[46]

Beck simply ignored Bailey and his lawyer and returned instead
to the writing process with Betty. He approached writing with the
same principles he had used for pimping; both were essentially acts
of strategic storytelling. Beck reasoned that the narrative had to be
entertaining and fascinating, but it also had to be logical and tightly
organized. "And, you had to answer, just as you do the whore, all of
the questions before they are asked. And, you can't be heavy-handed
with it. You have to do it in a casual way. But I didn't know this
was what they call painless exposition that the writing craft speaks
about. For every principle I used in *Pimp*, there is a literary name."[47]
Beck became more deliberate and systematic about his writing process now. He began by lying on his bed and staring up at the ceiling,
the process he had invented inside his prison cell at Chicago House
of Correction. He liked to write from two until seven in the morning. He discovered that in those quiet, late hours, he could stare up
at the ceiling and recall perfectly the voices of Baby Bell, Mattie
Cooper, Party Time, and dozens of other characters from his past.
He wrote down these snippets of conversation on anything he could
find: napkins, scraps of paper, and even paper plates. He recited his
vignettes in front of Betty to make sure that they sounded just right.
As he explained his process in an interview, "I write longhand and I
have my work typed up. And when I'm not in the physical process of
working, that is with pen in hand on paper, then I'm seeming to be
daydreaming. But I'm not. I'm reading on the ceiling characters for

yet another story. And I hallucinate their voices and try to get the texture of their voices so I can become acquainted with them. And great snatches of dialogue have been written on the ceiling already."[48]

Even though he was writing his life story, Beck was motivated by a number of literary, political, and personal concerns. He wanted to distinguish himself from other famous black authors of the era, who he felt pandered to white audiences. He was also determined to keep the style of the writing simple in order to reach as many working-class people as possible. He was a great admirer of James Baldwin, for instance, but he felt that he wrote for white, educated reviewers. "I decided I wasn't going to write for white critics. That's what my idol [Baldwin] did. It doesn't work. So I said to myself, 'You're going to write for the disadvantaged whites and blacks, on a fifth grade level.' "[49] Beck tried instead to model his story after the work of his hero Malcolm X, who himself had been a pimp in Detroit. *The Autobiography of Malcolm X* had come out a year prior, and Beck respected its radical stance toward white racism as well as its critique of black pimps. As he explained in an interview: "Pimps and whores today are anachronisms in the face of the kind of thing that has occurred in black America, since Malcolm X. He defined our enemies I should say. And our enemies are both within and without. Malcolm X defined the atrocity that pimpin' is. That the exploitation of the black woman is."[50] Beck wanted to take Malcolm X's ideas even further by exposing the pimp's poisonous influence in the black community, based on his own extensive experience. Finally and most importantly, Beck wrote his autobiography to atone for what he had done to his mother. Even though she was dead, he still felt guilty, and he hoped the act of writing would put that guilt behind him. As he wrote in the preface of his story, "Perhaps my remorse for my ghastly life will diminish to the degree that within this one book I have been allowed to purge myself. Perhaps one day I can win respect as a constructive human being. Most of all I wish to become a decent example for my children and for that wonderful woman in the grave, my mother."[51]

Betty and Beck worked together tirelessly writing up sections of the book. He wrote the vignettes up in longhand; she typed out

everything on the antiquated typewriter they had bought. They were
still searching for a publisher. One day, Betty spotted an ad in the
Sentinel. It was for a Los Angeles–based paperback publishing company called Holloway House. The ad read: "Black Writers Needed.
We are looking for black writers that have riveting stories about the
black experience." They decided to submit a short scene of about
twenty pages. It was a short story of Beck's life at the height of his
pimp success. It began: "Dawn was breaking as the big Hog scooted
through the streets. My five whores were chattering like drunk mag-
pies. I smelled the stink that only a street whore has after a long,
busy night. The inside of my nose was raw. It happens when you're a
pig for snorting cocaine. My nose was on fire and the stink of those
whores and the gangster they were smoking seemed like invisible
knives scraping to the root of my brain. I was in an evil, dangerous
mood despite the piles of scratch crammed into the glove compart-
ment."[52] It was devastating, original, and brilliant, but the book still
needed a name for the central character, a moniker that reflected his
ice-cold persona. Beck didn't want to use the handle he had actually
used when he was a pimp: Cavanaugh Slim. Protecting the anonymity of hustlers and sex workers was an important part of the code of
the streets, and so he wanted to use pseudonyms. "He is cold from
top to bottom," Beck said, describing the main character. "Like an
iceberg?" Betty asked. "Yes, that's it, like an iceberg," he replied.
Iceberg Slim was born.[53]

In September 1966, Beck walked into Holloway House's office
at 8060 Melrose Avenue in Hollywood with the first twenty pages
of what would become *Pimp: The Story of My Life*. Editor Milton
Van Sickle, a former metallurgist and electroplater, read the short
piece and was enthralled with its gutsy language and raw street sensibility. The company offered him a contract the same day. On September 22, 1966, Beck signed a deal with Holloway House. He had
two months to complete a manuscript of 100,000 words, and he
would be paid an advance of $1,500 in three separate installments
and about 4 cents per book in royalties. For an untested author, these
were pretty fair terms, and it was the most money that Beck had
ever made from legal means. He and Betty set out to complete the

manuscript at breakneck speed. He wrote and rewrote in longhand, and she typed up seven drafts of *Pimp* before they finally turned it over to the publisher. Van Sickle read the book and demanded only one change. He wanted a glossary to explain the street slang because he "at first couldn't understand what the hell he was talking about."[54] Holloway House never showed them the galleys, which made them both nervous. What if the book got lost in the shuffle? What if it didn't reflect the revisions and edits they had made? What if it never got published? Then one day in early 1967, a box of a dozen books arrived on their doorstep. The front cover featured an oil painting of a sinister-looking man, staring down impassively at a scantily clad woman. Emblazoned across the top in red and black letters were the words "*Pimp: The Story of My Life* by Iceberg Slim." The couple was ecstatic. They had published a book. "You shoulda seen the dance that I did," Betty later bragged. "And I said [to Beck], 'I told you, Goddamnit! Look at this. Didn't I tell you this was a book? Didn't I tell you?' And I sat down and started reading. I read the whole damn thing."[55]

CHAPTER 8

HOLLYWOOD (1967–1978)

In March 1967, Beck witnessed the publication of his autobiography, *Pimp: The Story of My Life*. It was a book that would transform contemporary black culture, laying the groundwork for blaxploitation films, street fiction, and gangsta rap. At the same time, *Pimp* would also indirectly influence future generations of would-be players by putting into print the dubious practices of the pimp book. In many ways, it was an odd book that did not fit neatly into any literary genre or marketplace. Although it was released in the midst of one of the most volatile periods in American history, *Pimp* made no direct references to the civil rights movement, the Black Power movement, the sit-ins, the riots, or any of the other struggles of that moment. Marketed as tabloid pulp literature—an exposé "of the raw, brutal reality of the jungle that lurks beneath the surface of every city"—it was not a book with an overt political message. Nevertheless, Beck's first-person confessional followed in a long African American autobiographical tradition, from the slave narratives of Frederick Douglass and Harriet Jacobs to the recent memoirs of Malcolm X and Claude Brown, in addressing the racial inequalities of American society. Beck narrates in gritty detail his life as a pimp both to warn young blacks about the dangers of a criminal life and to hold American society accountable for producing the pimp in the first place.

He announces in the first sentence of the preface, "In this book I will take you the reader with me into the secret inner world of the pimp. I will lay bare my life and thoughts as a pimp. The account of my brutality and cunning as a pimp will fill many of you with revulsion, however, if one intelligent, valuable young man or woman can be saved from the destructive slime then the displeasure I have given will have been outweighed by that individual's use of his potential in a socially constructive manner."[1] Over twenty-two chapters, Beck recounts his childhood in Rockford, his "street poisoned" teenage years in Milwaukee's Bronzeville, his prison sentences, his years pimping in Chicago, Cleveland, and Detroit, and finally, his conversion to the "square life." Although lacking the explicit Black Nationalist message of its closest contemporary, *The Autobiography of Malcolm X*, Beck's autobiography uses the pimp figure to bring attention to institutional white racism, urban segregation, and poor economic opportunities for blacks in the twentieth century. As he writes about his first encounter with a wealthy white suburb, "Ain't it a bitch? Ninety-eight percent of the black people back there in Hell will be born and die and never know the joys of this earthly Heaven. There ain't but two passports the white folks honor. A white skin and a bale of scratch. I sure got to pimp good and cop my scratch passport. Well at least I get a Cinderella crack at Heaven."[2]

For the first year, *Pimp* did not sell well. As Holloway House was a minor paperback press, it did not have access to major distributors. The book was sold at newsstands, local bookstores in Los Angeles, and small venues like liquor stores and barbershops. The *New York Times* refused to advertise *Pimp* because of its title, and no mainstream literary magazine or newspaper would review it. Holloway House tried alternative methods of bringing attention to the autobiography. It took out sensationalist ads in black newspapers such as the *Sentinel* that exclaimed: "Pimp's Secret Life: Brutal Reality of a Sexual Jungle." The company booked Beck for several speaking engagements at college campuses, and it put him on a number of talk shows, including *The Louis E. Lomax Show*, *The Dick Cavett Show*, and *Black Leader* with Robert Dorman. However, it was his appearance on *The Joe Pyne Show* on January 19, 1968, that finally brought Beck fully into the public eye. He actually went on the local Los Angeles talk show to promote his second book, *Trick Baby: The Story of a White Negro*, which he had published in December 1967. It is the fictionalized story of a black con man so light-skinned that he can pass for white, and it showcases various con games that Beck had encountered in Chicago during the 1940s. When he appeared on the show, he wore a mask that Betty had constructed for him. It was made of black fabric sewn over a pair of dark goggles, and the bizarre disguise looked like a cross between a gas mask and a black-face minstrel masquerade. The all-white audience sat in stunned silence as Beck joked with Pyne about his decision to give up the pimp life. "This is a better bag, as they say," he chuckled, referencing James Brown's hit song. It was an outrageous publicity stunt, and it worked. The next morning, audiences mobbed Pickwick Books in Hollywood, buying every copy of *Pimp* and *Trick Baby* off the shelf. Phone calls flooded the Holloway House office as people searched for places to purchase more books. As Bentley Morriss remembered it, "Half a dozen bookstores in Hollywood and Los Angeles had people waiting in line around the block to buy the book. And when they called and told me that, I didn't believe them, so I drove down to Hollywood Boulevard to see it. And it was a sight. It was like they were giving away something."[3] In only a few years' time, Beck's book would sell millions of copies, making him the most popular black author in America.

In the late 1960s, *Pimp: The Story of My Life* and *Trick Baby: The Story of a White Negro* provided new and original visions of black underworlds that few had seen and lived to write about. *Pimp* transcribes word for word the pimp book that Beck himself had used to capture prey, and it reconstructs the black urban neighborhoods in Chicago, Milwaukee, and Cleveland that had been destroyed by urban renewal. *Trick Baby* expands upon the depiction of mid-century Chicago created in *Pimp*, and in fact, it could be considered a loosely conceived sequel to Beck's memoir. The prologue of *Trick Baby* begins where *Pimp* ends, with Beck finishing out his sentence at the Chicago House of Correction in the early sixties. He meets White Folks, a con man whose white skin makes Beck think he is an undercover policeman. White Folks tells him, "I'm not white. I'm a Nigger hustler. My friends call me White Folks. My enemies call me Trick Baby. Blue Howard and I were pals, and played the con for twenty years."[4] The preface then gives way to the narrative itself, in which White Folks tells in first person the story of his childhood and his hustling days. *Trick Baby* represents a major step forward in Beck's development as a writer, as it successfully blurs the line between the autobiographical and the fictional. Beck substantiates White Folks's story as authentic in the preface, and then he goes on to ventriloquize that story himself in the body of the novel. In the last line of the preface, Beck invites his audience to suspend disbelief and, like him, just enjoy the tale of a master confidence man: "I lay there in the gloom forgetting my own troubles in the fascination of his story."[5]

At the plot level, *Trick Baby* is a novel that explores the theater of con artistry in Bronzeville during the halcyon days of the Chicago Renaissance, Albert "Baby" Bell, and the Jones Brothers. As Beck explained it to Joe Pyne in their interview, "The book is an incredible adventure story of the con, as it's played in the street. The verbatim dialogue. What the sucker says and what the con man's saying to weave the con spell."[6] In *Trick Baby*, cons come in all shapes and sizes. Some are relatively simple, such as the "belly-stick," where the convincer lures the mark into betting big at a rigged roulette wheel. There is also the "rocks" con, where a hustler sells fake diamond rings to a fence; he uses a real one to fool the buyer, and then switches it out for a counterfeit at the last moment. *Trick Baby* also explores more elaborate hustles, such as the "wire store" scam, in which an empty storefront is set up to look like a telegraph office. In this scenario, a roper brings in a mark to place a large bet on a horse race he claims he can rig by delaying the teletype race results to the books. The mark's own greed conspires against him, and he gives the roper all his savings in the hopes of cheating the system and making a fortune. The "drag" is a relative of the wire-store hustle; in this scheme, one con artist approaches a man on the street and points out his partner standing on the corner, who has just "found" a wallet stuffed with large bills. The two con men—pretending to be total strangers to one another—convince the mark that they will split the money three ways, so long as each of them puts up a bond of good faith. When the mark puts up his share, the two con men disappear into the shadows with his money to search for another sucker, a maneuver known as the "blowoff," or "final." Much like *Pimp*, *Trick Baby*'s message is a bleak one: "There are only two kinds of people in this whole wide world, grifters and suckers."[7]

Like all of Beck's works—which focus on con artists, pimps, prostitutes, boosters, and other outlaw characters—*Trick Baby* also uses the story of a black criminal to examine deeper issues of racial justice in America. *Trick Baby*'s narrative of a black hustler who can disguise himself as white follows in a long tradition of "passing" novels, where the black protagonist pretends to be white in order to escape the oppression of a racially divided society. Following the *Plessy v. Ferguson* decision of 1896—in which the Supreme Court effectively legalized racial segregation—numerous American writers wrote passing novels to protest America's discrimination under Jim Crow. Some of the more important authors in this camp include Mark Twain, Charles Chesnutt, James Weldon Johnson, Nella Larsen, Jessie Fauset, William Faulkner, Ralph Ellison, and Chester Himes. Passing in these books is represented as an indictment of a society that legally sanctions bigotry and promotes the betrayal of one's own race. Although the passage of the Civil Rights Act of 1964 and the Voting Rights Act of 1965 outlawed Jim Crow, *Trick Baby* updates the passing narrative to forecast a grim future for black people in the post–civil rights era.

At the novel's climax, White Folks, who has been passing in order to romance his way into the life of a wealthy white socialite, must attend a formal dinner with her at Chicago's exclusive Palmer House hotel. He is forced to witness and participate in a debate between a white racist police chief and a liberal white capitalist over the future of the so-called "nigra problem."[8] White Folks watches in silent horror as each man lays out his Orwellian solution to the black political struggles of the moment. The police chief's solution is to batter black protesters and civil rights advocates using force doled out by racist white policemen from the South. "I have known since my rookie policeman days," he proclaims, "that the nigras steal, rape, whore, pimp, and murder because they are basically criminally inclined. They're derived from inferior loins."[9] The capitalist's ideas are more sinister, as he reveals a "master plan" to separate educated

African American leaders from the black masses in order to neutralize them. He says, "There are really two ghettos. One is physical. The other psychological. Now it is true that we have selected certain niggers to wear white collars. Almost all of them do make physical escapes from the ghetto, with our assistance, of course. Our motives are first to give dramatic well-publicized reinforcement to our liberal image. Secondly, those niggers whom we seem to liberate are precisely those type of niggers who possess rare intellect and academic polish. We have to remove them from the seething black masses."[10]

For all the novel's attention to swindles such as the smack, the drag, the pigeon drop, and the flue, *Trick Baby*'s big reveal is that the true confidence game in America is white racism. Throughout the novel, White Folks passes as white in order to make temporary escapes from a prejudiced society, only to come face-to-face with the longest con of all, the deliberate and systematic oppression of black people. Faced with this dystopian reality, White Folks blows his cover, and he is ejected from the white society in which he has been passing. He goes on an alcohol-fueled bender, spiraling out of control, until he finally ends up in prison where he meets Beck. A story that nicely balances sensational street hustles and nuanced racial critique, *Trick Baby* illustrates Beck's growing mastery of literary forms, as well as his talent to combine sensational stories and political criticisms.

As Beck's fame as a writer grew in the late 1960s, he began to cultivate a public persona around Los Angeles. He increasingly saw himself as a spokesman for black urban America, and he used his knowledge of pimping as an unsuspected starting point to educate and inform. He joined the Los Angeles chapter of Operation Breadbasket, giving lectures there every Saturday. Martin Luther King Jr. had started the program in Atlanta in 1962, and the organization had opened a Los Angeles chapter just a few weeks before he was assassinated in 1968. The main purpose of the group was to weaken the white economic stranglehold on the black ghetto by boycotting businesses that did not employ black workers. Beck also joined the Open Door Program, an outgrowth of the Watts Writers Workshop. Sponsored by the Writers Guild of America, the Open Door Program was created to encourage minority writers in the profession of television writing. Furthermore, he got involved with the Performing Arts Society of Los Angeles, a program founded by the influential arts administrator Vantile Whitfield in 1964 to train inner-city youth in theater and performing arts. At these various venues, Beck mesmerized audiences with his lectures on a range of topics, including the history of the Puritans, theories of sexual repression and violence in contemporary America, and even the economics of supply and demand in the illegal sex trade. He explained that top pimps regarded women as a renewable resource and that they fashioned themselves as commodities brokers. Odie Hawkins, who had watched Beck as a teenager in Chicago, moved to Los Angeles in 1966 and attended various of these lectures. In his opinion, Beck was an even more talented orator than a writer; he had a magnetic effect that could not be translated to the page. "I have to say that his book, *Pimp*, and the others, never came close to capturing his true voice; the level of erudition, hipness, body language and nuances that his personal lectures conveyed."[11] Hawkins's belief was shared by many; the crowds went wild at Beck's lectures, and at their conclusion they would often mob him.[12]

During these formative years as a writer, Beck also focused on developing his skills as a serious author. Composing novels had come to replace the thrill he used to get from pimping, and he approached his new craft with the same intensity he had brought to the game. "Writing is better than pimping," he exclaimed in an interview. "In fact, it's better than being a doctor or a lawyer. I don't have to go to court, I don't have to go to the hospital to perform an operation. I have no equipment, man. Look, I don't even need paper; I'll write on the walls. All of my equipment is in my noggin. And another thing: writing has been a wonderful boon for me, psychologically. The vacuum of ego that existed when I could no longer pimp has been filled most adequately."[13] Beck worked constantly now, almost obsessively. When he was composing a book, he wrote sixteen hours per day, missed meals, ignored his children, and would go several days without bathing. Betty remembered that he was always hassling her about putting manuscripts together. He would say to her, "I need you. When can you come in here? I need you to come in here. I need you to help me. I need you to listen to me. I need you to—see if this plays. How does this sound to you? When can you type it up?"[14] Beck sat in his room and wrote chapter after chapter in longhand. Then he and Betty acted out the dialogues in front of the kids as a kind of living-room theater. They wrote and rehearsed and revised and rehearsed again until it was perfect. As his daughter Camille recalled many years later, "I remember from the time I was four years old watching this show. We didn't have TV. It was like watching a play. He would act out all the parts and then say to her, 'Okay, now you take this one.' Male or female. It didn't matter."[15]

Following the success of the first two books, these were good years for the family. They moved into a two-bedroom house at 1235 West Ninetieth Street. It was a bit cramped, but it had a yard where the kids could play, and for the first time, Beck and Betty felt a sense of stability. As Betty recalled, "We had that little two-bedroom house. We had a kitchen. We had a living room, and we had a bathroom, and a laundry room. I had a washing machine. Have you ever seen one . . . of those washing machines with the rollers? That was my washing machine. And I washed all of our clothes and everything in that washing machine."[16] Perhaps pining for his pimp lifestyle, he purchased a 1948 Lincoln Continental, a tank of a car with a twelve-cylinder engine and an enormous chrome grill. He also bought a gigantic Great Dane named Leana. Betty taught herself how to cook, and Beck playfully joined his kids in stealing food while she prepared meals. "He loved it when I was in the kitchen fixing a big holiday meal or something like that," Betty later said. "He would come in and all my children do the same thing. Pick, pick, pick . . . And I'd smack him with a spoon. He just wanted to be around me."[17] Betty also learned how to sew, and she started making all the clothes for the children. When Beck saw her work, he asked her to make clothes for him. He missed his sparkling pimp wardrobe, and now that he was an author and a public personality, he wanted something spectacular again. Betty remembered, "He described what he wanted, and I sat down with a pencil and newspaper and I cut out a pattern and I made a shirt. That shirt—well, all hell broke loose. It was non-ending. Silk pajamas to velour robes, it never stopped."[18] She would eventually make him dozens upon dozens of outfits in all styles and colors. Soon Beck had everything from a sky blue leisure suit with wide lapels to an electric pink suit that looked like aluminum foil.

In 1968, Beck embarked on his third novel. He had developed a recognizable prose style and had successfully written about what he knew, but he wanted to push beyond the limits of his street crime novels. "I knew that if I were really to become a writer," he admitted later, "I had to develop some versatility."[19] The result was *Mama Black Widow*, a groundbreaking book that focuses on the life of Otis Tilson, "an incredibly comely and tragic homosexual queen."[20] Inspired no doubt by his literary hero James Baldwin, *Mama Black Widow* is one of the few African American novels during this period to deal explicitly with homosexual characters and themes. Although Beck did not overtly identify as gay himself, he acknowledged that there was a certain fluid sexuality in the pimping profession that had prepared him for the writing of the novel. "I've always suspected, even in my own case, that one of the elements of attraction is that a woman in The Life can somehow have her lesbian tendencies gratified, her latent homosexuality gratified by the pimp's latent homosexuality, by the female quotient in his personality."[21] Like *Trick Baby*, *Mama Black Widow* begins with Beck encountering his friend Otis, which serves as a pretext for Otis to tell his story. In the preface, Beck encourages him, "I guarantee all you need to do is tell your story like it is to prove a thousand points about this black hell and the poisonous pus of double standard justice, racial bigotry and criminal economic freeze-out, infecting and grotesquely bloating the hideous underbelly of white America's shining facade of democracy and freedom and opportunity for all."[22]

What follows is a powerful work of literary naturalism that hews closely to the tradition of Richard Wright's protest novel *Native Son*. Naturalism is a literary practice that uses realist representations to reveal how the environment and social conditions have an overwhelming effect on the individual. *Mama Black Widow* focuses on the Tilson family, who migrate to Chicago in the 1930s from a sharecropping plantation in Mississippi. Like many Southern transplants, they find that the city is not the promised land as advertised, but rather a "desolate concrete wilderness."[23] Through Otis's first-person narration, the novel bears witness to the violent destruction of each family member in a world of abject poverty and brutal racism. As one character sums it up, in Chicago "a nigger is like a mop head or toilet brush. The white folks use him to clean up their puking and droppings until he wears out. Then they simply press another hungry nigger into service. They never really see him or realize he is a human unless he steals from them or kills one of them. Then they drop the full weight of their double standard law and bury him in prison or barbeque him in the electric chair."[24] All of Otis's family members meet a horrific fate. After the father cannot find suitable work because he is barred from union jobs, he drinks himself to death. Carol, one of Otis's sisters, bleeds out after her mother tries to perform an abortion on her. Bessie, Otis's other sister, chooses a life of prostitution when she cannot see any alternative opportunities. She is killed gruesomely by a white john, who "had hacked off her nose to the whitish bone of the bridge, and her lips had been raggedly slashed away to give the awful visage a grisly bloodstained grin. Where her breasts had thrust, there were blackened stumps."[25] Finally, Otis's older brother, Junior, gets sentenced to ninety-nine years in prison when he kills the pimp responsible for Bessie's death. At the end of the novel, only Otis and his mother, Sedalia, remain, and in her madness and guilt over the loss of her family, she tries to stab him in the throat with a pair of scissors.

Mama Black Widow interweaves these stories of black victimization with a snapshot of gay life in Bronzeville from the 1940s to the 1960s, a subculture within a subculture. Published in 1969, the year of the Stonewall Riots, the novel offers a rare glimpse into the world of gay black men in the era prior to the gay liberation movement. Speakeasies and Black and Tan clubs in Chicago's South Side had been popular hangouts for interracial couples, homosexuals, cross-dressers, and sex workers since the 1920s. During Beck's prime years as a pimp in Chicago, he no doubt crossed paths with these sexual communities, as there was significant overlap among them. As his protagonist, Otis, describes it, "The night people were crawling Madison Street like maggots on a corpse. Thickly painted queers and whores, white, black and yellow, jiggled corrupt behinds inside loud minidresses. They leered dirty smiles at the shabby tricks prowling for an orgy for five bucks. Black pimps with brutish faces stalked the turf in long flashy cars."[26] Like the rest of his family, Otis is persecuted by this dangerous world. As a boy, he is sexually molested by his pastor, and when he dresses in drag as an adult, he is harassed by the police, beaten by other black men, and repeatedly raped. In the face of such overwhelming violence, Bronzeville's gay community is one of the few places that Otis finds temporary refuge. As he says, "I felt cozy and intoxicated, but not only because of the pills and drinks I had taken. There was somehow a sweet and wonderful atmosphere of equality and brotherhood among queers. I guess they were so despised and discriminated against in the straight world that in mutual anguish and suffering they found emotional sanctuary among themselves."[27] In some ways, *Mama Black Widow* follows a formula that had been successful for Beck's two earlier works. Through the eyes of a black antihero, the book represents Chicago's street culture of the pre–civil rights era in vivid and brutal detail. At the same time, *Mama Black Widow* moves even further beyond the autobiographical boundaries of *Pimp* (as well as the quasi-autobiographical boundaries of *Trick Baby*) to illustrate the genius of an author pushing past the limits of writing about the life he himself lived to evoke a subterranean world that had all but disappeared from view.

—

By 1971, Beck had sold two million books, making him the best-selling black author in America, according to his publisher.[28] He was a minor celebrity now in Los Angeles. When he walked through the streets of South Central, people recognized him. They ran up to him wanting to get an autograph and to hear his advice on how to pimp. He had real power to influence people now, and he wanted to use it. *Pimp, Trick Baby,* and *Mama Black Widow* were tremendous literary accomplishments, but the political message in each was veiled behind the stories of pimping, con artistry, and underground subcultures. Beck was ready to write something more overtly radical, something that reflected the emerging militancy of the African American political movements of the time. Martin Luther King Jr. had been assassinated in April 1968; after that, riots broke out in over one hundred cities in America. His death also coincided with black America's waning faith in nonviolent protest and civil disobedience as the most potent methods of effecting change. Declining blue-collar employment and rising crime rates in many cities, including Los Angeles, forecasted a bleak future for urban African Americans. The Black Power movement filled the space left in the wake of King's leadership; the late 1960s and early '70s witnessed the rise of more militant black organizations, such as the Black Panther Party. In 1967, Stokely Carmichael published his influential *Black Power*; a year later Tommie Smith and John Carlos raised their fists from the winner's podium at the Olympics in a Black Power salute; and in 1969, H. Rap Brown published his activist autobiography, *Die Nigger Die!* Los Angeles was a particularly active headquarters for black radicalism. Influential black thinkers like Bunchy Carter and Angela Davis rose to national fame with their revolutionary stances against white power, while the Los Angeles chapter of the Black Panther Party showed unprecedented heroism when a handful of members held off hundreds of LAPD officers in a five-hour gun battle at their Central Avenue office. Beck saw these events unfolding around him, and he decided to publish his response from the perspective of an ex-pimp. After all, he admitted to an interviewer, "These are times when you must choose sides if you're going to be a black writer."[29]

In 1971, he published *The Naked Soul of Iceberg Slim*, a collection of essays, vignettes, and personal deliberations. It was modeled on W. E. B. Du Bois's pioneering *The Souls of Black Folk* and James Baldwin's *The Fire Next Time*. Beck regarded Baldwin in particular as a personal muse; he called him an "awesome" presence that he felt "hovering over [his] shoulder."[30] Beck dedicated the book to his heroes in the fight for black equality: the champion boxer Jack Johnson, Malcolm X, Angela Davis, Huey Newton, Bobby Seale, George Jackson, and "all the street niggers and strugglers in and out of the joints."[31] From the opening pages, Beck characterizes America as a kind of prison, and his book seeks to analyze its design from the perspective of an insider. "I want to say at the outset that I have become ill, insane as an inmate of a torture chamber behind America's fake facade of justice and democracy. But I am not as ill as I was, and I am getting better all of the time."[32] Over the course of fifteen chapters, Beck weighs in on a range of topics including the history of lynching, the potential for black revolution, the social and psychological causes of pimping, the class divide in America, Western standards of beauty, and racism in the prison system. Although dealing with complex political, social, and philosophical issues, he sets out to connect with the general black public by reaching as many readers as possible. As he says in *Soul*, "I believe that in these times a black writer is a success only when the black masses can relate to his work and to him with respect and a strong sense of kinship. I believe a black writer in these times who shuns or loses kinship with his people is early doomed to dry up and die as a writer. He needs for his creative survival a living, throbbing lifeline to his people, for with only the impersonal and fawning quicksand favor of the white public, his writer's juices will drain away."[33]

Like Du Bois and Baldwin before him, Beck did not restrict himself exclusively to the essay form to express his ideas, but drew on personal experiences to frame his larger views. *Soul* includes stream-of-consciousness musings composed while walking through his neighborhood, a letter from a fan seeking advice on the writing process, and his own letters, short vignettes, and outright polemics. He provides short stories spanning from his childhood to his current life in Los Angeles, which not only fill in significant gaps in his autobiography, but also serve as parables for his growing activist consciousness. He relates a story from his teenage years in Milwaukee about the first time he fell in love, which also serves as an illustration about class conflict in the black community. He tells a tale about saving a young girl from a "gorilla" pimp in Chicago, which turns out to be a larger meditation on racial self-hatred in a consumer-driven society. Perhaps the most powerful story he tells is about when, as a child, he had witnessed his father stand up to a drunk and abusive "Big

Bill" Thompson. Contemplating how his father got away with defying the mayor of Chicago, he writes, addressing Robert Sr. directly, "Perhaps, in that galley arena with no gangster lackeys or hoodlum cops around to crush your challenge, he showed craven cowardice and camouflaged his terror with hysterical laughter. Who knows, Papa, but that maybe all the power-gluttonous architects of repression and racism in America have yellow neon stripes glowing on their backs as they cower behind their police and soldiers."[34] Starting from a deeply personal story about his father, Beck concludes that the white power structure is a flimsy facade barely held together by a repressive police and military force. It is a theme that runs throughout *Soul,* and, echoing Stokely Carmichael, Angela Davis, and Huey Newton, Beck ultimately calls for the overthrow of white political and economic power. As he eloquently sums it up: "America is being led to her death by racist power junkies coasting on a stupid trip— the fatal fantasy that soldiers and police can destroy with clubs and guns an indestructible force: the hunger of the human soul for dignity, justice, and freedom."[35]

Unsurprisingly, some of Beck's most insightful essays are his analyses of the pimp game and its relationship to larger race and gender dynamics in American society. In the remarkable piece "Rapping About the Pimp Game," he provides detailed explanations of the rules and parameters of The Life. "He's a gutter god," Beck explains of the pimp, "who puts his emotions and sex drive into a kind of commercial cold storage. He never gets sweeter than the amount of a particular whore's money. The codes, the rules, the attitudes of pimping are passed along to new young pimps who, if imaginative, will discover something new and cunning to add to the pimp book."[36] Beck not only provides descriptions of how the pimp snatches up young victims, but as an ex-player he also cleverly shows how he has transformed the rundown into a speech to deter young people from the game. "Pimping is for dudes who are suckers for jail cells and smack dealers," he tells an aspiring pimp from his neighborhood. "You think pimping is a beauty contest? You think you can fuck? There are johns, tricks in the streets that can lay your whore and suck her cunt so good she'll have convulsions with diarrhea. You take that cream puff young broad to the city and in six weeks some slicker will pump her rotten with H [heroin], and you'll be flat-ass busted waiting for your folks to send you the fare back home. I wouldn't lay a bet you won't wind up a puddle of shit and blood in some alley."[37] In *Soul*, Beck turns the pimp rundown on its head, revealing how his gift for persuasion can be repurposed to dissuade would-be pimps and prostitutes.

Soul then goes even deeper to expose the origins of pimping as rooted in American racism. In his essay "Racism and the Black Revolution," Beck hypothesizes that pimping is the result of the overvaluation of white female sexuality, what he calls the "mythic white supercunt." Not only was the sanctity of white womanhood used as a convenient excuse to lynch black men beginning in the late nineteenth century; the white woman as the exclusive measure of beauty has carried over into the twentieth century in television, movies, magazines, and other forms of consumer culture. As a consequence, Beck theorizes, the black woman is more susceptible to the false charms of the pimp. "Because she is an overshadowed underdog, essentially deprived of the chance to win herself a dependable, desirable man and thereby security and a sense of self-esteem, she is an easy mark for the gaudy black pimp and his hypnotic castles in the air."[38] Ironically, this psychosexual dynamic promoted by white racist thought also motivates that very same racist to seek out the black prostitute—the embodiment of taboo. In Beck's experience as a pimp, he witnessed many white men secretly leaving their ideal suburban lives to troll the streets of the black ghetto in search of the very thing that they supposedly despised most. He writes, "The sadistic racist becomes the whimpering sexual masochist only because his guilt overwhelms his hatred for the black race. The racist submits his quivering body to beatings and feces of the black woman. Eagerly, joyously, he roots his ecstatic nose into a black cunt to stain himself, punish himself. With balls near bursting, he will leave pleasant nests (and the alabaster supercunt) in suburbia to comb the booby-trapped ghetto for a black female object—his instrument of torture."[39]

While deeply critical of the white power structure, including the capitalist state, the prison industrial complex, and the police,

Beck saves his sharpest criticisms for the black middle class, whom he regards as opportunists and con artists who take advantage of the black masses. "Uncle Tom comes forth in many hats and shapes—politician, preacher, greedy, glory-grabbing nigger socialite and the plain power addict. But all are outlaw whores in the stable of the white power structure and suck a mixture of shit and money from the bung hole of the Master as the murderous noose of race and poverty chokes their brethren."[40] He condemns a black starlet who denies her connection to the black race after crossing into the Hollywood mainstream. He denounces Professor Walter Bailey, who had tried to cheat him out of fair compensation while writing *Pimp*. He targets black landlords who exploit their tenants with firetrap apartments, deacons and lawyers who bilk the elderly out of their life savings, and politicians who aspire to little more than the bourgeois lifestyle of their white counterparts. At the end of one essay he wonders, should an armed revolution occur, whether the middle class will be the first target of the uprising: "Will the contempt and disdain that many middle-class blacks feel for lower caste blacks increase and deepen the distrust and hostility that the black masses feel for their privileged brothers? Will Black Revolution first shed the blood of black middle-class predators of the ghetto?"[41]

It is therefore no surprise that *Soul* ultimately celebrates the Black Panthers as the future hope for black people. "Black Panthers are the authentic champions and heroes of the black race,"[42] he writes in his essay "The Black Panthers." The antithesis of pimps or the black middle class, the Panthers are for Beck the genuine actors in the struggle for black freedom. As he expresses it after a visit to the Black Panthers' headquarters, "I had the sobering realization that unlike the hundreds of non-Panther black youngsters who had recognized me on the street and admired me as a kind of folk hero, because of my lurid and sensational pimp background, the Panther youngsters were blind to my negative glamour and, in fact, expressed a polite disdain for my former profession and its phony flash of big cars, jewelry and clothes. Their only obsession seemed to be the freedom of black people."[43] This encounter with the Panthers leads him to take up a radical stance against white America. At one point in *Soul*, he even identifies with the extreme solution posed by one fallen member of the Black Panther Party, writing, "If we have to kill every man, woman, and child who stands in our way, then fuck it. If we have to destroy the world in order that the universe will not be polluted, then fuck it. We will not allow ourselves the luxury of life at the expense of freedom . . . It is by the gun that we have been enslaved and it will be by the gun that we will be liberated."[44]

Beck exploited every opportunity to get his messages to the people. He took long walks in order to discourage people away from The Life. When hustlers approached him on the street, looking for advice on how to pimp, he did everything he could to demystify pimping. "Just hordes of youngsters approach me on the street," he told one interviewer. "And they try to pick my brain for the hidden treasures they think are buried inside my skull. And I always slap their wrists before they reach for it."[45] He held "rap sessions" at colleges, public libraries, and community centers throughout the country, including the Venice Branch Library, the Afro Arts Book Center, Los Angeles City College, Malcolm X College, Loop Junior College, and San Jose State. He wrote opinion pieces criticizing the work of fellow black writers he felt damaged the cause of radical African American thinking. In October 1972, he published a response to future Pulitzer Prize–winning author James Alan McPherson, whose short story "The Silver Bullet" had appeared earlier in *Playboy* magazine. He wrote, "Since your author's principal objective is apparently 'soul-shit' satire, this admittedly paranoid street nigger must react icily to 'Bullet.' McPherson's is fraudulent symbolism that characterizes all so-called black urban youth gangs and black nationalists as predatory buffoons. I can only hope that my reaction to the 'Silver Bullet,' if not shared is at least understood."[46] He appeared on *Black Journal*, a weekly show that featured news, skits, interviews, and profiles about black issues. In the episode titled "The Black Pimp," which aired November 2, 1971, Beck returned to the Palm Tavern in Chicago, where he had learned the pimp trade from Albert "Baby" Bell. Here he outlined how his failed life as a pimp ultimately led to his revolutionary consciousness. As he proclaims at the end of the interview, "I'm here tonight appearing before you a well individual. Free of the street poison that put me into the kind of position where I brutalized and exploited our black queens. You have to have a realization that when you exploit your own kind, that you are in effect, counter-revolutionary. That you are hobbling and crippling the struggle of black people, for freedom and dignity."[47] Beck gave interviews in the *Chicago Defender, Washington Post, National Observer, Sepia, Black Collegian*, and *Washington Free Press*, celebrating the work of the Black Panthers and repeated many of his ideas from *Soul*. Beck some-times went even further than his heroes in promoting black mili-tancy, stating at one point, "Since the Panthers have so much moxie, since they're not afraid to die, since they're capable of projecting great terror, why didn't they go underground and form a completely secret organization, with a spy network and all? They could take over this whole country and no one would stop them. If the white man heard that an elaborate black espionage organization existed, he would think, 'No nigger is that smart' and go back to sleep. But these youngsters have no time to listen to older black men."[48]

It might come as a surprise that at the same moment that Beck was at his most famous and had sold millions of books, he was strug-gling to make money. The royalty checks he received from Holloway House were shrinking in size, even as he was growing in popularity. The royalty statements themselves were grossly inadequate; some-times they consisted of a single piece of paper with the names of the books listed and arbitrary dollar amounts next to them. As Holloway House editor and novelist Emory Holmes joked, "The royalty state-ments at Holloway House are really comical, because they are really a farce and have no bearing to reality. I'm happy when my beer money comes in the form of my royalties."[49] Although Beck had been—to borrow the language of the pimp game—Holloway Houses's "bot-tom" writer in 1967 with the publication of *Pimp*, by the early 1970s, the company had come to employ a number of authors writing pimp-themed novels. Donald Goines's *Whoreson*, Randolph Harris's *Trick-shot*, Odie Hawkins's *Ghetto Sketches*, Andrew Jackson's *Gentleman Pimp*, and Joseph Nazel's *Billion Dollar Death (Iceman #1)* were all released before 1974, establishing Holloway House as the preemi-nent publisher of "black experience" novels. The company paid many of its new authors, such as Goines, half of what it gave Beck for an advance, and some wrote as much as a book a month to make a living. Holloway House at this time also launched *Players* magazine. Edited by Watts Writers Workshop poet Wanda Coleman, and featuring regular columns by essayist Stanley Crouch and future chairman of the NAACP Julian Bond, *Players* was originally an upscale, black-themed *Playboy* that capitalized on the popular pimp and hustler images. In other words, by the early 1970s, Holloway House had built a successful business around Beck's creative output and ideas, and it no longer really needed him to be the foundational writer in its literary stable.

Beck's financial situation got so bad that it became difficult for his family to survive. There were four kids now, with the birth of the youngest daughter, Misty, in 1970. The old typewriter that Betty had used to write the first four books broke down, and they had to harass the company to give them another one. Beck even resorted to hustling a bit on the side to make ends meet. He made extra money by selling television boxes full of bricks out of the back of his car. He would set up a working TV on a street corner, and then sell brick-filled TV boxes to unsuspecting customers. On October 2, 1971, Beck wrote to Holloway House complaining of inconsistent royalty statements and low pay.

> *This letter probably represents the most urgent invitation for your self examination and reevaluation of your business philosophy, ethics, and basic morality than any communication written or vocal that you have received since your debut as a publisher (and accountant, secret partner in violation of State and Federal Law).*
>
> *Many years ago I flinched as a hack at Leavenworth Penitentiary slammed the steel barred door of a cell behind me. I had been an egomaniac in the free world, so consequently I stood stupidly, staring about at the reality of my grim new disaster situation. But I remember how the full impact of my fall and the claustrophobic horror of my dilemma was blunted, made unreal by the need of my raging ego mania to deny that I*

myself had been and was the long term stupid asshole who had egoed myself into the penitentiary.

I lay in that steel box for a month in shock before I was able to give my self a merciless psychic enema for the discovery that simply my own ego clouded judgment and evaluation of a crucial phase of my life and business affairs (illicit) and of a person (the victimized whore) vitally and inextricably tied into these hard realities and my own fate. My long-range value booby trap judgmental disaster had sprung from contempt for the vital person's potential and intelligence, my pathetic arrogance and my blinding gluttonous greed.

[To] state a simplistic but nevertheless valid premise, we could say that life itself (and particularly for that of the business man, illicit or so-called legal) is a chain of value judgments of the people and the situations which touch the total spectrum of our needs, our commercial interests, our existences. Ultimately we become successes or failures or even convicts as a direct result of how eruditely, how precisely we judge, evaluate, and gauge the present or future significance (and potential) of the people links involved in our chain of life situations. Small wonder that life is the most convoluted, treacherous game that we play. Our flawed judgments, our hoodlum egos, our contempt, our stupidity, our greed can mine the game with terror, misery and probably business extraction.

You have, for years now, represented a most traumatic problem in my life and in the lives of my deprived young children, in the life of their mother, the woman I love. Never before in my frustrating and unsatisfactory relationship with Holloway House have I had the compelling desperation to resolve the long term problem that has been reinforced and amplified by my receiving your so called royalty reports which were transparently fraudulent and an insult to even my moderate intellect.

A few questions for you relative to these, your most recently clumsy "sleights of ledger" which starkly confirm again the fact of illegal juggling of my account and conspiracy to withhold

*from me my legal rights to accurate (the actual number of
printings and sales of my books) royalty reports and to receive
promptly all monies due me from the sales of my books. These
rights are clearly defined within our book contracts.*

*Are you so self destructively contemptuous of my intelligence
that you expect me to believe the absurd figure of 352,519
printed copies of "PIMP," a book familiar to millions of people?
Why would your firm be motivated to [redesign] the cover
and increase by nearly 40% the price of an elderly paperback
(which a court of civil law would probably find unprecedented)
which has given me minimal monetary returns? Why did
you delete the important royalty report element of what
printing "PIMP" and "MAMA BLACK WIDOW" are now
in? Why do you report to me that a mere 131,053 copies of
"MAMA BLACK WIDOW" have been printed when I have
in my fat dossier of our predacious relationship (me victim)
the legal proof that "MAMA BLACK WIDOW" went into
a more than 80,000 copy second printing a very few days
after it's first printing 2½ years ago? Why and how can you
remember to callously bill me for copies of "NAKED SOUL"
(ironically used to promote and nurture your interests and
again our predacious relationship) and have total amnesia for
the necessity to send me a royalty report on the commercially
spectacular "NAKED SOUL" (especially it's printing status)
which has inspired your firm to redesign all of my works in it's
image? Should I permit my family's and my existence to be
poisoned (ad infinitum) hobbled by your refusal to respect me,
to treat me fairly?*

*What is the solution to the problem that you people
represent? Should one achieve your utter destruction and
his financial justice in a civil court of law? Or should one
rendezvous with the merciless primeval creature that hunkers
in the nightmarish pit of crimson abandon that exists in the
psyche of every man?*

*Why do you persistently inflict the indignity of fraudulent
royalty reports upon me? You have four successful works of*

mine that were created with my blood and agony. I can not, I will not let you enjoy (in blissful indifference) the monies from the fruit of my suffering while denying me and my family the minimal comforts and quality of existence that I as a talented and productive human being and father am entitled to make possible for them and myself. Why must I make you aware for instance of the fact that the $2,283.41 that you sent will have to be sent immediately on Monday for a used car of function. And for a used refrigerator and for a used table and chairs that will not collapse while my children are eating?

WHAT ARE YOU PEOPLE GOING TO DO?

I NEED EVERY LEGAL DOLLAR THAT I HAVE EARNED.

THIS FAMILY OF SIX HUMAN BEINGS NEED 800.00 A MONTH

TO SURVIVE AS HUMAN BEINGS.

I WANT WHAT YOU OWE ME.

Robert Beck

As this impassioned letter makes clear, Beck had ironically become the victim of a system of exploitation he had once imposed on sex workers. Although the sex trade and the book business are clearly not equivalent, it is also apparent that from Beck's point of view, Holloway House was making massive profits from his work without paying him his due compensation. While Bentley Morriss claimed, "They [the authors] always received the amount of money that they should have received. We did an honest job. We never took advantage of our authors," Beck's letter tells a different story.[50] The company audaciously reported to newspapers and magazines that it had sold millions of copies of his books, at the same time telling Beck it had sold only a few hundred thousand. By the early 1970s, America's most famous pimp was seemingly being pimped by the commercial literary marketplace that had made him a star.

It was not Holloway House, but Hollywood that came to Beck's financial rescue. In 1972, Universal Pictures bought the rights to *Trick Baby* for a reputed $25,000. It was the height of the blaxploitation era, a moment when Hollywood was making films that glamorized the ghetto and elevated the black pimp, drug dealer, and detective to the status of folk heroes. These films exploded on the American scene after the release of Melvin Van Peebles's independent movie *Sweet Sweetback's Baadasssss Song* in 1971. The story centers on Sweetback, a sex worker who is arrested by white police officers for a crime he didn't commit. When Sweetback witnesses the police brutalizing a young revolutionary from a Black Panther–like organization, he murders the two cops and goes on the run. After a series of escapes and sexual adventures, Sweetback finally eludes the police, crossing the border into Mexico. At the end of the film, a message blazes across the screen: "A baadasssss nigger is coming back to collect some dues." Although white critics mostly dismissed the film, it was a huge success in black neighborhoods. It became the most profitable independent film made to that point, grossing over $10 million by the end of the year. Huey Newton said it was the first revolutionary black film ever made, and it became required viewing for Black Panther Party members. After studios saw the enormous commercial potential of a black-themed film, they rushed to create their own versions. It was also 1971 that witnessed the release of *Shaft*, about a black detective of the same name. The film famously saved MGM from financial ruin, and it spawned two sequels, *Shaft's Big Score* and *Shaft in Africa*, as well as an Academy Award–winning score by Isaac Hayes. Many other black-themed films followed in this early period, including *Super Fly* (1972), *Across 110th Street* (1972), *Slaughter* (1972), *Hammer* (1972), *Black Caesar* (1973) *Blacula* (1972), *The Mack* (1973), *Coffy* (1973), *Cleopatra Jones* (1973), and dozens of others. By the time *Trick Baby* hit theaters in December 1972, blaxploitation was a well-established genre of popular film.

The sale of *Trick Baby* immediately vaulted Beck into an entirely new level of success. For a brief moment, it gave him a chance to relive the glory days as a pimp. Betty remembered the day he got the money from the studio. "He got that $25,000, and he came home with it. He cashed the check and brought it all in cash naturally and called me in his room and said, 'Shut the door.' I said, 'I can't right now. I don't know what the kids are doing.' 'Well go put them somewhere and shut the door.' And he threw a full-length white mink coat out on the bed and all these hundred dollar bills. He said, 'So, what do you think of that?' I said, 'We can get the hell out of this house.' And I said, 'So, what is this?' He said, 'A white mink coat.' And I said, 'I never told you I wanted a white mink coat. I don't like coats.' 'You're gonna wear this one.' So I got a $10,000 white mink coat out of the $25,000."[51] With their newfound wealth, they moved out of their cramped house on Ninetieth Street into a much bigger place on Iris Drive. It was a three-story house in the Hollywood Hills that had a balcony on the third floor where Beck could write and look out at the famous HOLLYWOOD sign about two miles away.

In late 1972, *Trick Baby* hit theaters nationwide. It was directed by Larry Yust, a relatively unknown director whose only previous work was his short film based on Shirley Jackson's chilling short story "The Lottery," about a small town whose residents ritualistically stone one member of the community to death. Anchoring *Trick Baby* was the famous voice and character actor Mel Stewart, best known for his role as George Jefferson's brother, Henry, in the television series *All in the Family*. The film also included a number of up-and-comers, including Kiel Martin, who would later go on to star in the cop drama *Hill Street Blues*, and Vernee Watson-Johnson, who would appear in hundreds of television episodes and films, including *Welcome Back, Kotter; The Fresh Prince of Bel-Air;* and *Days of Our Lives*. In Los Angeles, *Trick Baby* was screened at the Pacific Pantages, Tower, and Baldwin Theaters, as well as the Olympic, Compton, and Vermont drive-ins. In Chicago, it played at Loew's Palace, the Republic, and the Loop Theater, and was shown at the DeMille and Juliet Theaters in New York. In Philadelphia, *Trick Baby* set the record for the largest opening-day gross, making over $11,000.

For a brief moment, Beck and Betty got to feel like Hollywood royalty. At the Los Angeles premiere, they walked the red carpet; Betty wore the white mink coat he had given her. Because they couldn't find a babysitter, she later snuck out the back of the theater to take care of the kids, who were waiting in the Lincoln parked down the block. After that, Beck went on tour to promote the film. Because he hated to fly, he traveled by train to Chicago, New York, Boston, Philadelphia, and up and down the East Coast. Reviewers did not care for the film, mostly because the white screenwriters poached only surface street elements from Beck's original novel. One critic complained, "*Trick Baby* is only occasionally entertaining and too deeply couched in gutter level rhetoric,"[52] while another protested, "If there is anything to praise in this bastardized version of Iceberg Slim's novel, it has not come from the screen collaborators, for they have watered down, misadapted, and ultimately messed up Iceberg Slim's original work."[53] Three ministers from Chicago even protested the film's screening, calling it "racist and unfit to be seen by anyone."[54] Beck also wasn't entirely happy with the adaptation, but he was proud to have his book on the screen. He felt it was still better than a lot of the run-of-the-mill blaxploitation films out there, and he had hope that it would launch him into a commercially successful phase of his career. "The film has the artistic values that so many black critics of so-called contemporary black films have decried a lack of. I think this flick was put together so well that these characters are human beings rather than just super-niggers on the screen moving from one violent scene to another."[55]

With literary success, money from the film, and a new home, it seemed like life was taking a turn for the better for Beck, Betty, and the kids. But there were fissures in the marriage that were beginning to widen as time went on. After the success of the film, the couple took the kids on their first real vacation up and down the California coast in an RV. Beck filled the motor home with dozens of outfits, shoes, and hats of every color. It was so full of his stuff that there was hardly room for anything else. However, once they got on the road, he never left the RV. He hated the sunshine and felt uncomfortable interacting with crowds of people, so he stayed inside wearing his pajamas and reading books. They drove everywhere from Disneyland to the beaches in San Diego, and yet Beck spent the entire vacation sitting in parking lots. He left the RV only once, on the eighth day, when Betty convinced him to take a shower at a public restroom in San Diego. As the months and years went on, Beck's experience from his time as a pimp wore on the family in other ways. He was distant with his kids, and he didn't allow them to go to school because he feared for their safety. They would enter the school system only years later, after the couple split up. Beck also held on to some old-fashioned ideas about the division of labor in the house: he expected Betty to do all of the typing, sewing, cooking, and cleaning. He even had her install electric windows in the Lincoln and reupholster its seats. Betty still liked to drink whiskey regularly, and Beck had taken up smoking weed while he wrote in the upstairs attic. At times, when they were both intoxicated, they fought ferociously. Beck stood over her, trying to intimidate her with his height. She countered that she didn't like his "goddamn pimp bullshit." When the fights got really heated, he fled for fear of things getting physical. He drew the boundary there; he would never strike her. Through all of these conflicts, the writing somehow kept them together for a while longer. As the Becks' oldest daughter, Camille, remembered, "He loved her. He loved her because they had that work ethic. They had a very powerful thing that happened between them when those books were being put into production . . . She's typing, he's acting it out. And she'd start acting it out. And the work ethic that they had together was incredible."[56]

By the mid-1970s, Beck seemed poised for breakout success. He had sold 3.5 million copies of his books, 1.75 million of which were *Pimp*.[57] He had a major blockbuster film attached to his name, he gave interviews in national publications, and he was recognized on the street by the fans of his books. However, it started to become clear that the success Beck and Betty had been hoping for was the very thing tearing the relationship apart. For one, he kept her out of the public eye. He didn't take her to his readings, public lectures, or parties. In interviews, when he was asked about her racial identity, he evaded the question by claiming that she was Creole or Cajun, which he joked "makes for some rather good cooking and devotion and love."[58] He defended himself to Betty, claiming that he was protecting her from retaliation from the white media or the Black Pan-thers. However, as his fame increased, Beck spent more time away from home, and his behavior became more difficult to justify. As their youngest daughter, Misty, characterized it, "He was definitely out of the house a lot when the books began to take off. That was the distance between my parents. He was off becoming a writer. Actually, a pimp again, is what she would say. He is back out there, and she's left at home with four kids."[59] The fame and attention that Beck enjoyed as an author proved as seductive as the pimp life he had once left behind. As he himself admitted in one of the last inter-views he ever gave, "When you've been a pimp for as long as I have, it's in every pore, in every atom of your being. And it is only through illusion that you convince yourself that it's dead. You know in your secret heart that the monster might very well be activated by exter-nal forces. And then I was a junkie, you see. And afflicted with the permanent imprint of the junkie, and all of the spin-out phantasma-goria, the lusting, even when one had kicked one's habit. There's a lusting, lusting for that feeling, that sensation, because there is no sensation—even the hell of the writer when he's in the throes of cre-ation, as magnificent as that is—that can compare with the chemical rush of a speedball. But one is therapeutic and one is hemlock."[60]

According to some sources, at nearly sixty years of age, Beck went back to pimping one final time. Others claim that he took to run-ning around with a number of women. He wasn't pimping; he was cheating on Betty. What is known for sure is that by the mid-1970s, Beck was hanging out at Los Angeles's infamous Parisian Room, a haunt for musicians, pimps, and black celebrities. Located on the corner of Washington and La Brea, the Parisian Room had become a local hotspot as early as 1962. It was decorated with murals created by Frank Bowers, a Los Angeles artist who painted pop art for dive bars and tiki lounges in exchange for his unpaid bar tabs. Entertain-ers who regularly came through the Parisian included Count Basie,

Sarah Vaughan, T-Bone Walker, Sam Fletcher, Jimmy Witherspoon, Arthur Prysock, as well as local drag queen sensation Sir Lady Java, who was billed as "Prettiest Man on Earth."

Jazz legend Red Holloway often emceed at the Parisian, and he wowed listeners by wading into the crowd playing his electric sax. He opened and closed the joint, and throughout the night he "held court," announcing the arrival of pimps and black "royalty" to the crowd. They often rewarded him with sixty-five-dollar bottles of champagne, and they tipped him up to a hundred dollars to play songs. It was a bravado atmosphere reminiscent of 1940s Bronzeville or Paradise Valley, and Beck fit right in. He ultimately became such a fixture at the Parisian that he and Holloway even recorded an album together, titled *Reflections*. After hours, they often reminisced about Chicago, where they had both lived in the 1950s, and one day, Beck told him that he wanted to do a recording of pimp toasts. Holloway introduced him to Lou Drozin, the owner of Laff Records, which put out albums by Redd Foxx and Richard Pryor. In 1976, Beck recorded four toasts with the Red Holloway Quartet playing jazz improvisations in the background. With the personal and brilliant track "Mama Debt" anchoring the album, *Reflections* went on to influence rappers, including Ice-T, and it predated hip-hop originals such as "Rapper's Delight" and "The Message" by a few years.

In Holloway's version of events, Beck was also pimping out of the Parisian, a story that many in his family reject. The now-deceased Holloway was known as somewhat of a bullshitter, and we have his account of Beck's time at the club from only a single interview. It is entirely possible that Holloway made up this whole story in order to appear that he was a more intimate friend of the legendary Iceberg Slim. According to Holloway, he was in charge of keeping the pimps in line; physical violence was not tolerated in the club. When he met Beck, he knew his reputation from his books, so he reportedly gave him the same speech that he gave all the newcomers. "Now listen if you gonna kick your ladies' ass, that's your business, but you don't do it in here, you know. If you got something to do you take it outside."[61] As Holloway told it, Beck followed the same routine each time he came to the Parisian. He started by sitting at the front of the club with the other pimps at a large circular table, but as the evening wore on, he hunkered down in a booth in the back to collect money from women. He liked the booth, he reported, because his prostitutes could visit him through the back door without being noticed. He kept three women at once, and none was over the age of twenty-five. He dressed them in new, expensive outfits, and he sent them to the beautician once a week. He made arrangements with porters from different hotels in Hollywood to broker deals between his workers and johns, and for this service, they got a small cut. His women were required to bring him at least $500 a night, and they often came back with $1,000. He never wore the same suit twice to the club, and he tipped the waitresses so much money—up to $100 a night—that they fought over who would get his section. The player-haters were jealous of him, but he let everyone know that he carried a gun in an ankle holster just in case they doubted how dangerous he still was.

Even while pushing sixty, Beck also supposedly followed the code of the pimp that he had immortalized in his books, much to the amusement of his other patrons. A woman from Hollywood Hills had been coming to the Parisian for years, for instance, trying to pick up famous black musicians and personalities. She took an interest in Beck, bought him a drink one night, and invited him back to her place. He agreed, and as they were about to leave, he said, "Well, wait a minute, we haven't talked about the financial arrangements." Not understanding the rules of the pimp game, she replied, "Well, I'm not gonna charge you anything." He told her, "I know, but I'm gonna charge you." When she asked him, "What are you crazy?" he answered, "Well, I would be crazy if I'm gonna fuck for free." She stormed out of the place and never came back. As everyone laughed, Beck announced to the bar, "That bitch got a lot of nerve, she think I'm just gonna fuck for nothing."[62] Holloway also claimed that there were other incidents where Beck was as dangerous as the Cavanaugh Slim of old.

I'm on a break here and I hear this commotion. "Bitch, what the fuck!" And I say, "Oh shit." And I run back there in the

back to see what is going on, you know, and I said, "Slim!"
And he said, "I know. I know. I know." So he jumps up and
goes to the toilet. So I go in behind him, because I wanted to
ask him what was goin' on. So I see him take something, and
then I saw his money, and he threw it in the commode and he
flushed it down. I said, "Man what the fuck are you doin?" He
said, "This bitch gave me fifty fuckin' dollars, and she'd been
gone all day." So I said, "Oh you could have gave me that fifty."
So anyway, he went back over there, and he said, "Bitch where
the fuck you been all day?" She said, "Well, I had my period
and I just didn't feel well." He said, "You ain't got lockjaw have
you? You better get the fuck outta here."[63]

Despite being old enough to be the father, or even grandfather, of
his prostitutes, Holloway testified, Beck returned to the pimp game
with the same ferocity that had made him notorious in Chicago. If
these stories are true, he had betrayed the memory of his mother,
Mary, and he had betrayed his marriage. While he had started writing to absolve himself of the terrible life he had lived as a pimp, his
success as an author had tragically brought him full circle back to
the game.

However, these stories seem pretty far-fetched—particularly
Holloway's claims about the money Beck was making and the way
he was dressing his women. They very well might be true, but
according to his own daughters, Beck was not pimping again. He
was cheating on Betty, perhaps even with prostitutes. According to
Misty, "My dad stopped pimping. There was no reason to pimp. My
dad would've probably written about that in one of his books. He
was pretty much a reformed pimp. I have to say 150% that is not
true. My mom was psychotic. There was no way. I mean, yeah, he
had sex with other women, but making money off of them? Uh-uh.
Reformed. Pimping them and having sexual relations with them is
totally different. Pimping them is making money off of them, while
they're on their backs. Maybe he did have sex with whores and stuff,
but he stayed in a room like a recluse, even with my mother. I mean
honestly there's no way."[64] Beck's oldest daughter, Camille, was less

sure about the extent of his treachery, though she remembered that her father openly flaunted his philandering at home. He brought a variety of women to the house, which he called his "publicists" and "assistants." As she characterized it, "He used to move these hookers into the house. They were supposed to be his assistants. But there was a lot of traffic between the rooms."[65]

Whether Beck was sleeping with these women or taking money from them or both is really beside the point. The real issue for Betty was that her husband's actions undermined everything they had built together for sixteen years. He was spending more time away from home, and she became overwhelmed by the responsibility of raising four kids on her own. She was homeschooling them, but with all the responsibilities of motherhood and keeping up with the housework, she had uneven success. She drank more and started taking pills. Again, to quote Misty, "My mom stayed home 90 percent of the time. She was the head of the house. She was the person who gave discipline. She was the person who made meals. Rules. Again, my father was not home a lot, during the book tours and stuff. One of the reasons why my mom was so upset with him is that she did want a little bit of the limelight and kind of wanted to travel and do things with him. It kind of wore on her. She helped a lot with the writing and she made his clothes. And she is left home with four kids. I believe a lot of depression set in at that time."[66]

In the midst of these family conflicts, Beck's writing suffered noticeably. Following the success of the *Trick Baby* film, he started gearing his books explicitly toward the commercial market in the hopes of capitalizing on his success with the film. In 1977, he published *Long White Con*, a sequel to *Trick Baby*. Like most sequels, *Long White Con* is not as good as the original, and it is by far his weakest artistic effort. Told in third person, it reads more like a screenplay than his earlier, first-person novels, and it lacks all the intimacy and urgency of its predecessor. *Long White Con* is also littered with flashbacks, scenes lifted verbatim directly out of *Trick Baby*, which feel like filler. In this story, White Folks and a team of con artists pretend to be treasure hunters, searching for a life-size statue encrusted with jewels created by an Aztec king. They befriend a wealthy mark at the very moment they "discover" the statue in a dummy ghost town that is up for auction. The team sets up the mark to make his own "discovery" of millions in cash hidden away beneath the feet of the statue. When the statue and land go up for auction, the mark buys them for hundreds of thousands of dollars, which he pays directly to the swindlers. Set in the rural mining country of the Southwest and featuring an implausible scam at the center of the plot, *Long White Con* just doesn't have the same feel of realism as Beck's Chicago novels. There are of course flashes of the old Beck, when he threads together stories of con artistry with critiques of a racist society. For instance, at one point, White Folks plans to seduce Christina Buckmeister—coal, banking, and real estate heiress—so that he can marry her and use her fortune as financial reparations for slavery. "He'd punish her for the hopelessness and starvation in black ghettos, for his dead black mother. For all the blacks ever imprisoned in holds of slaveships. He'd punish her for being spoiled, pampered, aggressive, beautiful and rich."[67] However, these moments are few and far between, and in large part, *Long White Con* reads like a flat attempt to create a ready-made screenplay for a filmable sequel to *Trick Baby*.

A much better effort was Beck's *Death Wish: A Story of the Mafia*, also published in 1977, which is a fictionalized account of the Chicago mob's infamous takeover of the African American policy rackets. In the early 1940s, Ed Jones of the Jones Brothers served time at Terre Haute Federal Penitentiary with Sam Giancana, a soldier for the Chicago Outfit, who would later become mob boss in the 1950s. In a misplaced gesture of friendship, Jones told Giancana all about the policy rackets, and when they were both released from prison, Giancana decided to take over the business. He had Ed Jones kidnapped and eventually ransomed for $100,000; afterward, the Jones family boarded a train heading for Mexico to live the rest of their lives on their estate. Through the late '40s and early '50s, the mob assassinated and intimidated the remaining policy kings with bullets and dynamite. The last black policy king who refused to negotiate or cave under the Outfit's pressure was the famous Teddy Roe. His defiance of the white mob made him a folk hero among Bronzeville citizens; he and his family were shot at, his friends were killed, his house was bombed, and yet he told Giancana he would rather die than hand policy over to the mob. When Roe was finally killed on August 4, 1952, a reported 50,000 people attended his funeral to pay their respects to the last man in Bronzeville to stand up to the mob. In the early 1970s, the FBI caught Giancana admitting on tape, "I'll say this. Nigger or no nigger, that bastard went out like a man. He had balls. It was a fuckin' shame to kill him."[68]

Beck lived in Chicago through much of this takeover, and as Albert "Baby" Bell's protégé, he no doubt had secondhand knowledge of much of the violence. *Death Wish* is an expansive and ambitious novel representing these events, with dozens of characters and a number of complex plots involving mafiosi, voodoo zealots, youth gangs, and an underground revolutionary force known as the Warriors. Although a number of characters compete for center stage, the novel's hero is clearly Willie Poe, a figure based on Teddy Roe, and reputedly "the only nigger in the history of the world that ever stuck his black ass out and told the Mafia to kiss it. He is the greatest and baddest on the planet."[69] After the mafia murders Poe, a group of black militants form the Warriors to take their revenge. The group buys a vacant church and builds a network of secret tunnels underneath it called the Free Zone. There, the organization recruits an interracial squadron of five hundred soldiers, which it trains in guerrilla maneuvers and mastery of weapons. With the help of a voodoo priestess, the Warriors set out to kill all the mafia men in Chicago. An all-out war ensues, and at the end of the novel—like a Shakespearean tragedy—there are only a handful of survivors. Blending historical fact and speculative fiction, *Death Wish* cleverly provides a fictionalized exploration of the question that Beck had pondered with the Black Panthers nearly ten years earlier: "Why didn't they go underground and form a completely secret organization, with a spy network and all?"

However, for all of its imagination and complex plotting, *Death Wish* suffers from problems similar to those that plague *Long White Con*. The book reads more like an unwieldy screenplay treatment than a novel. There are so many characters, many of which lack depth, that it is difficult to distinguish them from one another. Further, the dialogue of the Italian mobsters doesn't ring quite true, which is distracting considering they populate half of the novel. As Beck explained it later in an interview, he had actually conceived *Death Wish* first as a screenplay. However, he couldn't get it produced by Universal Pictures, because his radical politics got in the way of his desire to make money. "I had an idea. It was called *Death Wish*. That wasn't the title of it. The publishers gave it that, because that wasn't my title. They gave it that title. And before we went, my agent, I said to him, 'Well I don't have an outline.' He says, 'You don't need an outline . . . You give them a verbal outline when you get in their office.' I did. There's [Ned] Tanen. You ever hear of him? Well he's the head of Universal. And he was sitting behind his desk, and he said, 'A great idea.' And his story consultant was there. And he says, 'We like it. Now listen, when do you want to start writing the screenplay? . . . Do you have any objections to writing it with Bob Garland?' Now Bob Garland happened to be white. Got me? Don't forget, I'm fresh out of the street now. I'm just learning how to . . . what do I know? I am full of all kinds of militant bullshit. My idol for Christ's Sake is Huey Newton, so you can see the trouble I was in. The Black Panthers. Those are my idols, OK? I said, 'For my solo shot, I would like to do it alone. I don't think I require [help].'"[70] Universal then passed on Beck's screenplay, so he wrote *Death Wish* as a novel. He tried to find a hardback publisher for it for years, but no one would touch it, as he was dismissed as a paperback writer. Reluctantly, he published again with Holloway House, where the book got the same treatment as his other works. Beck got his usual advance and royalties, the book was minimally edited, and its publication received little attention from the general public.

In the mid- to late 1970s, Beck became increasingly obsessed with trying to write screenplays, as this seemed like the only way he was going to make any money at his craft. When he was at home, he mostly hid out on the third floor of the house. The rest of the time he and Betty fought. She mockingly called him God when they argued, and one day she even pushed him down the stairs. When the police arrived, they just laughed when they saw a man of six feet two standing next to Betty, who was only five feet five. Not even the writing could keep them together anymore. She refused to type any of his screenplays. As she explained it, "We were not into writing short stories. We were not into writing scripts, movie scripts, or TV scripts. He knew nothing at all about lighting and sound and movement, of people from place to place . . . [I told him,] 'What the hell are we doing? Old as you are, old as I am, our old gray asses hanging down to the floor. And we're going to take up a new form of . . .' I said no. No, I'm not going to do it."[71]

In 1978, the money finally ran out from the books and the film, and that was the beginning of the end. Betty recalled, "And then I got a part-time job. And then he quit writing altogether. And then I told him, I said, 'Uh-uh. No, baby. We ain't pimping me, all right? I never paid a man's rent in my life, and I goddamn sure don't intend to start paying yours now. You either do what you know how to do, and let's get some money rolling in here or you lay on your own with your dead ass [and] I'm moving out with my children.' And I did."[72] Betty made good on her threat; she sold the white mink for a security deposit and first and last months' rent. She packed up her belongings and, taking her four children, she walked out of Beck's life forever.

CHAPTER 9

FINAL YEARS (1978–1992)

When Robert Beck and his common-law wife, Betty, split up in 1978, he was devastated. The breakup had been an ugly one; Betty destroyed many of his photos, and she threatened to throw burning matches into the Lincoln's gas tank if she ever saw it parked on the street. Beck was starting over again by himself, and at sixty years old, this was no easy task. His diabetes, which had developed a few years earlier, was beginning to take its toll on his health. He became fatigued more easily and his vision was starting to blur. Beck moved around Los Angeles for a couple of years with just a few possessions: his outfits, some photos, a few boxes of books, and his unpublished writings. He lived in a hotel in Hollywood for a while and then a small house in the West Adams neighborhood. Finally, he moved into the home of a friend, a schoolteacher who lived just off Crenshaw Boulevard in South Central. By the late seventies, he had virtually disappeared from public view. He gave no more interviews, and he published no more novels. Suddenly, almost inexplicably, Beck's moment in the limelight was over.

To make matters worse, he was broke. The blaxploitation era in Hollywood had passed, and the promise of making a movie version of *Death Wish* or a sequel to *Trick Baby* had evaporated. Beck's royalty checks from Holloway House continued to shrink. In the final six months of 1978, he was paid a mere $896.03 in royalties for his entire collection of works.[1] Driven by his financial desperation, he decided to publish one last book with the company in 1979, a collection of short stories. No other publisher would even look at his work. Holloway House had already released four of his short stories—"Airtight Willie & Me," "To Steal a Superfox," "Lonely Sweet," and "The Reckoning"—in *Players* in the late seventies. Beck submitted two more unpublished works: "Satin," a stock heist narrative, and "Grandma Randy," a horror story about a foster home manager who molests and murders children. Beck packaged these six stories together and published them as a collection called *Airtight Willie & Me*. It was the final book that he would publish in his lifetime, and it is by far the finest of his late fictional works he published with Holloway House. In many of the stories, he returns to the first-person narration and stylistic flourishes that made his early books *Pimp*, *Trick Baby*, and *Mama Black Widow* so intimate and riveting. For instance, in the collection's title story, Beck, fresh from prison, is double-crossed by his cellmate and street partner Airtight Willie after they pull the drag con together. At the end of the story, he waxes philosophical about the life of street crime, delivering one of his characteristic lines about it as a life of "cop and blow": "It was black ghetto Christmas. Saturday Night! Easy to cop a ho! I'd guerilla my Watusi ass into a chrome-and-leather ho den and gattle-gun my pimp-dream shit into some mud-kicker's frosty car. I pimp-pranced toward a ho jungle of neon blossoms a half mile away. Some ass-kicker was a cinch to be a ho short when the joints folded in the a.m."[2] Channeling the Iceberg Slim persona of a decade earlier, *Airtight Willie & Me* resurrects the dazzling prose and autobiographical vignettes that made Beck's works so irresistible in the first place. For fans of his gritty early work, *Airtight* was a fitting farewell from the man who invented the genre of black street fiction.

During this final era, Beck also produced pages and pages of other writings that he didn't publish, a stockpile of ideas that he worked up in various forms. Some of them were just quick character sketches, written on scraps of paper: "I am an ex–New York City detective and lawyer turned business man because of a shattered crotch courtesy of a shotgun blast fired by a member of a heist mob during an armored car caper." Others were even less fully formed, hieroglyphs that probably only Beck himself understood. One such statement read: "Hypocritical lunacy about the living sainthood of

Shirley Temple Black and all of the other soul deep hang-ups." He wrote outlines for short stories and ideas for novels that would never come to fruition. He was constantly inventing new methods for self-promotion and trying to think of a way to get out of the Holloway House machine. One of his most provocative ideas was to set up his own production company and promote the novels/screenplays of aspiring black writers in Hollywood. He scribbled this particular plan on the inside pages of a book titled *"Yellow Kid" Weil: The Auto-biography of America's Master Swindler.* The book itself tells the story of Joe Weil, a turn-of-the-century Chicago con artist who made a living using a combination of short and long cons. Beck greatly admired the book, and had borrowed from it liberally for both *Trick Baby* and *Long White Con.*

On the opening pages of Weil's book, Beck outlines his idea for "Iceberg Slim's Complete Rundown Kit," an instructional guide for fans on "how to write and turn your screenplays or novels into $$$$$."[3] Beck divides the Rundown Kit into parts that correspond with the stages of Weil's elaborate scams. The way that the outline is written, it is difficult to tell whether Beck is trying to promote writers or con them. Perhaps it is a little bit of both. There is the "Hook" section, in which Beck promises to "utilize his established contacts with the movie and television industries to personally promote and polish those ideas and scripts he considers rich in concept and $$$$$ potential."[4] He includes a "Prod" section, which entices buyers by telling them that the large demand for these kits "will make it impossible for Slim to ensure that the authors of superior scripts and ideas can get the best shot at the fame and fortune that the world has bestowed upon Iceberg Slim."[5] In the "Breakdown and Convincer" section, he asks potential customers to "Send the super bargain price of $10.00 to Iceberg Movie Productions in Hollywood, California for your literary rundown kit that you must agree would be a bargain at any price or Slim will refund your money and charge nothing."[6] Finally, in the "Close of Sale" portion, he promises, "Every prompt purchaser of the kit will receive under separate cover a copy of Iceberg's sensational screenplay soon to be a dynamite movie [and] can be used as a reference and model of successful form and packaging."[7] As a "Bonus Opportunity," Beck also asks that writers directly "enclose with your payment a brief confidential note as to why you believe your idea or completed work would be valuable on movie screens or in novel form for the human race and/or especially in the struggle of black people [and] you could be selected to spend an all expense luxury weekend as a guest of Iceberg Slim at the premiere of his latest film in fabulous Hollywood California."[8] At the time he wrote this in the mid- to late 1970s, Beck did not have much in the way of fame or fortune, any real Hollywood connections, or a movie production company. Seen in this light, the Rundown Kit reads like a pyramid scheme in which Beck hoped to capitalize on the popularity of the persona of Iceberg Slim and become a broker for undiscovered black writers. In other words, it appears that at one point Beck tried to beat Holloway House at its own game by creating his own stable of screenwriters and novelists. However, as he lacked the financial resources and industry relationships, Beck eventually abandoned this ambitious idea in frustration and went back to eking out a living with his meager royalties.

The most important unpublished manuscript that Beck produced during this period was his novel *Doom Fox*, a story of Los Angeles's black community from the end of World War II to the early 1970s. It was the first of three final novels that Beck would write about Los Angeles, but would remain unpublished during his lifetime. After releasing *Airtight Willie*, Beck decided he would rather hide his novel-length manuscripts away in a drawer than give them to Holloway House. *Doom Fox* presents Beck's more familiar voice and narrative style, featuring pimps, cutthroat gamblers, racist policemen, cunning prostitute boosters, and unwitting marks. At another level, the novel is much grander in scope and more experimental than anything he had attempted previously. It is the first and only of his novels written in the present tense, and it explores the intertwining stories of nearly fifty characters from three generations and a variety of diverse backgrounds and social classes. Some of the characters include Joe Allen Senior, who escapes to Los Angeles from the South after his imprisonment on a chain gang; Baptiste Rambeau, a gambler who at the age of three witnessed his whole family being murdered by a group of voodoo fanatics; Pretty Melvin Sternberg, the son of wealthy Beverly Hills socialites, who eventually murders a pimp named Whispering Slim; Delphine, a prostitute who struggles to maintain a sense of moral decency within the confines of her profession; and Reverend Felix, a faith healer and hypnotist, who claims he can cure cancer with powdered bat hearts.

At the center of the story is the unlikely hero Joe "Kong" Allen Junior, a heavyweight boxer whose honesty and ugliness make him an easy target for the con artists and gold diggers that populate the novel. In the opening pages, Joe cruises the famous Central Avenue corridor looking for some kind of affection amid the dive bars and blues clubs. As always, Beck's signature prose style evokes a secret world of urban life now long gone. "Jouncing bosoms that poke and peep from gauzy cleavages ache Joe's starved scrotum. He ducks into the Blue Pit Bar, a mecca for whores. A gamy meld of steamy crotches and clabbered perfume stings his nostrils. He seats himself at the crescent bar jammed with raucous whores, tricks, and hustlers. Pimps perch and swivel necks, hooded eyes aglitter in leather booths along the walls like gaudily featured vultures."[9] Like the stories of nearly all of the characters in this novel, Joe's ends tragically. His promising career as a heavyweight boxer falls apart; he spends ten years in prison after killing his wife's lover; and in the final scene of the book, his wife and son are murdered by a marauding LAPD squadron. After a gun battle with the police from his bedroom window, Joe turns the shotgun on himself and, resolving "to dream the sweetest dream there is," pulls the trigger.[10] Like Beck's other works, this novel is relentlessly violent, but there is something deeply sad about it, too. In *Doom Fox*, characters' petty passions, jealousies, and desires for revenge destroy their connections to family and community. Husbands cheat on their wives. Wives deceive their husbands. Fathers abandon their unborn children. Mothers leave their daughters to pursue shallow dreams of wealth. In the end, these acts of unfaithfulness lead to everyone's tragic death. The final image of the novel is an image of utter despair and loneliness, as Joe sits among the dead bodies of his loved ones aiming a shotgun at his own throat. Although a conventional Beck novel in some ways—populated by pimps, prostitutes, and con men—*Doom Fox*'s obsession with infidelity and crumbling family relationships seems to reflect a deeply personal sense of loss. Written just after his relationship ended with Betty, the novel consciously or unconsciously expresses Beck's sadness and guilt about his family life having fallen apart.

In 1980, after two years on his own, Beck's life changed dramatically for the better when he got a letter from a fan named Diane Millman. Diane was born in Los Angeles in 1943 and grew up in the Silver Lake neighborhood, a residential area in central Los Angeles, where Walt Disney built his first major studio in the 1930s. In her twenties, she moved around Los Angeles, living in the Leimert Park area and along Santa Barbara Avenue. By the late 1970s, she was a single mother of three who worked for the State of California, transcribing testimony of unemployment benefits cases. She was an avid reader, and had been especially impressed by Beck's latest novel, *Death Wish*. Somewhat on a whim, she decided to write him a letter, thanking him for his work. She included her phone number and was surprised when Beck called her. As Diane remembered it, "The time just happened to be right. I was just writing as a fan. I didn't know he had been separated for a couple years. He called and we started talking. We really clicked together."[11] They went on a few dates. Neither of them drank, so they stayed away from bars. They smoked a little weed now and then, but nothing excessive. They went to movies in Hollywood and Crenshaw, and they took long walks. Mostly they hung out at Diane's house in Silver Lake watching TV and talking. They were both deeply passionate about politics, and they often spent hours discussing subjects ranging from the Black Panthers to Ronald Reagan's presidency. One of their favorite pastimes was to go to the beach. Diane recalled, "We drove to the beach in his '48 Lincoln and just sat in the car and talked for a long time, with the sounds of the ocean in the background." Beck was also excited to find a reader for his newest work. He had decided not to publish it, but as an author, he still craved feedback from his readers. Diane was thrilled at the opportunity to read his unpublished manuscripts, so he showed her *Doom Fox*. "In fact," Diane later said, "we had a ritual at first, when we weren't together yet. He had me read a chapter each night to him over the phone just to get my reaction. And I read the whole book like that. I read the original typewritten manuscript."[12]

Beck loved to share his work with Diane, though he was adamant about keeping it away from Holloway House. As Diane explained it years after his death, "He NEVER wanted to give it to his publisher. He said to me, 'I would rather this gather dust on a shelf than to give it to the publisher.' [Holloway House] had robbed him for years. I did just that."[13] Five years after Beck passed away, Diane hired a literary agent, Faith Childs, who found an interested publisher for *Doom Fox*, Grove Press. Beck's old book contracts legally obligated her to offer Holloway House first look at the book, though she was not required necessarily to publish it with the company without an official offer and acceptance. The exchanges between her literary attorney and the legal counsel for Holloway House provide a captivating look at the publisher's sense of entitlement when it came to Beck's novels. On April 1, 1997, Diane's attorney, Brad Bunnin, sent a letter to Holloway House's lawyer Robert D. Wilner. In it, he explained that Diane was going to submit the book to other publishers, because of the company's failure to make an offer in writing after the required eight-week waiting period. The letter begins: "Diane Millman Beck asked me to review the publishing agreement between HH and her late husband, with specific attention to section 20. I've done so, and I've discussed the clause with Faith Childs, a prominent literary agent. We agree that the clause does not establish a right in Holloway House to acquire publishing rights to *Doom Fox* without a full process of offer and acceptance."[14] After a detailed explanation of the legal reasoning behind Diane's decision to hear offers from other publishers, Bunnin concludes, "Please consider that the manuscript for *Doom Fox* is hereby withdrawn. Mrs. Beck intends to submit the manuscript to other publishers. If Holloway wishes to acquire rights, it should submit a written proposal to the Faith Childs Agency, 132 West 22nd Street, 4th Floor, New York, NY 10011. Such an offer should, of course, adequately reflect the remarkable publishing history of Iceberg Slim's literary works."[15]

Just three days later, Holloway House's attorney Robert Wilner responded. Reflective of the company's generally cavalier attitude toward its authors, Wilner's opening line reads: "I am in receipt of your fax dated April 1, 1997, in the above-captioned matter. Since I did not receive it until the following business day, I am not viewing this as an 'April Fools' joke." The letter goes on to say that he and Holloway House "do not share your conclusion that the manuscript for *Doom Fox* is withdrawn." Wilner argues that the company did not have to make a formal offer that contains "material terms" because "industry custom, as well as past dealings with Robert Beck, establish those terms." He goes on to say that previous royalty payments and advances have been "consistent throughout my client's entire history of dealings with Robert Beck," and therefore "there is no reason to believe that there was any variance in the terms and conditions." Strangely, Wilner then questions whether Diane even owns the rights to the manuscript and whether Beck himself was the real author. The letter then concludes, with some menace, "I restate that from the actions of your office and your client, it is my considered opinion that the manuscript *Doom Fox* is not withdrawn and you are not free to submit it to any other publisher. Please govern yourself accordingly."[16]

A week later, on April 10, Bunnin responded with what would be the final letter in the exchange. It begins with a question that Beck himself had probably been wondering all along in his dealings with Holloway House: "If Holloway House wishes to acquire publication rights to Iceberg Slim's last book, wouldn't it be fitting for the publisher to approach the transaction in a spirit of generosity and friendly cooperation, with due regard for its long relationship with Robert Beck? An offer that adequately reflects the earnings of past books and the fact that this is Mr. Beck's last book, with a significant advance, would have been evidence of that spirit. Instead, the publisher seems to have taken for granted that the extraordinarily small advance and original mass market paperback royalties would be a part of any deal, but they are not acceptable to Mrs. Beck, who indeed owns the rights to the work." The letter takes on Wilner's arguments line by line, pointing out that "industry custom simply doesn't fulfill missing material terms for a complex contract" and that the "history of past dealings between an author now deceased and your client do not establish a contract for a new work." At the end of the letter, Bunnin proposes a compromise on behalf of Diane, inviting Holloway House to make an offer in the form of a complete contract. Diane would have the right to accept or reject that contract. He concludes with a partially veiled threat of his own: "As Holloway House's lawyer, you have a real opportunity to encourage your client to offer a fair deal to Mrs. Beck. I urge you to let them know that generosity and cooperation will serve all parties better than any attempt at intimidation or interference, the consequences of which would be unfortunate for all concerned."[17] Holloway House never responded, but instead launched a public campaign to discredit the book's authenticity after it was published. The company even persuaded Beck's daughter Camille to file a lawsuit against Diane. The lawsuit was later thrown out of court, dismissed as having no merit, and Diane was free to publish *Doom Fox* with Grove Press in 1998. It was the first Robert Beck novel to be published in nearly twenty years. It would be nearly two more decades before the posthumous release of Beck's next novel, *Shetani's Sister,* in 2015.

—

By the middle of 1981, Beck and Diane had grown much closer, and she invited him to move in with her at her house in Silver Lake. A year later, they were married. Beck still liked his privacy, so he took up residence in the small apartment adjacent to the main house. Together, they built a quiet, peaceful life. They watched TV at night and took walks. However, Beck developed diabetic neuropathy, causing him a great amount of pain in his legs, and it made walking extraordinarily difficult. Diane arranged for him to see a specialist at the UCLA Medical Center, and it took months for the pain to subside. In the meantime, he stayed at home, working on new short stories and novels. He enjoyed reading the fan mail that Holloway House forwarded along. Many of the letters were from men who had read his books while serving time in prison. Some of them resembled mini-essays that spanned a variety of topics, including black history, political struggles, and the art of fiction. Others praised him for his inspiring works, and they often sought advice on how to write novels themselves. Beck and Diane read these letters together, and he tried to respond to as many of them as he could. The following exchange is a typical one between Beck and his readers:

Mr. Beck (Or if I may Bob)

I have just finished reading "The Naked Soul." I found it to be very interesting. I didn't write this letter to try and run game on you. I wrote this letter because I have a problem in which I trust you can help.

I want to write a book that will reach people just as you have, but I wish to write about a totally different subject: I wish to write about crack.

I will try to be brief as I fill you in on why I am saying this.

Presently, I am an inmate in _____ Prison. I am twenty-one years old. I am married. I have been selling crack for three years, and I was a user.

I have seen how crack destroys people's lives, their homes, and their hopes for the future, but most of all, I experienced the hurt. I felt that if I put what I experienced on paper it could enlighten people to what the life on the "inside" of crack is like. This way it could reach the would-be sellers and the would-be users and hopefully the present users and sellers.

You lived longer as a pimp than I as a drug dealer, but some of the things I witnessed and went through would curl the very hairs on the President's lower posterior. I want to go into it all. The cops, whores, thieves, beggars, life, death, children, the elderly, the jails, etc.

"Only those with experience can teach."

Crack has ruined my life, left me on a near divorce, no family to turn to, a second prison term and almost lifeless on many accounts as a dealer and a user.

To me, if just one person would read the book I am hoping to write and be spared the hardships I would feel much better than I do.

On page 60 of "The Naked Soul," you said, "that a pimp's

life is perhaps the worst life anybody could have. He is feared,
hated, and walks a greased wire with hell on one side and
death on the other from pimps, his victims, their parents, or
relatives." My brother you are close, a pimp may come second,
but a crack dealer comes first.

Bob, I sincerely hope you can see what I am saying and
decide to offer your help. I would be most gracious to you for it.
I also, alongside of how to go about writing it, [want to know]
how to get Holloway House to publish it. I chose Holloway
because a lot of people read books put out by them. I for one
own every book written by D Goines also seven books plus the
one I have related to that were written by you as well as a few
others that are home in the living room on the book shelves.

Please consider what I have said and reply.
Thank you,

Beck replied:

Dear ———,

I appreciated your interest in my books. Your motivations
for writing a book about your crack experiences are admirable.
[Penciled in later: "Crack is at present a highly topical subject
that affords an insider like yourself a chance to get your story
published."] You can prepare a vivid brief chronological outline
(2–3 pages neatly typed) of your story highlights. You can send
it to the editor at Holloway House with a typed cover letter
explaining your motivations for telling your stories. ———, the
other way to go is to use the above outline to write your novel
and send the complete work to Holloway House. Perhaps your
story would have more impact written in the first person. In
writing your story use as much as possible those characters and
situations that enhance excitement and interest for readers. Be
brief with pre adult bio segments unless you have determined
that certain of these experiences (parental failure) are causal
in the later traumas of your life. Keep your sentences crisp
and release as many ego restraints and inhibitions as you can

when you start your journey. In a biographical work, to confess
imperfection and vulnerability on the page is to charm and win
the empathy of readers. Get down _____! Good luck.
Sincerely Yours
R.B.

P.S. Because I have been in less than perfect health this letter
was delayed

With the exception of his declining health, Beck's life as an older man suited him. He and Diane established a domestic regularity that worked for them. And although he had no intention of publishing, he still wrote with great passion; the ritual of putting words to paper became more important than the product. He experimented with a broad range of ideas. He wrote a variety of short stories, including "Dandy Dipper," a brilliant and compact narrative about an aging pickpocket who is released from prison after two decades, only to land himself right back in jail when he can't resist ripping off two young hustlers. It is a story about the seductive pull of the criminal life, an addiction with which Beck was intimately familiar. He created an outline for a book titled *Hear No Evil* about a satanic cult who brings about the birth of the Antichrist, and he wrote the opening of a novel called *I Love You . . . Goodbye* about a young woman who seduces a powerful corporate executive, only to tell him she must "move to the ecstasy of the next conquest." However, these were merely writing exercises compared to his masterpiece, *Shetani's Sister*, the second of his Los Angeles novels, completed around 1983. A cross between detective fiction and the pimp literature that made him famous, *Shetani's Sister* is a significant departure from his earlier works in a number of ways. It of course provides the familiar Beckian glimpse into Los Angeles's criminal underworld, that "sidewalk parade" of "half naked hookers, square pushovers, and sissies clog[ging] the streets and bars. Sex, crime, booze, and dope ruled the treacherous night. The melded odors of bargain colognes and steamy armpits rode the sweltering air like a sour aphrodisiac for gawking male bangers."[18]

However, Beck's final commentary on the pimp figure completely destroys any kind of romanticism that he ever might have associated with the figure. Two standard antiheroes drive the narrative. Sergeant Russell Rucker is a vice detective who struggles with alcoholism and a fierce temper, but attempts to clean up prostitution and police corruption in LA. His foil is Shetani, a twenty-five-year veteran pimp from Harlem, who controls a stable of sixteen prostitutes with violence and daily doses of heroin. Chapter by chapter, the novel alternates between the perspectives of the pimp and the detective, until their worlds finally collide in a violent and spectacular conclusion at the end of the novel. Unexpectedly, the book ultimately sympathizes with the white detective and demonizes the pimp—a radically different kind of stance for a Beck novel. Shetani is portrayed as a murdering psychopath who kills his women, his friends, and anyone else who gets in his way. Detective Rucker, on the other hand, represents Beck's most concentrated attempt to write a white character—a policeman, no less—with a sense of complex interiority and morality. Such a shift represents Beck's desire to move beyond what he considered a narrow political focus in his writing. To be able to create a three-dimensional white police officer, the object of hatred among many black Americans, including himself, was for Beck the highest expression of artistry. As he stated in an interview just a few years earlier, "I don't try to persuade. I used to be political. When I first started writing. Nothing is worse than to write with a tendency like that. You can't be a true artist. That's what hobbled most of the young black writers that came up in the '60s. They couldn't achieve catharsis. In other words, one must—if he's black or any ethnic—if he's aware of the inequities of this society, purge himself, have that catharsis through his writing, in order to approach the pristine peak that the artist, the true artist, knows. An artist has to be objective. I can draw a policeman now and get empathy if a policeman occurs in a story of mine. You see, if you never achieve a catharsis, inevitably, you would draw the policeman one-dimensionally as a pure beast. You don't make him human. Because your prejudice has obscured it. And strangulated art."[19]

In spring of 1985, Beck decided to move back to South Central, to a small studio at 4835 Crenshaw Boulevard. He and Diane were still happily married. He just preferred the solitude of the apartment. When he was a pimp with a stable, he'd had his own suite in a hotel. Even after he and Betty were married with the kids, he'd kept his own room. Now, nearing the end of his life, he preferred to be alone again. Beck's last residence was located in a modest two-story walkup. The room was no pimp pad like the days of old; it was small but neat. It was fitted with a Murphy bed, and Beck replaced it with a king-size bed so he could have a larger space to spread out his materials and write. There was just enough room left over in the efficiency for a few chairs. He piled his books and papers all around the tiny apartment, and put up a few photos of his daughters on the headboard and one of Diane on the dresser. He kept the rest of his photographs in a suitcase until Diane organized them for him in an album. There were large windows facing east, and from there he could look out at the neighborhood. Most days, he liked to sit in his recliner by the front window with a pair of binoculars and watch the people walking down the street. He was well known in the neighborhood, especially by the old-timers who remembered his books from the late 1960s. Some of the guys from the block even brought him weed as a show of respect. Most days, he smoked a little weed and wrote. He listened to jazz—his favorite musician was Arthur Prysock—and became a huge fan of the Lakers, never missing a game when they were on TV. He also liked to watch conservative talk shows, so that he could see what the enemy was thinking.

It was also during this time that the diabetic neuropathy flared up again, and he stopped taking his long walks. His kidneys started to fail, and he had to go on dialysis. A small medical van took him to his appointments three times a week, and Diane picked him up afterward in her 1972 Cadillac. Even though he was sick, Beck still dressed up in all of his finery for doctor visits. He wore a suit and a leather cap on top of his head to cover his growing bald spot. During the week, Diane brought him groceries, and she drove him around the Crenshaw neighborhood in his 1948 Lincoln. Driving it made her nervous, as it was even larger than her Cadillac. As they made their way through the streets of Los Angeles, fans recognized him in the passenger seat, and they ran up to pay their respects. Perhaps the most devastating part of Beck's failing health was that his eyesight started to go bad. When Diane took him to get his license renewed, he was nearly blind in one eye, so she stood in front of him signaling the letters. They had a laugh about that later. But the loss of vision severely curtailed his reading and writing, which, for Beck, was anything but funny. Diane recalled, "After we were together five years, his kidney started to go bad. He really couldn't read much. I would read him the books that I loved and he liked. He didn't go blind, but his eyes weren't good."[20]

Beck also struggled during these years to maintain ties with his children, though these relationships were complicated in various ways. After all, in prisons and certain sections of the black community, he was known as the most famous pimp of all time. No doubt that notoriety had a powerful impact on his kids. Each of them dealt with it in different ways. His stepson, Robin, refused to meet or talk to him at all. Melody came to visit him often at his apartment, and when he was on dialysis she met him at the hospital to sit and talk. Beck's youngest daughter, Misty, knew her father the least, as her parents had split when she was just a child. As a teenager, she sometimes skipped school with her friend Tiffany to visit him, taking the bus from Hollywood to Crenshaw. He lived across the street from a Church's Chicken fast-food joint, and he would give them money to buy lunch. Over the meal, he would lecture them about skipping school and warn them against the dangers of pimps and doing drugs. Misty was mostly well behaved, but like most teenagers, she tested a few boundaries. At fifteen, for instance, she and Tiffany were cited for underage drinking. Beck and Diane went to court with them to offer their support. Beck sat in the courtroom—the first time he had been in one in twenty-five years—while Diane, Misty, and Tiffany met with the judge in her private chambers. As Diane put it, she "read the girls the riot act" in front of the judge, and they seemed sufficiently frightened that the judge let them off with a warning. It was the last time Misty would be in trouble with the law.

While Beck met some challenges as a parent with these kids, it was nothing compared to the difficulties he faced with his oldest daughter, Camille. She was as beautiful as she was unpredictable, and at a young age she had left home and started running the streets. She had absorbed all of the dangerous parts of her father's personality, and by the time she was in her teens, she was "street poisoned," as Beck called it. She worked at Carney's famous hot dog and burger joint on Sunset Boulevard, where she met rich older men who supported her financially. By the time she was nineteen, Camille was living a fast Hollywood lifestyle, snorting cocaine regularly and hanging out with celebrities. She became a drug courier for a high-level cocaine dealer, transporting drugs up the Eastern Seaboard. In September 1983, Camille and her boyfriend Brian C. Bennett were arrested for possession of eleven kilograms (nearly twenty-five pounds) of cocaine at the Staples Mill Road Amtrak station in Richmond, Virginia, a popular stopover for drug smugglers between Florida and New York.[21] She was held on a million-dollar bond in Henrico County jail. Somehow she made bail, but she was not allowed to leave the state. Before the trial, Camille fell from the seventh-floor balcony of a hotel. Her left arm was broken in several places, and she spent three days in a coma, but miraculously, she lived. According to Camille's account, when she woke up, she asked her father to talk to the prosecutor in the case, and he apparently made a convincing plea for her freedom. "That's my daughter and I love her. That man, he took her to the wrong place, and brought her back to the wrong place. She didn't have nothing to do with narcotics."[22] The combination of Beck's arguments and Camille's severe injuries worked in her favor. In January 1984, she received a five-year suspended sentence.[23] Whether she jumped from that balcony in a suicide attempt, or was pushed by her boyfriend in order to keep her quiet, is a matter of some dispute. It is not a story to be told here, but one that will be revealed in Misty Beck's forthcoming autobiography.

Although Beck had a somewhat troubled relationship with his own children at the end of his life, he still tried to be a father figure to many young fans who read his books. The most famous of these admirers was the undisputed heavyweight champion of the world, Mike Tyson. Beck met Tyson in 1988, shortly after he had become champion and married actress Robin Givens. While Tyson was partying one night at a Los Angeles club with Leon Isaac Kennedy, star of the cult classic *Penitentiary* films, the actor offhandedly mentioned he knew Beck. Tyson was a devoted reader, and he had been a fan of Beck's work for years. He wanted to meet him, so Kennedy took him to the Crenshaw apartment the next day. As Tyson remembered their first meeting, "I sat down and talked with him for seven hours straight. We talked about his life and his books. I thought he would talk like a crude street guy but he was very erudite and spoke nobly. He enunciated each syllable precisely."[24] At this moment, Tyson realized that he and Beck had a lot in common. Although Tyson had a reputation as an illiterate street thug, he was in fact well read in a variety of subjects. He loved the works of Oscar Wilde, Charles Darwin, Machiavelli, Leo Tolstoy, Alexandre Dumas, Adam Smith, and Friedrich Nietzsche, and he studied the lives of historical figures such as Alexander the Great and Vladimir Lenin. Tyson admired Beck's book knowledge as well as his street sensibility; he also respected his style. After all, Beck was the first black man he knew to wear ascots and French cuffs.

Tyson started making regular trips to see him. Sometimes he came alone. Other times, he brought with him his manager, Don King, or friends before going out to the clubs. Beck ran these rap sessions like a college course. He sat on his bed in his silk pajamas, while Tyson and his companions parked at his feet, raising their hands in order to ask him questions. Beck explained lessons from the pimp book, he lectured Tyson on his troubled relationships with women, and he pushed him to think more deeply about his unconscious drives and motivations. As Tyson recalled, Beck told him one day, "You're going to leave here and have women problems all your life, because you'll just fuck anything. And then you want to give them all full speed ahead, you want to give them all everything you got. You just will always have women problems, boy. I see you're into satisfying every woman and you're going to lose at that every time. You let them invade your mind . . . You're going to always have some kind of connection with them or they're going to have some connection with you, because you have to satisfy that feeling. And that's very dangerous. Dangerous to yourself. You put that pressure on yourself, you don't feel good, you don't satisfy the woman. That's a problem with your mother. There's some connection that you had with your mother."[25] Beck's insights about Tyson's dangerous relationship with women were prophetic. The next year he was publicly accused of assault by his wife, Robin Givens, and a few years after that, he was convicted of raping Desiree Washington and ultimately served three years in prison. It was because Tyson had just entered prison, in April 1992, that he missed Beck's funeral a few weeks later. Tyson lamented, "I wish I would have met him before I married Robin. He would have set my ass straight."

Over the next few years, Beck and Tyson maintained a close bond, though Beck always kept a cool distance. Despite Tyson's numerous invitations, he didn't go to any of Tyson's fights. He would have to dress up in one of his leather suits, and he was too old to go through the trouble. Although Tyson was by this point a multimillionaire, surrounded by sycophants, Beck wasn't really interested in his money. According to Tyson, he seemed content to live out the rest of his life quietly and modestly in his small apartment. The only time Beck asked for his help was when planning his own funeral. He didn't want to be buried in the ground, because he was afraid that the roaches and bugs would get to him there. "I'm beautiful," he told Tyson. "I don't want them eating my eyes." As a final gesture of respect, Tyson claimed he gave Beck $25,000 so that he could have a casket placed in the wall at Forest Lawn Memorial Park. A genuine pimp to his last days, Beck didn't say "Thank you" for the money. He just said, "Wow, man." As Tyson fondly recalled, "That's why I loved him. He kept it real until the end. I think he expected me to say 'Thank you' for giving him my money."[26]

Even in his ill health, Beck still played the role of mentor to the kids in the neighborhood. Gone were the days when he walked for miles, seeking out young hustlers on the street and steering them away from The Life. By the late 1980s, he struggled just to breathe while walking up the single flight of stairs to his apartment. At that point, he didn't go out much. According to Paula Wood, the manager of the building where Beck lived, he was quiet and kept to himself for the most part. He sometimes gave children from the neighborhood a few quarters, and he provided them with little tasks to keep them productive and out of the heavy gang activity that continued to spread through the city. He took a particular interest in talking to Wood's son, Sterling Blanche, who everyone knew as "Key." He was known to run with a rough crowd, and Wood hoped that Beck might be able to help him stay away from street life. This was not to be, as Blanche was eventually arrested and sentenced to life in prison on multiple counts of armed robbery.

As he got older, Beck grew increasingly concerned about the disturbing changes occurring in LA during the eighties and their implications for young black men like Blanche. Over the course of just a few decades, Los Angeles had become what one urban historian has called "Fortress L.A.," a repressive police state with few job opportunities outside of low-paying service work or illegal industries. Since the Watts Riots of 1965, police had increased the level of surveillance, implementing the first wide-scale use of aerial surveillance helicopters and inventing the SWAT team. For a brief moment, the Black Panthers provided people with the hope of a political front united against the forces of injustice and oppression, but the organization was effectively dismantled by the LAPD and FBI's COINTELPRO program. In the early 1970s, "Crippin'," a new gang identification, emerged in the wake of the loss of the Panthers, and signaled a transformation of black urban culture in the city. Inheriting the Panther style and militancy, the Crips perverted the Black Power messages of community control by emphasizing violence as a means to secure it. With increasing black-on-black violence in the late 1970s, the "Bloods" organized as a defensive response against this aggressive new form of gang culture. The famous Crips-versus-Bloods rivalry was born.

In the 1980s, the combination of black unemployment and the growth of the crack cocaine industry fueled gang participation and filled California jail cells. In 1982, a Colombian cartel rerouted massive quantities of cocaine from Florida to California, turning Los Angeles into the nation's distribution center for cocaine. As jobless rates among young black men soared to 45 percent at this time, gang participation and selling drugs became one of the last resorts for working-class blacks to make a living.[27] South Los Angeles, for instance, lost 70,000 high-wage industrial jobs between 1978 and 1982 alone,[28] as automobile assembly, tire manufacturing, and steel production factories closed in steady succession.[29] By the mid-1980s, hundreds of independent crack houses set up business in LA, employing somewhere around 10,000 people, according to the LAPD.[30] Highly addictive, cheaper, and more dangerous than its powdered counterpart, crack came to dominate the Los Angeles scene in the eighties. A national panic ensued, as the media presented overblown and racist images of crack babies, welfare mothers, and black "delinquents." Lawmakers rushed to create ever more repressive laws, which clearly targeted blacks and Latinos. For example, a person convicted of selling five grams of crack cocaine (worth about $125) would receive a mandatory sentence of five years, while it would take five hundred grams of powdered cocaine (worth $50,000) for the convicted individual to receive the same amount of time.[31] Due to the hypervigilant criminalization of the drug trade during the 1980s, the American prison population doubled, and almost half of the population was African American.[32] By 1990, a quarter of all young black men were in prison, on parole, or under surveillance of the criminal justice system,[33] and Los Angeles held the dubious distinction of having the largest urban prison population in America.[34]

In Los Angeles, Chief Darryl Gates's militarized police force terrorized black citizens in an all-out assault on working-class communities. The police and Sheriff's Department initiated curfews, entrapments, and outright harassment of non-Anglo youths. Over a dozen people died as the result of illegal chokeholds administered by LAPD officers, which Chief Gates defended by explaining, "We may be finding that in some blacks when [the chokehold] is applied the veins or arteries do not open up as fast as they do on normal people."[35] In 1988, Gates implemented the Operation Hammer program, a task force whose overzealous raids of black communities infringed on the civil rights of countless minorities, and resulted in the deaths of unarmed teenagers and senior citizens.[36] Under this regime, black teenagers could be picked up for "looking suspicious"—that is, black—and then have their names and addresses logged in the LAPD anti-gang database.[37] By 1988, California blacks made up the largest percent of any ethnic group in the state prison system. The 1980s was a watershed moment in which blacks were subjected to ever more vigilant forms of police and state control. Beck saw these changes, and he put the blame squarely on the shoulders of the New Right. As he said in the last interview he ever gave, "Our dear friend Reagan. He's the one who turned this flood tide of not caring, and he's responsible in my opinion for the reactivation of overt racism to the extent and degree that it now flourishes. Reagan, from what I can understand, he was just a yes man for powerful corporate interests. The country really went backward, man! And you know for a fact . . . any rational person knows that there's no way that the so-called gang culture could have become what it is today . . . if just the minimal opportunity that existed prior to Reagan's administration had been enforced."[38]

Although he didn't know it at the time, Beck's works inspired the most powerful artistic response to America's new police state: gangsta rap. The two most influential gangsta-style rappers, Ice-T and Ice Cube, both named themselves after Iceberg Slim, and they styled their antiestablishment messages and hardcore confessionals of violent street life after Beck's street fiction. Tracy "Ice-T" Marrow grew up in New Jersey, but moved to Los Angeles after his parents passed away. At Crenshaw High School, he hung out with a Crips set at the same time he was reading the works of Beck and Donald Goines. Soon he started imitating Beck to entertain his friends, making up his own rhymes. "I used to write these long rhymes—this was before beats was involved in it—because I was familiar with Iceberg Slim and what the players used to do called toastin'."[39] After releasing the underground sensation "The Coldest Rap" in 1982, Ice-T went on to record what is widely acknowledged as one the defining songs of gangsta rap, "6 'N the Mornin'." Updating Beck's stories and pimp toasts to represent the realities of black life in South Central Los Angeles, the song introduced many of the images that would become standard rap fare: pimping women, police harassment, gang violence, flaunting wealth, and prison life. A sample of any stanza from the track sounds like it could have been lifted directly out of *Pimp*:

> *Hit the boulevard in my A.M.G. [Mercedes]*
> *Ho's catchin' whiplash tryin' to glimpse the T*[40]

Beck also deeply influenced gangsta rap's other main innovator, O'Shea "Ice Cube" Jackson. The man who coined the term "gangsta rap,"[41] Ice Cube was a brilliant lyricist who put the genre on the map when he joined the controversial group Niggaz Wit Attitudes (N.W.A). In 1988, N.W.A released its *Straight Outta Compton* and brought gangsta rap into mainstream consciousness. With the songs "Straight Outta Compton" and "Fuck tha Police" anchoring the album, *Straight Outta Compton* announced the arrival of a new, openly defiant kind of hip-hop. Ice Cube penned most of the lyrics for these songs, and like the narratives of Iceberg Slim, they tell the story of black urban America caught in a crisis of gang warfare, crime, police repression, and violence against women. As he raps in "Fuck tha Police," which is probably the group's most infamous song,

> *Fuck the police comin' straight from the underground*
> *A young nigga got it bad 'cause I'm brown*

Gangsta rap spoke back in subversive and clever ways to America's racist power structures, and in response, various law-enforcement agencies took swift action. The police refused to provide security at N.W.A's concert tour, and the FBI's assistant director of public affairs famously sent a letter to the group's distributor, Priority Records, stating: "Advocating violence and assault is wrong, and we in the law enforcement community take exception to such action."[42] Such controversies did not inhibit gangsta rap's growth, but rather made it the most popular and lucrative musical genre of the 1990s. Later musicians like Snoop Dogg, Notorious B.I.G., 2Pac, and Jay-Z would draw inspiration from Ice-T and Ice Cube, as well as from Iceberg Slim, to turn rap into the most significant mouthpiece for black urban culture in the past twenty-five years.

At the same moment that gangsta rap was emerging as the preeminent form of popular dissent among black youth, the man who had centrally influenced the genre had almost entirely disappeared from the American scene. But even at seventy, Beck was still hard at work, crafting one last novel in response to the nation's decline under Reaganomics and the crack epidemic: *Night Train to Sugar Hill*. Because of his poor health and failing eyesight, he relied on Diane's help more than ever to put together the manuscript. As she said, "I was Slim's typist . . . He wrote longhand, and I transcribed it into the computer. If I felt, at rare times, that a sentence or paragraph edit would work better, I spoke to him about it. And he edited his longhand copy. *Night Train* he did write when we were together. He dictated a lot of this to me, as his eyes were very poor because of diabetes."[43] When Beck finished the novel in 1990, he gave two copies in sealed envelopes to Camille and he told her, "Publish this after I am gone. Just don't let Bentley Morriss get it."[44] However, Camille died of a methamphetamine overdose in 2010, and *Night Train to Sugar Hill* remains the last of Beck's major unpublished works to this day.

Set against the backdrop of LA's contemporary gang violence and drug trade, *Night Train to Sugar Hill* is a deeply introspective novel in which Beck reflects on the meaning of his life from the perspective of a dying man. At the center of the story is seventy-five-year-old Baptiste Landreau O'Leary, whom Beck admits in the prologue "is the author's alter ego." In this "fictionalized social drama," Baptiste is surrounded by "composite characterizations of real people who have been given pseudonyms." There are no one-to-one correspondences between the real people from his life and the characters on the page, only dreamlike associations where archetypal characters bear faint resemblance to people he encountered throughout his lifetime. Isaiah, Baptiste's surrogate son and best friend, is California's former Golden Gloves champion, and he bears a glancing resemblance to Mike Tyson, whom Beck was regularly mentoring at the time he wrote the book. Sabina, the white woman from Austin, Texas, who moves to the ghetto and marries Isaiah to escape the sexual abuse of her own father, has some characteristics of Betty, but these similarities run only skin deep. Baptiste's late wife, the "loyal lovable" Deanna, appears to be inspired by Beck's then current wife, Diane, but there are too few details given to know for sure. Even Baptiste himself, who resembles Beck in a variety of important ways—he is

hurled against the wall by his father at a young age; he is visited by
nightmares about his mother his whole life; he suffers from a defective heart, kidneys, and eyesight as an old man—is more of a fantasy
of the man Beck wishes he could have been. Baptiste lives in Beverly
Hills, he finances an inner-city gym for aspiring athletes, and most
important, he single-handedly saves Los Angeles from the crack epidemic plaguing the black community at the conclusion of the novel.

At the opening, Baptiste and Isaiah attend the funeral of a murdered gang member named Leroy, an event that provides the context
for the rest of the novel. Delivering Leroy's eulogy, the reverend acts
as a thinly veiled spokesperson for Beck himself, who blames right-
wing conservatives for the crisis facing black America: "The racist
policies of Ronald Reagan, George Bush and the Republican party
must share the blame with the killer of Leroy and all of the others. It
pains my soul that some of us are so politically naïve . . . any nigger
in America who votes for the enemy Republican party is stupid, mis-
informed, or afflicted with the Uncle Tom need to be punished and
to kiss the ass of his master. Wake up to the truth!"[45] The novel then
bears witness to the destructive effects of the crack cocaine industry
that has been allowed to flourish under Reagan's regime. Sabina's son
Eric, a rising star in the city's boxing circuit, dies from an overdose
of crack that he has stolen from his mother. Isaiah, seeking revenge
for the boy's death, tries to murder the neighborhood crack dealer,
Freddy, and instead is himself killed. In order to protect himself, the
city's top drug distributor, Portillo, poisons both Freddy and Sabina
by lacing their crack with cyanide.

Witnessing all this death around him, Baptiste decides to kill
Portillo. It is a final act of murder that he hopes will interrupt the
flow of drugs into South Central and stem the violence, at least for a
while. At the end of the novel, he delivers a dramatic speech to the
members of his boxing gym and their parents. Throwing up a Black
Power salute reminiscent of Malcolm X, he says, "There is a rampant
misconception among certain white people that most black people
have a genetic predisposition toward dope and crime. You and a
majority of others are living proof that such a theory is garbage . . . I
am going to take radical action against crack cocaine in South Cen-

tral."[46] Baptiste manages to kill Portillo, and with only a few hours of life left, he boards a train to New York in the hopes of seeing his only daughter, Opal. He carries with him a copy of his unfinished autobiography, a massive document that he completes on the train ride just before he finally passes away. "He had been absolutely candid about the good and the bad he had done in his lifetime," the narrator reports. "He had included a detailed account of Portillo's murder and why. Opal would not submit it to her agent friend until after his death—which was soon, he knew."[47] When the police catch up with him in New York, Baptiste is already dead, and the only thing that remains is the autobiography. The police pass the tome off to his daughter, thinking that it has no significance to their investigation. In this way, *Night Train* offers a meta-commentary on Beck's own struggles with his life of crime, his rage at the nation's indifference to African American struggles with racism and poverty, and his hopes that his writing might offer answers for those who read it carefully. Beck, sensing that his life was coming to a close, concludes his last novel with the fantasy that he might have some part in saving black America through his books. It seems a fitting ending for the author who gave voice to those who lived at the margins of urban America throughout the twentieth century.

At the end of his life, Beck was in extremely poor health. He certainly didn't lecture anymore, and he didn't really go out into the streets. As his eyes continued to fail, Diane read to him books that she loved, including the hard-boiled detective novel *Blue Belle* by Andrew Vachss. The author would later cite Beck as a major influence. By this point, Beck had an enlarged heart, and he was blind in one eye. Diane pushed him around in a rickety wheelchair, which tended to fall apart. The days of his dialysis treatments were especially difficult. When he climbed the flight of stairs back to his second-story apartment, he sometimes had to rest for a few minutes between steps. He had never been an affectionate man, even when he had been healthy. He did not freely give out hugs and kisses. At the end of his life, he was so fragile that he became even more formal, offering handshakes. Diane knew he was getting closer to the end, and so she asked Bentley Morriss to increase one of his royalty checks. She kept this from her husband, because she knew he would have too much pride to ask for such a thing. Morriss consented and fronted her $1,500. Through it all, Diane reported, "Slim never complained, not once, about his health."[48] Although he believed "it was lights out when you die,"[49] he maintained stalwart dignity in the face of imminent death. He also retained a wicked sense of humor, despite the dire circumstances. Diane remembered, "We were in Beverly Hills one day—his kidney doctor had referred him for a visit with another doctor. He was in a wheelchair. After the appointment, I was pushing him across a street. In the middle of the street one of the footrests came off. I picked it up and continued to the other side. When we got there he said, 'If Scoby [a Milwaukee friend] could just see me now—no suit, no tie, in a raggedly wheelchair, being pushed by a white woman.' "[50]

On the morning of April 30, 1992, the second day of the Rodney King riots, Beck was deathly ill at Brotman Medical Center. He watched his city burn on the television from his hospital bed. It looked like the start of the black revolution that he had always half hoped, half feared would come. Gangrene had set in on his foot. Beck had picked at a callus on his foot, and it had gotten infected. He hadn't told anyone about it until it was too late. The doctors told him he would die if they didn't take at least part of the leg. Beck was unsure. Even though he had gotten old, he still thought of himself as a "pretty motherfucker."[51] He wanted to keep the leg. He decided to let them administer some tests, which would indicate how far the gangrene had progressed. The results would be ready the next day. He asked Diane to wash his hair, and she did so while they watched the images of horror flicker across the television screen together. She left before lunch and called him in the afternoon to check in. Melody worked only a few blocks away from the hospital, so she came by to visit. Camille was living in Michigan at the time, having just given birth to her first daughter, so she was indisposed. Misty, meanwhile, was attempting to make her way to the hospital. However, Los Angeles was completely locked down on a dusk-till-dawn curfew, and she couldn't get there through the chaos. At 7:00 p.m., Beck ate a hamburger for dinner. A few minutes later, he suffered cardiac arrest. The hospital staff worked for thirty minutes in an effort to revive him, but he had passed away. Because of the riots, his body was held at the hospital for five days before it could be transported to the funeral home. On Saturday, May 9, 1992, Beck's funeral was held at the Angelus Crenshaw Chapel. Well over a hundred people filled the church, including football great Jim Brown and actor Leon Isaac Kennedy. Of course, Beck's children were there, as were Diane and her children. Even Betty showed up to pay her final respects. Diane's daughter Leah sang a heartfelt rendition of Carole King's "Way Over Yonder," and the mourners played "Mama Debt" from Beck's *Reflections* album, so that they could hear Beck's commanding voice together one last time. When the service was over, they transported his body to Forest Lawn Memorial Park in Glendale, where he was laid to rest in an aboveground mausoleum, just as he had wanted. The epitaph etched on his gravestone (and later repeated by author Andrew Vachss in his book *Shella* as a tribute to Beck) was a simple but elegant expression of the enduring impact that his life and his works still have on those who read or knew him: "Iceberg Slim. Truth, Still Shining Down."

For nearly fifty years, Robert Beck's works have quietly, from the underground, transformed African American literature and culture. There would have been no street literature, no blaxploitation, no hip-hop the way that we know them today without *Pimp: The Story of My Life*. We might appreciate Beck's contributions to American life more fully if we consider the everyday people who he moved. About a month after his funeral, a letter dated June 8, 1992, arrived at his apartment. In a long, heartfelt confession, the author poured out his appreciation for all that Beck had inspired him to do. News had not yet reached him of Beck's passing, and the letter is all the more poignant because of it. It sums up Beck's life, his works, and the hidden world of glamour, struggle, and sorrow that he tried to make transparent to all of us. Because of that, this letter is perhaps the most eloquent eulogy of all for the man who will always be known best as Iceberg Slim.

Dear Brother Beck, respected elder.

This letter is way overdue. Please forgive the lateness, but I do have this flaw of procrastinating. I just turned 40 on May 27th of this year. Back during the summer of 1970 when I was 18, I read Pimp: The Story of My Life. *And over the next year I read* Trick Baby, Mama Black Widow, *and* The Naked Soul of Iceberg Slim. *And over the following years I read* Death Wish, Long White Con, Airtight Willie and Me. *As well as some articles you wrote for* Players Magazine. *I would like to thank you so very much for your writings.*

First I would like to thank you, because your writings inspired me to read more. And that was so important for a person who was not inclined to read . . . The expanding of my ability to read got me through college. My grandparents were sharecroppers in South Carolina and Georgia. My mother and her brothers and sisters busted their backs in those fields as children, and as adults put out the same kind of energy in the factories of the Northern cities. And to be the first of their line to receive a college diploma made me very proud. For it gave vindication to their years of work and love for their children. Thank you for the part you played in that process . . .

I only played on the fringes of the underworld. I never allowed myself to get truly involved with any illegal activities. Yes there were times deals were in the process, and the money to be made was a lot, and a guy with the right money and reputation could have all kinds of things. But the lesson of your life experiences stayed in my mind. What's that Slim said? Out of all that shit he did, all of that time in jail, all of those risks of injury and death, all of that emotional abuse he did to others and himself, and when the whole thing was over with, he did not have a dime more than when he started . . .

By the way, back in May of 1989, I won some money on the Kentucky Derby. I took some of the month and did something I always wanted to. I bought a 7-day Greyhound bus pass. I toured several cities in the Midwest. When I arrived in Milwaukee, I felt like Malcolm X visiting Mecca. This was the

week of July 4th. That afternoon I traveled the city. Strange,
except for the wider streets, your area of Milwaukee looked
very similar to the area of Newark that I first recall as a child.

I stood at 7th and Vliet, and 7th and Apple. The area has
been renovated, but I pictured what it must have seemed like
to you at twilight in the spring. I saw Roosevelt School, and
imagined you as a teenager sitting on the steps with some sweet
girl on a Sunday afternoon.

The next day I went to Chicago. I had been there once as a
14 year old. But that was 4 years before I was introduced to
your writings. So I did not have the same view of things then
that I would have later. I got up at 6 o'clock in the morning. I
caught a bus from my Loop hotel to the Southside. I certainly
was not going to carry my ass there at night, because I might
not be left with any ass to carry back.

I saw 47th Street. I saw 63rd Street. I saw Cottage Grove
Avenue. I saw Calumet Avenue. Sure a lot of the buildings
were abandoned, burned out, and deteriorating. But it did not
matter a bit. I shut my eyes and pictured it as it must have
been when you saw it in the late 1930s and 1940s, and how
Louis Armstrong must have seen it in the 1920s and 1930s.

I could see the flashing lights. I could hear the music, the
fast pounding jazz and the sweet easy blues. I could see the
handsome men in the sharp looking suits. I could see the pretty
women all done up in their fashionable dresses. I could see the
smiles, and oh yes the cars. Hey Ice, I hope I'm not being too
romantic about a time and place I did not know first hand.

At this point I'm going to do you a favor. I'm going to close
out this letter. If there is one sin I know I'm guilty of, it is
a habit of overwriting. In closing I just want to say that I
appreciate your work. I hope your health is good. And I hope
you are enjoying the exchange of love between your friends,
family and yourself. As I write this, it is early June. Father's
Day is approaching. Happy Father's Day.

ACKNOWLEDGMENTS

I have been working on this book for more than ten years, and during that time I have received the support of many people. Colleagues like Kenneth Warren, Eric Lott, Jennifer Wicke, Eric Rasmussen, Mike Branch, Greta de Jong, Dennis Dworkin, Scott Casper, Deborah Achtenburg, H. Bruce Franklin, Sean McCann, and Frankie Y. Bailey encouraged me during various stages of the research and writing process. My close friends Erin James, Cathy Chaput, Jim Webber, Lynda Walsh, Madeline Chaput, Beckett Senter, Patrick Walsh, Sean Jaureguito, Rei Magosaki, Ben James, Jamie Farley, Amber Yoder, and especially Andrea Stevens all contributed to this project in indispensable ways.

I want to express my deepest gratitude to Diane Millman Beck, Robert Beck's gracious wife. Her generosity of spirit and willingness to share her memories of her husband with me over the years made this book possible. In that time, Diane has become a dear and honored friend, and I cannot even begin to repay her kindness. I also received support from Beck's youngest daughter, Misty. She spent hours on the phone with me, telling fascinating stories and helping me set the historical record straight about her father's legacy. I have appreciated her honesty, warmth, and, most of all, trust in my writing. Thanks, too, to Paula Wood, Beck's landlord during the last seven years of his life; she provided key insights about the man in his final years.

I owe a debt to a number of individuals who were involved with Holloway House Publishing Company and who aided me in reconstructing the history of the company and the writers who published there. Bentley Morriss sat down for several discussions over the years, and he has been encouraging of my research for a decade. I also had the good fortune to interview and develop relationships with many talented authors who worked for Holloway House, including Roland Jefferson, Emory Holmes, Odie Hawkins, and the late Wanda Coleman.

Jorge Hinojosa, director of the documentary *Iceberg Slim: Portrait of a Pimp*, was remarkably generous in sharing rare interviews and files he had collected about Beck. Over the years, he invited me into his home countless times to review his extensive archive. Jorge often encouraged me to sit down for meals with his family, and sometimes he even invited me to sleep in his guest room after long days of researching. I have come to regard him as a valued friend, and I am eternally grateful for his comradeship and his contributions to this book.

Many librarians, researchers, and archivists at various institutions helped me immeasurably over the years by tracking down school and prison records, rare historic newspapers, and unique photos. Thanks to Cara Adams, archivist at the Mayme A. Clayton Library and Museum in Culver City, California; Joyce Higgins, president of the Northern Illinois chapter of the Afro-American Historical and Genealogical Society; David Ruffin, board member of the Rockford, Illinois, Ethnic Heritage Museum; Jean H. Lythgoe and Janice E. Carter, librarian assistants at Rockford Public Library; Colette McConoughey, student records technician in the Rockford Public School District; Kevin Abing, archivist at the Milwaukee County Historical Society; Ms. Foster at Lincoln High School in Milwaukee; Elaine Herroon, the subject librarian at Cleveland Public Library; Ellen Keith at the Chicago History Museum Research Center; Lt. John Berg of the Milwaukee County Prison; and Philip J. Costello, Clerk of the Circuit Court in Cook County. I owe a special debt of gratitude to Lee Grady, the reference archivist in the Library-Archives Division at the Wisconsin Historical Society. Mr. Grady worked tirelessly to uncover Beck's prison and psychiatric records that had previously been locked away for seventy years.

As always, many graduate students provided valuable assistance in writing this book. Landon Lutrick conducted important research in the early stages of the project. Jonathan Katalenic worked diligently and under strict deadlines to make sure all of the footnotes were cited correctly and that the manuscript was formatted properly. He also tracked down information on small, but important details that made all the difference in reconstructing the most accurate and compelling portrait of Beck's life possible. My good friend Josh Culpepper kindly donated his time and inimitable editing skills, preparing the entire manuscript for publication in exchange for a few beers and a first edition of Ernest Hemingway's *The Old Man and the Sea.*

Finding a publisher for *Street Poison* was no easy task, and I would like to thank my agent Matthew Carnicelli for working so diligently for the past five years to find a home for my books. He helped me land a contract for my first monograph, *Pimping Fictions*, he guided me in the creation of a compelling and saleable proposal for *Street Poison*, and he helped me negotiate the turbulent process of publishing a trade book. Matthew has in many ways been my biggest supporter over the years, and I could not ask for a better agent and a wiser friend. Special thanks also to Gerald Howard, my editor at Doubleday. Along with his endlessly helpful editorial assistant, Jeremy Medina, Gerry has been an enthusiastic guide on this journey toward publication. Gerry's insightful comments on drafts, his savvy about the complex world of publishing, and his indefatigable excitement about the project have made *Street Poison* a book I am proud to publish.

Finally, I would like to thank my closest family. My best friend, Johann Sehmsdorf, has been a constant companion in the struggle to answer life's most important questions over the past twenty years. Lastly, I dedicate this book to my sister Jessie Gifford and her wife, Jen Gifford. You both constantly remind me of the power that laughter has to create and sustain love.

NOTES

CHAPTER 1: CHILDHOOD

1. Lovett, *African American*, 74–75, 89.
2. United States Census Bureau, "Twelfth Census of the United States—1900 Population," June 18, 1900.
3. United States Census Bureau, "Thirteenth Census of the United States—1910 Population," April 16, 1910.
4. Lovett, *African American*, 126.
5. "Mid-Frolic Social Club," *Nashville Globe*, April 13, 1917: 3.
6. "In Honor of an Ionian Club," *Nashville Globe*, Jan. 12, 1917.
7. "Mid-Frolic Social Club," *Nashville Globe*, Jan. 26, 1917: 5.
8. "In Honor of Miss Mary Brown," *Nashville Globe*, Sept. 21, 1917: 5.
9. Lovett, *African American*, 89.
10. Ibid., 249, 251.
11. Grossman, *Land of Hope*, 4.
12. United States Draft Card, "Robert Moppins," Aug. 29, 1918.
13. Drake and Cayton, *Black Metropolis*, 64.
14. "Ghastly Deeds of Rioters Told," *Chicago Defender*, Aug. 2, 1919: 14.
15. Hughes, *Big Sea*, 33.
16. Mumford, *Interzones*, 38.
17. Slim, *Pimp*, 20.
18. Ibid., 21.
19. Ibid.
20. Koblin, "Portrait," 50.
21. Slim, *Pimp*, 19.
22. Ibid., 15.
23. Ibid., 21.
24. Molyneaux, *African Americans*.
25. Chapman, *That Men Know*, 54; and Jaffe, "Race Line," 7–42.
26. United States Census Bureau, "Thirteenth Census of the United States—1910 Population," April 16, 1910.
27. "Royal Cleaning and Pressing Shop," *Rockford Republic*, Sept. 18, 1920: 13.
28. "Forest City Cleaners and Hatters," *Rockford Republic*, Sept. 22, 1925: 11.
29. "Solicitors for Federation Are Finishing Work," *Rockford Morning Star*, Dec. 2, 1921.
30. "Colored Citizens Discuss Housing Problems in City," *Rockford Morning Star*, Jan. 14, 1920: 4.

31. "Colored Club to Have Baseball Team," *Rockford Morning Star*, April 11, 1922: 10.
32. "Lawn Party Tonight at Thatch Residence," *Daily Register Gazette*, July 2, 1927: 14.
33. "A.M.E. Churches in Conference September 21 to 25," *Daily Register Gazette*, Sept. 16, 1927: 5.
34. "Debate Politics at Church," *Rockford Republic*, Nov. 2, 1928: 6.
35. "Christmas Dinner at Allen Chapel Free to All in Need," *Daily Register Gazette*, Dec. 20, 1929: 2.
36. "Frank Brown," *Rockford Morning Star*, April 1, 1931: 9.
37. Slim, *Pimp*, 22.
38. "Moppins, Robert," Roosevelt Junior High School Enrollment Card, Jan. 26, 1931.
39. "Best Spellers at Roosevelt High Selected," *Rockford Register-Republic*, March 7, 1931: 9.
40. Caunes, "Interview with Iceberg Slim."
41. Bukowski, *Big Bill*, 19, 148.
42. Slim, *Naked Soul*, 48.
43. Ibid., 46.
44. "Peerless Improved Club," *Chicago Defender*, May 17, 1930: 19.
45. Slim, *Pimp*, 22.
46. Caunes, "Interview with Iceberg Slim."
47. Ibid.
48. Slim, *Pimp*, 25.
49. Ibid.
50. "Thank You," *The Crusader*, July 23, 1954: 2.
51. Slim, *Pimp*, 28.
52. Moore, "Inside Story," 35.

CHAPTER 2: EDUCATION

1. Slim, *Pimp*, 27.
2. Ibid., 30.
3. Jones, *Selma*, 15.
4. Trotter, *Black Milwaukee*, 156.
5. Ibid., 70.
6. Pollard and Arijotutu, *African-Centered*, 26.
7. Laffin, *Milwaukee*, 16–17; and Vick, "From No Street," 41.
8. Geenen, *Milwaukee's Bronzeville*, 7–9.
9. Vick, "From Walnut Street," 36–40.
10. Jones, *Selma*, 19–21.
11. Slim, *Naked Soul*, 97.
12. Slim, *Airtight Willie*, 71.
13. Ibid., 9.
14. Ibid., 101.
15. Slim, *Pimp*, 30.
16. Ibid., 33.
17. Ibid., 36.
18. Ibid., 39–40.
19. Ibid., 38.
20. Ibid.

21. Ibid.
22. Ibid., 39.
23. Ibid.
24. Ibid., 36.
25. Ibid., 33.
26. Ibid., 31.
27. Slim, *Naked Soul*, 98.
28. Federal Bureau of Investigation, "70734—Robert Lee Maupins," no date.
29. Lincoln High School, Milwaukee, "Maupins, Robert," May 21, 1935: 1.
30. Ibid.
31. *The Quill*, 55.
32. Federal Bureau of Investigation, "70734—Robert Lee Maupins," no date.
33. Slim, *Naked Soul*, 99–100.
34. Slim, *Pimp*, 42.
35. Grandison, "Landscapes," 334–67.
36. Rampersad, *Life*, 63.
37. "Student Manual," Tuskegee, AL: Tuskegee Institute, 1933, 3.
38. Slim, *Pimp*, 42.
39. Ibid., 42.
40. Hurston, "Characteristics," 361.
41. Slim, *Pimp*, 42.
42. United States Penitentiary, Leavenworth, "United States v. Robert Lee Maupin," July 12, 1945, 24.
43. Slim, *Pimp*, 44.
44. Caunes, "Interview with Iceberg Slim."
45. Ibid.

CHAPTER 3: PRISON

1. Slim, *Pimp*, 59.
2. Trotter, *From a Raw Deal*, 4.
3. Slim, *Pimp*, 45.
4. Ibid., 66.
5. Ibid., 63.
6. Slim, *Naked Soul*, 57.
7. Ibid., 59.
8. Ibid., 67–68.
9. Slim, *Pimp*, 64.
10. Still, *Milwaukee*, 482–83.
11. Davis and Schweitzer, "Policy of Good Design," 105–6.
12. State Board of Control of Wisconsin, "Mental Examination—Maupin, Robert Lee," Feb. 2, 1939: 1.
13. Ibid.
14. United States Penitentiary, Leavenworth, "United States v. Robert Lee Maupin," July 12, 1945: 24.
15. Slim, *Pimp*, 60.
16. Ibid., 61.
17. Ibid.
18. Ibid., 63.
19. Ibid., 61.
20. Ibid., 65.

21. Ibid., 62.
22. Ibid.
23. Wisconsin State Reformatory, "Robert Lee Maupins," Dec. 23, 1938: 1.
24. State Board of Control of Wisconsin, "Mental Examination—Maupin, Robert Lee," Feb. 2, 1939: 1.
25. Slim, *Pimp*, 48.
26. Ibid., 48.
27. Telzrow, "Punishment," 24–33.
28. *150 Years*, 7.
29. Slim, *Pimp*, 49.
30. Ibid.
31. State Board of Control of Wisconsin, "Physical Examination—Maupin, Robert Lee," Jan. 1939: 1.
32. State Board of Control of Wisconsin, "Mental Examination—Maupin, Robert Lee," Feb. 2, 1939: 1.
33. Ibid., 1–2.
34. Slim, *Pimp*, 52.
35. Ibid.
36. Ibid., 50.
37. Ibid., 53.
38. Telzrow, *Wisconsin*, 29.
39. Slim, *Pimp*, 49–50.
40. Ibid., 53.
41. Wisconsin State Reformatory, "Robert Lee Maupins," Dec. 23, 1938: 1.
42. Slim, *Pimp*, 56.
43. Ibid.
44. State Board of Control of Wisconsin, "Mental Examination—Maupin, Robert Lee," Aug. 16, 1939: 1.
45. Ibid., 1–2.
46. Slim, *Pimp*, 59.
47. Vick, "From Walnut Street," 70.
48. Trotter, *From a Raw Deal*, 206.
49. Geenen, *Milwaukee's Bronzeville*, 9.
50. Vick, "From Walnut Street," 67.
51. Trotter, *From a Raw Deal*, 206.
52. V. C. Benevue, "Milwaukee, Wisc.," *Chicago Defender*, Mar. 4, 1944: 17A.
53. State Board of Control of Wisconsin, "Request for Permission to Leave State—Robert Lee Maupins," Jan. 5, 1940: 1.
54. Slim, *Pimp*, 45.
55. Ibid., 46.
56. Ibid.
57. State Board of Control of Wisconsin, "Mental Examination—Maupins, Robert Lee," Jan. 21, 1941: 1.
58. Slim, *Pimp*, 47.
59. Ibid., 47.
60. "The Story of the Wisconsin State Prison," 7–8.
61. Ibid., 4.
62. Lee, *Wisconsin State Prison*, 2–4.
63. "Lions Club," *Stevens Point Daily Journal*, April 28, 1939: 3.
64. Lee, *Wisconsin State Prison*, 5.
65. Ibid., 4–5.
66. Biennial Report of the Wisconsin State Prison, 5–9.

67. Ernesto Rodriguez, and Ted Vogel, *In the Iron Cage: The True Story of Ernesto R. Rodriguez*. Full text online at http://www.ironcagebook.com.
68. Lee, *Wisconsin State Prison*, 1.
69. Ibid.
70. Burke, *Wisconsin State Prison*, 1.
71. Lee, *Wisconsin State Prison*, 2–3.
72. Burke, *Wisconsin State Prison*, 8.
73. Slim, *Pimp*, 74.
74. Ibid.
75. "Waupun Prisoners Refuse to Eat as Protest on Food," *Stevens Point Daily Journal*, Aug. 5, 1940: 1.
76. "$3,000,000 Body, 30 Cent Engine," *Capital Times*, Oct. 30, 1941: 4.
77. "New Prisoners' Song Is Heard: 'Give Us a Chance—We'll Fight,'" *Wisconsin State Journal*, Mar. 26, 1942: 6.
78. "Waupun Prisoners Support Red Cross, Buy Defense Stamps," *Capital Times*, Jan. 28, 1942: 4.
79. Waupun State Prison, "Robert L. Maupins," Aug. 27, 1941: 1.
80. State Board of Control of Wisconsin, "Mental Examination—Maupins, Robert Lee," Jan. 21, 1941: 1.
81. Ibid.
82. Ibid., 2.
83. Slim, *Pimp*, 74.
84. Ibid., 74.
85. Ibid., 80.
86. Ibid., 81.
87. Ibid., 84.
88. Ibid., 315.
89. Ibid., 75.
90. Ibid., 74–75.

CHAPTER 4: CHICAGO

1. Slim, *Pimp*, 61.
2. Ibid.
3. Ibid., 86–87.
4. Ibid., 80.
5. Federal Bureau of Investigation, "Report on Convicted Prisoner by United States Attorney—Robert Lee Maupin," May 24, 1945.
6. Slim, *Pimp*, 81.
7. Ibid.
8. Ibid., 83.
9. Ibid., 85.
10. Ibid., 81.
11. Slim, *Naked Soul*, 58.
12. Slim, *Pimp*, 139–40.
13. Ibid., 114.
14. Ibid., 115.
15. Ibid.
16. Ibid.
17. Ibid., 116.
18. Ibid., 78.
19. Ibid.

20. Ibid., 89.
21. Hirsch, *Making*, 4.
22. Ibid., 25.
23. Drake and Cayton, *Black Metropolis*, 90–91.
24. Lemann, *Promised Land*, 71–73.
25. Bone and Courage, *Muse in Bronzeville*.
26. Thompson, *Kings*, 105.
27. Ibid., 105–6.
28. Ibid., 151.
29. Drake and Cayton, *Black Metropolis*, 524.
30. Thompson, *Kings*, 54–57.
31. Chepesiuk, *Black Gangsters*, 152–56.
32. Slim, *Pimp*, 103.
33. Ibid., 104.
34. Ibid., 107.
35. "Al Gainer and Dave Clark on Yankee Stadium Card: Chicago Will Be at the 'Big Fight' by Rail, Air, and Auto," *Pittsburgh Courier*, June 13, 1936: A7.
36. Al Monroe, "Everybody Goes—When the Wagon Comes!" *Chicago Defender*, May 2, 1936: 8.
37. Earl J. Morris, "Grand Town Day and Night: Christopher Columbus, a Rhythm Cocktail," *Pittsburgh Courier*, March 28, 1936: A7.
38. Earl J. Morris, "Grand Town Day and Night: Operator 25 Digs Up Some Ethiopia Dirt—Exclusive!" *Pittsburgh Courier*, Jan. 18, 1936: A6.
39. Harry Smith, "Swingin' the News," *Chicago Defender*, July 5, 1941: 20.
40. Al Monroe, "Swinging the News," *Chicago Defender*, March 14, 1942: 19.
41. Ted Watson, "Big Jim Cooper Puts on Ritz," *Chicago Defender*, Dec. 28, 1974: A5.
42. "Delisa Shooting Case Fizzles Out at Hearing," *Chicago Defender*, Sept. 10, 1938: 6.
43. "Baby Bell Pleads Intoxication; Freed," *Chicago Defender*, June 6, 1942: 7.
44. Ole Nosey, "Everybody Goes—When the Wagon Comes," *Chicago Defender*, June 12, 1943: 12.
45. Ole Nosey, "Everybody Goes—When the Wagon Comes," *Chicago Defender*, July 3, 1943: 12.
46. Al Monroe, "Swinging the News," *Chicago Defender*, June 6, 1943: 17.
47. L. Davis, "About Justice in Baby Bell Case," *Chicago Defender*, Aug. 28, 1943: 14.
48. Thompson, *Kings*, 217.
49. "Bar Association Elects Euclid Taylor," *Cleveland Call and Post*, Aug. 30, 1941: 1B.
50. "Seek Three Officers for Rape," *Atlanta Daily World*, Nov. 7, 1932: 1A.
51. "Judge Refuses to Give Youth to Dixie Sheriff," *Chicago Defender*, Nov. 18, 1933: 13.
52. "Euclid Taylor Elected Head of Bar Group," *Chicago Defender*, Aug. 30, 1941: 5.
53. "Policy King Has $5,000 Casket," *Baltimore Afro-American*, Jan. 21, 1939: 2.
54. "Blackburn, Joe Louis' Trainer, Is Acquitted," *Atlanta Daily World*, March 11, 1936: 1.
55. Thompson, *Kings*, 266.
56. Earl J. Morris, "Grand Town Day and Night: Operator 25 Digs Up Some Ethiopia Dirt—Exclusive!" *Pittsburgh Courier*, Jan. 18, 1936: A6.
57. Slim, *Pimp*, 99.

58. Langston Hughes, "From the International House, Bronzeville Seems Far Far Away," *Chicago Defender*, June 11, 1949: 6.
59. "The Black Pimp."
60. Slim, *Pimp*, 194–95.
61. Ibid., 195.
62. Blair, *I've Got to Make*, 166.
63. Slim, *Pimp*, 215.
64. Ibid.
65. Ibid.
66. Ibid.
67. Ibid., 196.
68. Ibid.
69. Ibid., 197.
70. Ibid.
71. Ibid., 215.
72. Ibid., 170.
73. Slim, *Airtight Willie*, 10.
74. Caunes, "Interview with Iceberg Slim."
75. Slim, *Pimp*, 165.
76. Abrahams, *Deep Down*, 97–172.
77. Wepman, Newman, and Binderman, *The Life*, 1–16.
78. Caunes, "Interview with Iceberg Slim."
79. Slim, *Pimp*, 167.
80. Ibid., 115.
81. Ibid., 183.
82. Ibid., 218.
83. Ibid., 219.
84. Ibid.
85. Caunes, "Interview with Iceberg Slim."
86. Koblin, "Portrait," 54.
87. Slim, *Pimp*, 114.
88. Ibid., 179.
89. Hinojosa, interview with Odie Hawkins.
90. Slim, *Pimp*, 117.
91. Ibid., 223–24.
92. Ibid., 225.
93. Caunes, "Interview with Iceberg Slim."

CHAPTER 5: LEAVENWORTH FEDERAL PENITENTIARY

1. Slim, *Pimp*, 227.
2. Ibid.
3. Ibid., 159.
4. Ibid.
5. Ibid., 232.
6. Ibid., 233–34.
7. Ibid., 234.
8. Ibid., 235.
9. Ibid.
10. Ibid., 243.
11. United States Penitentiary, Leavenworth, "Report on Convicted Prisoner—Maupin, Robert Lee," July 12, 1945.

12. United States Penitentiary, Leavenworth, "Associate Warden's Report—Maupin, Robert Lee," July 6, 1945.
13. United States Penitentiary, Leavenworth, "Report on Convicted Prisoner—Maupin, Robert Lee," July 12, 1945.
14. Federal Bureau of Investigation, "Record of FBI No. 1470734," no date.
15. Slim, *Pimp*, 246.
16. United States Penitentiary, Leavenworth, "United States v. Robert Lee Maupin," July 12, 1945.
17. United States Penitentiary, Leavenworth, "Report on Convicted Prisoner—Maupin, Robert Lee," July 12, 1945.
18. Earley, *Hot House*, 30.
19. Benson, "Prison of Democracy," 1–11.
20. Earley, *Hot House*, 25–26.
21. Slim, *Pimp*, 246–47.
22. United States Penitentiary, Leavenworth, "Medical—Initial Examination and Correlated History—Maupin, Robert Lee," June 9, 1945.
23. United States Penitentiary, Leavenworth, "Vocational and Educational History—Maupin, Robert Lee," no date.
24. United States Penitentiary, Leavenworth, "Psychiatric—Maupin, Robert Lee," July 6, 1945.
25. Ibid.
26. United States Penitentiary, Leavenworth, "Associate Warden's Report—Maupin, Robert Lee," July 6, 1945.
27. United States Penitentiary, Leavenworth, "List of Relatives and Approved Correspondents—Maupin, Robert Lee," July 12, 1945.
28. United States Penitentiary, Leavenworth, "Marital Status Report—Maupin, Robert Lee," June 23, 1945.
29. United States Penitentiary, Leavenworth, "Good Time Board Meeting. Maupins, Robert Lee—No. 61956," July 3, 1945: 1.
30. Ibid., 2.
31. Ibid.
32. Ibid., 3.
33. Ibid.
34. LaMaster, *U.S. Penitentiary*, 93.
35. Slim, *Pimp*, 247.
36. Ibid., 247.
37. Ibid., 247–48.
38. Ibid., 248.
39. Slim, *Naked Soul*, 196.
40. Ibid., 57–58.
41. Johnston, *Leavenworth*, 208.
42. Slim, *Pimp*, 249–50.
43. Davis, "Iceberg Slim," 97.
44. Slim, *Naked Soul*, 95.
45. Iceberg Slim, "Mama Debt." *Reflections*, Infinite Zero, 1994, CD.
46. Slim, *Airtight Willie*, 45.
47. Ibid., 46.
48. Ibid., 47.
49. Iceberg Slim, undated letter to a fan, currently in author's collection.
50. Slim, *Pimp*, 228.
51. United States Penitentiary, Leavenworth, "Report on Convicted Prisoner—Maupin, Robert Lee," July 12, 1945.

52. United States Penitentiary, Leavenworth, "Release Progress Report—Maupin, Robert Lee," August 7, 1946.

53. United States Penitentiary, Leavenworth, "Special Progress Report—Maupin, Robert Lee," July 24, 1946.

54. Slim, *Naked Soul*, 18.

55. United States Penitentiary, Leavenworth, "Parole Progress Report—Maupin, Robert Lee," Oct. 1945.

56. United States Penitentiary, Leavenworth, "Special Progress Report—Maupin, Robert Lee," July 24, 1946.

57. Slim, *Pimp*, 250.

CHAPTER 6: ON THE ROAD

1. Slim, *Pimp*, 232.

2. Ibid., 250.

3. Slim, *Airtight Willie*, 13.

4. Slim, *Pimp*, 251.

5. Reckless, *Crime*, 544.

6. Slim, *Pimp*, 257.

7. Slim, *Pimp*, 260.

8. Claussenius, *House of Correction*, 25.

9. "Denies Escape from City Jail 14 Years Ago," *Chicago Daily Tribune*, April 9, 1961: 4.

10. Slim, *Airtight Willie*, 73.

11. State of Wisconsin Municipal Court: Milwaukee County, "State of Wisconsin v. Mattie Maupins," May 29, 1951.

12. The State of Wisconsin State Department of Public Welfare, "Re: Maupins, Mattie WHW #2471," March 24, 1952.

13. Slim, *Pimp*, 267.

14. Ibid., 268.

15. Ibid., 269.

16. Ibid., 267.

17. Ibid., 268.

18. Ibid.

19. Wisconsin Home for Women, "Mattie Maupin—(1) WHW 2269 (2) WHW 2471," no date.

20. Ibid.

21. Wisconsin Home for Women, "Mattie Maupins—Notes for Dr. Dredge," June 15, 1951.

22. Wisconsin Home for Women, "Letters Sent—Maupin, Mattie," Sept. 21, 1951.

23. Wisconsin Home for Women, "Mattie Maupins—Notes for Dr. Dredge," June 15, 1951.

24. The State of Wisconsin State Department of Public Welfare, "Re: Maupins, Mattie WHW #2471," March 24, 1952.

25. Wisconsin State Department of Public Welfare Division of Corrections, "Social Investigation Summary—Maupins, Mattie—MHW #2471," July 1953.

26. Texas Prison System Bureau of Classification, "Mattie Maupins #136284," March 8, 1956.

27. Jones, *Selma*, 24–25.

28. Hirsch, *Making*.

29. Slim, *Pimp*, 270.

30. Borden, *Detroit's Paradise*, 7–10.

31. Wolcott, *Remaking Respectability*, 102.
32. Borden, *Detroit's Paradise*, 9.
33. Wolcott, *Remaking Respectability*, 111, 175.
34. Williams, *Detroit*, 34.
35. Goines, *Whoreson*, 7–8.
36. Sugrue, *Origins*, 47–51.
37. Slim, *Pimp*, 270–71.
38. Ibid., 271.
39. Ibid.
40. Ibid., 272.
41. Ibid., 273.
42. Hirsch, *Making*, 47.
43. Slim, *Pimp*, 275.
44. Kushner, *Ghetto*, 46.
45. Phillips, *Alabama North*, 133.
46. Ibid., 57–97.
47. Kushner, *Ghetto*, 48–50.
48. Himes, *Quality*, 18.
49. Kerr, *Derelict Paradise*, 125.
50. Ibid., 158.
51. Ibid., 129.
52. Slim, *Pimp*, 285.
53. Ibid., 282.
54. Slim, *Airtight Willie*, 35.
55. Davis, "Iceberg Slim," 100.
56. Moore, "Inside Story," 34.
57. Slim, *Pimp*, 275.
58. Ibid., 285.
59. Taylor, *Forging*, 28.
60. Ibid., 188.
61. Ibid., 175–84.
62. Slim, *Pimp*, 224–25.
63. Ibid., 225.
64. West, "Sweet Talk," 79–80.
65. Ibid., 79.
66. Slim, *Pimp*, 289.
67. Ibid., 291.
68. "Walker J. Butler," *Chicago Daily Law Bulletin*, June 10, 1960: 6.
69. Slim, *Pimp*, 298.
70. Stern, "Chicago House," 23.
71. Slim, *Pimp*, 301.
72. Ibid., 303.
73. Ibid., 305.
74. Robert Beck, Correspondence to Warden of the Chicago House of Correction, no date, print. Courtesy Diane Beck.

CHAPTER 7: LOS ANGELES

1. Slim, *Pimp*, 283.
2. Slim, *Naked Soul*, 24.
3. Ibid., 18–19.

4. Slim, *Pimp*, 309.
5. Slim, *Naked Soul*, 27.
6. Ibid.
7. Ibid., 25.
8. Slim, *Pimp*, 305.
9. Moore, "Inside Story," 35.
10. Slim, *Naked Soul*, 37–38.
11. Sides, *L.A. City Limits*, 11.
12. Davis, *City of Quartz*, 162.
13. Sides, *L.A. City Limits*, 57–130.
14. Davis, *City of Quartz*, 399–401.
15. Slim, *Pimp*, 310.
16. Betty Beck, personal interview with Jorge Hinojosa, 2008.
17. Ibid.
18. Ibid.
19. Ibid.
20. Ibid.
21. Ibid.
22. Moore, "Inside Story," 32–33.
23. Betty Beck, personal interview with Jorge Hinojosa, 2008.
24. Ibid.
25. Slim, *Pimp*, 305.
26. Ibid., 312.
27. Betty Beck, personal interview with Jorge Hinojosa, 2008.
28. Milner, "America's No. 1 Pimp," 20.
29. Betty Beck, personal interview with Jorge Hinojosa, 2008.
30. Ibid.
31. Gilstrap, "The House," 87–99.
32. Bentley Morriss, personal interview with Jorge Hinojosa, 2008.
33. Gifford, *Pimping Fictions*, 48.
34. Emory Holmes, personal interview with Jorge Hinojosa, 2009.
35. Betty Beck, personal interview with Jorge Hinojosa, 2008.
36. Ibid.
37. Ibid.
38. Davis, "Iceberg Slim," 101.
39. Betty Beck, personal interview with Jorge Hinojosa, 2008.
40. "Annual Men's Day," *Los Angeles Sentinel*, Sept. 24, 1959: B11.
41. "Workshops Set for State Drug Confab," *New York Amsterdam News*, Oct. 10, 1970: 12.
42. Slim, *Naked Soul*, 141.
43. Ibid., 140–41.
44. Ibid., 143.
45. Ibid.
46. G. Edmond Hayes to Robert Beck, Oct. 5, 1966, print. Courtesy Diane Beck.
47. Moore, "Inside Story," 35.
48. Davis, "Iceberg Slim," 104–5.
49. "Ex-Convict," 17.
50. "The Black Pimp."
51. Slim, *Pimp*, 17.
52. Slim, *Pimp*, 11.
53. Mark Skillz, "The Hustle—The Story of Robert Beck aka Iceberg Slim," *Davey*

D's Hip-hop Corner—Hip-hop and Politics, Feb. 5, 2010, http://hiphopand politics.com/2010/02/05/the-hustle-the-story-of-robert-beck-aka-iceberg -slim.

54. Milner and Milner, *Black Players*, 287.
55. Betty Beck, personal interview with Jorge Hinojosa, 2008.

CHAPTER 8: HOLLYWOOD

1. Slim, *Pimp*, 17.
2. Ibid., 146.
3. Gifford, *Pimping Fictions*, 50.
4. Slim, *Trick*, 9–10.
5. Ibid., 10.
6. Pyne, "Interview with Iceberg Slim."
7. Slim, *Trick*, 126.
8. Ibid., 247.
9. Ibid.
10. Ibid., 249–50.
11. Ian Whitaker, interview with Odie Hawkins, 160.
12. Cleaver, "Fond Memories," 116.
13. Milner, "America's No. 1 Pimp," 17.
14. Betty Beck, personal interview with Jorge Hinojosa, 2008.
15. Camille Beck, personal interview with Jorge Hinojosa, 2008.
16. Betty Beck, personal interview with Jorge Hinojosa, 2008.
17. Ibid.
18. Ibid.
19. Anderson, "No More Baubles," 27.
20. Slim, *Mama*, 11.
21. Salaam, "Psychology of the Pimp," 88.
22. Slim, *Mama*, 12.
23. Ibid., 61.
24. Ibid., 63.
25. Ibid., 173.
26. Ibid., 28.
27. Ibid., 33.
28. Dickey, "Iceberg Slim," 63.
29. Anderson, "No More Baubles," 27.
30. Davis, "Iceberg Slim," 108.
31. Slim, *Naked Soul*, dedication page.
32. Ibid., 17.
33. Ibid., 219.
34. Ibid., 49.
35. Ibid., 165.
36. Ibid., 57.
37. Ibid., 55–56.
38. Ibid., 175.
39. Ibid., 177.
40. Ibid., 185.
41. Ibid., 146–47.
42. Ibid., 154.
43. Ibid., 153.
44. Ibid., 163.

45. "The Black Pimp."
46. Iceberg Slim, "Letter to the Editor," *Playboy*, Oct. 1972, print.
47. "The Black Pimp."
48. Milner, "America's No. 1 Pimp," 19.
49. Emory Holmes, personal interview with Jorge Hinojosa, 2009.
50. Bentley Morriss, personal interview with Jorge Hinojosa, 2008.
51. Betty Beck, personal interview with Jorge Hinojosa, 2008.
52. James P. Murray, "Black Moviemaking Booms; Award-Winners Increase," *New York Amsterdam News*, March 17, 1973: C7.
53. Rossi Jackson, "The 'Trick Baby' May Be on You," *New Pittsburgh Courier*, March 3, 1973: 17.
54. Tony Griggs, "Clerics Call Film Racist," *Chicago Defender*, Feb. 5, 1973: 3.
55. Ellis, "Iceberg Slim," 39.
56. Camille Beck, personal interview with Jorge Hinojosa, 2008.
57. West, "Sweet Talk," 75.
58. Davis, "Iceberg Slim," 106.
59. Misty Beck, personal interview with Jorge Hinojosa, 2008.
60. Davis, "Iceberg Slim," 104.
61. Red Holloway, personal interview with Jorge Hinojosa, 2009.
62. Ibid.
63. Ibid.
64. Misty Beck, electronic correspondence to Justin D. Gifford, Sept. 14, 2014.
65. Camille Beck, personal interview with Jorge Hinojosa, 2008.
66. Misty Beck, personal interview with Jorge Hinojosa, 2008.
67. Slim, *Long*, 73.
68. Chepesiuk, *Black Gangsters*, 95.
69. Slim, *Death*, 106.
70. Caunes, "Interview with Iceberg Slim."
71. Betty Beck, personal interview with Jorge Hinojosa, 2008.
72. Ibid.

CHAPTER 9: FINAL YEARS

1. Holloway House Publishing Company, "Royalty Statement—Iceberg Slim," March 31, 1979, courtesy Diane Beck.
2. Slim, *Airtight Willie*, 25.
3. Slim, *Iceberg Slim's Complete Rundown Kit.*
4. Ibid.
5. Ibid.
6. Ibid.
7. Ibid.
8. Ibid.
9. Slim, *Doom*, 5.
10. Ibid., 240.
11. Diane Beck, electronic correspondence to Justin D. Gifford, July 20, 2013.
12. Diane Beck, electronic correspondence to Justin D. Gifford, July 21, 2013.
13. Diane Beck, electronic correspondence to Justin D. Gifford, July 11, 2013.
14. Brad Bunnin to Robert D. Wilner, April 1, 1997, print. Courtesy Diane Beck.
15. Ibid.
16. Robert D. Wilner to Brad Bunnin, April 4, 1997, print. Courtesy Diane Beck.
17. Brad Bunnin to Robert D. Wilner, April 10, 1997, print. Courtesy Diane Beck.
18. Slim, *Shetani's*, 8.

19. Davis, "Iceberg Slim," 102.
20. Diane Beck, electronic correspondence to Justin D. Gifford, July 17, 2013.
21. "Police Dispatch," *Richmond Times-Dispatch*, Sept. 22, 1983: C5.
22. Camille Beck, personal interview with Jorge Hinojosa, 2008.
23. "Police Dispatch," *Richmond Times-Dispatch*, Jan. 20, 1984: C4.
24. Tyson, *Undisputed*, 156.
25. Ibid., 158–59.
26. Ibid., 159.
27. Davis, *City of Quartz*, 305.
28. Gooding-Williams, *Reading*, 122.
29. Quinn, *Nuthin'*, 43.
30. Davis, *City of Quartz*, 314.
31. Ibid., 288.
32. Reeves and Campbell, *Cracked*, 41.
33. Gooding-Williams, *Reading*, 127.
34. Kelley, *Race Rebels*, 193.
35. Ibid., 184.
36. Davis, *City of Quartz*, 274–75.
37. Kelley, *Race Rebels*, 202.
38. Goad, *ANSWER Me!*, 21.
39. Light, *Vibe*, 116.
40. Ice-T, "6 'N the Mornin'," *Rhyme Pays*, Sire/Warner Bros. Records, 1987.
41. Quinn, *Nuthin'*, 10.
42. Borgmeyer and Lang, *Dr. Dre: A Biography*, 39.
43. Diane Beck, electronic correspondence to Justin D. Gifford, July 11, 2013.
44. Camille Beck, personal interview with Jorge Hinojosa, 2008.
45. Slim, *Night*, 7–8.
46. Ibid., 122.
47. Ibid., 134.
48. Diane Beck, electronic correspondence to Justin D. Gifford, July 11, 2013.
49. Ian Whitaker, interview with Misty Beck, 128.
50. Diane Beck, electronic correspondence to Justin D. Gifford, Aug. 14, 2014.
51. Ian Whitaker, interview with Misty Beck, 137.

BIBLIOGRAPHY

Slim, Iceberg. *Airtight Willie & Me*. Los Angeles: Holloway House Publishing Company, 1979.
———. *Death Wish*. Los Angeles: Holloway House Publishing Company, 1977.
———. *Doom Fox*. New York: Grove Press, 1998.
———. *Iceberg Slim's Complete Rundown Kit*. Courtesy Diane Beck.
———. *Long White Con*. Los Angeles: Holloway House Publishing Company, 1977.
———. *Mama Black Widow*. Los Angeles: Holloway House Publishing Company, 1969.
———. *The Naked Soul of Iceberg Slim*. Los Angeles: Holloway House Publishing Company, 1971.
———. *Night Train to Sugar Hill*. Copyright Robert Beck, 1990. Care of Diane Beck.
———. *Pimp: The Story of My Life*. Los Angeles: Holloway House Publishing Company, 1967.
———. *Shetani's Sister*. Copyright Robert Beck, 1986. Care of Diane Beck.
———. *Trick Baby*. Los Angeles: Holloway House Publishing Company, 1967.

BOOKS AND ACADEMIC ARTICLES
150 Years of Inmate Work Programs. Madison, WI: Wisconsin Bureau of Correctional Enterprises, 2003.
Abrahams, Roger D. *Deep Down in the Jungle: Black American Folklore from the Streets of Philadelphia*. New Brunswick, NJ: Folklore Associates, Inc., 1964.
Benson, Sara M. "The Prison of Democracy: U.S. Legal Culture and the Idea of Leavenworth Penitentiary." Diss. University of California, Santa Cruz, 2011.
Blair, Cynthia M. *I've Got to Make My Livin': Black Women's Sex Work in Turn-of-the-Century Chicago*. Chicago: University of Chicago Press, 2010.
Bone, Robert, and Richard A. Courage. *The Muse in Bronzeville: African American Creative Expression in Chicago, 1932–1950*. New Brunswick, NJ: Rutgers University Press, 2011.
Borden, Ernest H. *Detroit's Paradise Valley*. Charleston, SC: Arcadia Publishing, 2003.
Borgmeyer, John, and Holly Lang. *Dr. Dre: A Biography*, Westport, CT: Greenwood Press, 2007, 39.
Bukowski, Douglas. *Big Bill, Chicago, and the Politics of Image*. Urbana: University of Chicago Press, 1998.
Burke, John C. *Wisconsin State Prison Rules for the Government of Prisoners*. Wisconsin State Prison, 1943.

Chapman, Barbara. *That Men Know So Little of Men*. Rockford, IL: Rockford Public Library, 1975.

Chepesiuk, Ron. *Black Gangsters of Chicago*. Fort Lee, NJ: Barricade Books, 2007.

Claussenius, G. A. *The House of Correction of the City of Chicago: A Retrospect Covering Half a Century of Endeavor from the Founding of the Institution to the Present Time, 1871–1921*. Chicago: City of Chicago, 1922.

Davis, Mike. *City of Quartz: Excavating the Future in Los Angeles*. New York: Vintage Books, 1990.

Davis, Valerie J., and Jackie Schweitzer. "The Policy of Good Design: Quilt Designs and Designers from the WPA Milwaukee Handicrafts Project, 1935–1942." *Uncoverings* 32 (2011): 103–21.

Drake, St. Clair, and Horace R. Cayton. *Black Metropolis: A Study of Negro Life in a Northern City*. New York: Harcourt, Brace and Company, 1945.

Earley, Pete. *The Hot House: Life Inside Leavenworth Prison*. New York: Bantam Books, 1992.

Geenen, Paul H. *Milwaukee's Bronzeville: 1900–1950*. Charleston, SC: Arcadia Publishing, 2006.

Gifford, Justin. *Pimping Fictions: African American Crime Literature and the Untold Story of Black Pulp Publishing*. Philadelphia: Temple University Press, 2013.

Gilstrap, Peter. "The House that Black Built." *The Misread City: New Literary Los Angeles*. Eds. Scott Timburg and Dana Gioia. Los Angeles: Red Hen Press, 2003. 87–99.

Goad, Jim. *ANSWER Me!: The First Three*. San Francisco: AK Press, 1995.

Goines, Donald. *Whoreson*. Los Angeles: Holloway House Publishing Company, 1972.

Gooding-Williams, Robert. *Reading Rodney King/Reading Urban Uprising*. London: Routledge, 1993.

Grandison, K. Ian. "Landscapes of Terror: A Reading of Tuskegee's Historic Campus, 1881–1915." *The Geography of Identity*. Ed. Patricia Yaeger. Ann Arbor, MI: University of Michigan Press, 1996. 334–67.

Grossman, James R. *Land of Hope: Chicago, Black Southerners, and the Great Migration*. Chicago: University of Chicago Press, 1991.

Himes, Chester. *The Quality of Hurt: The Early Years—The Autobiography of Chester Himes*. New York: Doubleday, 1972.

Hirsch, Arnold. *Making the Second Ghetto: Race and Housing in Chicago 1940–1960*. Chicago: University of Chicago Press, 1998.

Hughes, Langston. *The Big Sea: An Autobiography*. New York: Hill & Wang, 1993.

Hurston, Zora Neale. "Characteristics of Negro Expression." *The New Negro: Readings on Race, Representation, and African American Culture 1892–1938*. Eds. Henry Louis Gates and Gene Andrew Jarrett. Princeton, NJ: Princeton University Press, 1995. 355–64.

Jaffe, Chris. "The Race Line to Rockford." *Journal of the Illinois State Historical Society* 103.1 (Spring 2010): 7–42.

Johnston, J. H., III. *Leavenworth Penitentiary: A History of America's Oldest Federal Prison*. Leavenworth, KS: J. H. Johnston, III, 2005.

Jones, Patrick D. *The Selma of the North: Civil Rights Insurgency in Milwaukee*. Cambridge, MA: Harvard University Press, 2010.

Kelley, Robin D. G. *Race Rebels: Culture, Politics, and the Black Working Class*. New York: Free Press, 1996.

Kerr, Daniel R. *Derelict Paradise: Homelessness and Urban Development in Cleveland, Ohio*. Amherst, MA: University of Massachusetts Press, 2011.

Kushner, Kenneth L. *A Ghetto Takes Shape: Black Cleveland 1870–1930*. Urbana: University of Illinois Press, 1976.

Laffin, Kathy. *Black Milwaukee: A Developmental History*. Milwaukee, WI: T. S. Collection of the Milwaukee Public Library, 1970.

LaMaster, Kenneth. *U.S. Penitentiary Leavenworth*. Charleston, SC: Arcadia Publishing, 2008.

Lee, Oscar. *Wisconsin State Prison Rules for the Government of Prisoners*. Wisconsin State Prison, 1932.

Lemann, Nicholas. *The Promised Land: The Black Migration and How It Changed America*. New York: Alfred A. Knopf, 1991.

Light, Alan, ed. *The VIBE History of Hip Hop*. New York: Three Rivers Press, 1999.

Lovett, Bobby. *The African American History of Nashville, Tennessee: 1780–1930*. Fayetteville, AR: University of Arkansas Press, 1999.

Milner, Christina, and Richard Milner. *Black Players: The Secret World of Black Pimps*. New York: Bantam Books, 1972.

Molyneaux, John L. *African Americans in Early Rockford, 1834–1871*. Rockford, IL: Rockford Public Library, 2000.

Mumford, Kevin. *Interzones: Black/White Sex Districts in Chicago and New York in the Early Twentieth Century*. New York: Columbia University Press, 1997.

Phillips, Kimberley L. *Alabama North: African American Migrants, Community, and Working Class Activism in Cleveland, 1915–45*. Urbana: University of Illinois Press, 1999.

Pollard, Diane S., and Cheryl S. Arijotutu. *African-Centered Schooling in Theory and Practice*. Westport, CT: Bergin and Garvey, 2000.

The Quill. Vol. 15. Milwaukee, WI: Lincoln High School, 1935.

Quinn, Eithne. *Nuthin' but a "G" Thang: The Culture and Commerce of Gangsta Rap*. New York: Columbia University Press, 2004.

Rampersad, Arnold. *The Life of Langston Hughes*. Oxford: Oxford University Press, 1986.

Reckless, Walter Cade. *The Crime Problem*. New York: Appleton-Century-Crofts, 1955.

Reeves, Jimmie L., and Richard Campbell. *Cracked Coverage: Television News, the Anti-Cocaine Crusade, and the Reagan Legacy*. Durham, NC: Duke University Press, 1994.

Sides, Josh. *L.A. City Limits: African American Los Angeles from the Great Depression to the Present*. Oakland: University of California Press, 2006.

Stern, Max. "The Chicago House of Correction: A History and Examination of Recent Statistics Regarding Persons Committed to It." MA thesis, University of Chicago, 1932.

Still, Bayrd. *Milwaukee: The History of a City*. Madison, WI: The State Historical Society of Wisconsin, 1948.

"The Story of the Wisconsin State Prison." Waupun, WI: Wisconsin State Prison, 1939.

Sugrue, Thomas. *The Origins of the Urban Crisis: Race and Inequality in Postwar Detroit*. Princeton, NJ: Princeton University Press, 2005.

Taylor, Quintard. *The Forging of a Black Community: Seattle's Central District, from 1870 Through the Civil Rights Era*. Seattle: University of Washington Press, 1994.

Telzrow, Michael E. "Punishment and Reform: The Wisconsin State Reformatory." *Voyageur: Historical Review of Brown County and Northeast Wisconsin*. 18.2 (2002): 24–33.

————. *Wisconsin State Reformatory*. Charleston, SC: Arcadia Publishing, 2009.

Thompson, Nathan. *Kings: The True Story of Chicago's Policy Kings and Numbers Racketeers*. Chicago: The Bronzeville Press, 2006.

Trotter, Joe William, Jr. *Black Milwaukee: The Making of an Industrial Proletariat, 1915–45*. Champaign: University of Illinois Press, 2007.

————. *From a Raw Deal to a New Deal: African Americans 1929–1945*. Oxford: Oxford University Press, 1996.

Tyson, Mike. *Undisputed Truth*. New York: Blue Rider Press, 2013.

Vick, William Albert. "From Walnut Street to No Street: Milwaukee's Afro-American Businesses, 1945–1965." MA thesis. University of Wisconsin, Milwaukee, 1993.

Wepman, Dennis, Ronald B. Newman, and Murray B. Binderman. *The Life: The Lore and Folk Poetry of the Black Hustler*. Philadelphia: University of Pennsylvania Press, 1976.

Williams, Jeremy. *Detroit: The Black Bottom Community*. Charleston, SC: Arcadia Publishing, 2009.

Wolcott, Victoria W. *Remaking Respectability: African American Women in Interwar Detroit*. Chapel Hill: University of North Carolina Press, 2001.

INTERVIEWS

Anderson, Monroe. "No More Baubles: One Time Procurer Turns to Prose—and Still Sells." *National Observer*, Dec. 4, 1971. Reprinted in *Iceberg Slim: The Lost Interviews with the Pimp*. Ed. Ian Whitaker. UK: Infinite Dreams Publishing, 2009.

"The Black Pimp." Interview. *Black Journal*. Nov. 2, 1971.

Caunes, Antoine de. "Interview with Iceberg Slim." *Rapido*. March 11, 1988.

Cleaver, Jim. "Fond Memories of a Different Man." *Los Angeles Sentinel*, July 9, 1992. Reprinted in *Iceberg Slim: The Lost Interviews with the Pimp*. Ed. Ian Whitaker. UK: Infinite Dreams Publishing, 2009.

Davis, Nolan. "Iceberg Slim: Pimping the Page." *Players* 4.1 (1977). Reprinted in *Iceberg Slim: The Lost Interviews with the Pimp*. Ed. Ian Whitaker. UK: Infinite Dreams Publishing, 2009.

Dickey, Fred. "Iceberg Slim Portrays Grim Life." *San Jose Mercury News*. April 30, 1972. Reprinted in *Iceberg Slim: The Lost Interviews with the Pimp*. Ed. Ian Whitaker. UK: Infinite Dreams Publishing, 2009.

Ellis, Joe. "Iceberg Slim Is Warming Up to Life." *Chicago Defender*, Dec. 16, 1972. Reprinted in *Iceberg Slim: The Lost Interviews with the Pimp*. Ed. Ian Whitaker. UK: Infinite Dream Publishing, 2009.

"Ex-Convict Now Movie Author." Interview. *Boston Herald*, Feb. 5, 1973.

Hinojosa, Jorge. Interview with Odie Hawkins. *Iceberg Slim: Portrait of a Pimp*. Film. Dir. Jorge Hinojosa. Final Level Entertainment, 2012.

Koblin, Helen. "Portrait of a Pimp." *Los Angeles Free Press*, Feb. 25, 1972. Reprinted in *Iceberg Slim: The Lost Interviews with the Pimp*. Ed. Ian Whitaker. UK: Infinite Dreams Publishing, 2009.

Milner, Richard B. "America's No. 1 Pimp Tells It Like It Is!" *Rogue Magazine* 18 (June 1969). Reprinted in *Iceberg Slim: The Lost Interviews with the Pimp*. Ed. Ian Whitaker. UK: Infinite Dreams Publishing, 2009.

Moore, Bob. "The Inside Story of Black Pimps." *Sepia Magazine*, Feb. 1972. Reprinted in *Iceberg Slim: The Lost Interviews with the Pimp*. Ed. Ian Whitaker. UK: Infinite Dreams Publishing, 2009.

Pyne, Joe. "Interview with Iceberg Slim." *The Joe Pyne Show*. Aired Jan. 19, 1968.

Salaam, Kalamu ya. "The Psychology of the Pimp." *The Black Collegian*, Jan./Feb. 1975. Reprinted in *Iceberg Slim: The Lost Interviews with the Pimp*. Ed. Ian Whitaker. UK: Infinite Dreams Publishing, 2009.

West, Hollie I. "Sweet Talk, Hustle, and Muscle." Interview with Iceberg Slim. *Washington Post*, 1973. Reprinted in *Iceberg Slim: The Lost Interviews with the Pimp*. Ed. Ian Whitaker. UK: Infinite Dreams Publishing, 2009.

Whitaker, Ian. Interview with Misty Beck. *Iceberg Slim: The Lost Interviews with the Pimp*. Ed. Ian Whitaker. UK: Infinite Dreams Publishing, 2009.

———. Interview with Odie Hawkins. June 18, 2009. *Iceberg Slim: The Lost Interviews with the Pimp*. Ed. Ian Whitaker. UK: Infinite Dreams Publishing, 2009.

INDEX

ABOUT THE AUTHOR

Dr. Justin Gifford is an associate professor of English literature at the University of Nevada, Reno. His teaching and research focus on American and African American literature. His book *Pimping Fictions: African American Crime Literature and the Untold Story of Black Pulp Publishing*, the first literary and cultural history of black street fiction, was a 2014 finalist for both the Edgar Allan Poe award for literary criticism and Phi Beta Kappa's Christian Gauss Award for scholarship.